AN
AFFAIR
OF STATE

AN

AFFAIR
OF STATE

THE INVESTIGATION, IMPEACHMENT, AND TRIAL OF PRESIDENT CLINTON

Richard A. Posner

Harvard University Press
Cambridge, Massachusetts
London, England

Copyright © 1999 by the President and Fellows of Harvard College
All rights reserved
Printed in the United States of America

Second printing, 1999

Library of Congress Cataloging-in-Publication Data
Posner, Richard A.
An affair of state: the investigation, impeachment and trial
of President Clinton/Richard A. Posner.
p. cm.
Includes bibliographical references and index.
ISBN 0-674-00080-3 (hardcover : alk. paper)
1. Clinton, Bill, 1946– —Impeachment.   2. Trials (Impeachment)—
United States.   3. Impeachments—United States.   I. Title.
KF5076.C57P67   1999
342.73'062—dc21   99-24307

Contents

Dramatis Personae

Monica Lewinsky	White House intern, then employee; Clinton girlfriend and witness in his Senate trial
William Clinton	President of the United States
Kenneth Starr	Independent Counsel, investigating the President
Betty Currie	The President's personal secretary
Evelyn Lieberman	Deputy White House Chief of Staff
Paula Jones	Plaintiff in a sexual harassment suit against Clinton
Susan Webber Wright	District judge in the Jones case
Bill Richardson	U.S. Ambassador to the United Nations
Vernon Jordan	Washington lawyer; Clinton friend and witness in his Senate trial
Ronald Perelman	Chairman of the executive committee of Revlon, Inc.
Sidney Blumenthal	Assistant to the President; witness in Clinton's Senate trial
Webster Hubbell	Former Associate Attorney General
Linda Tripp	Pentagon employee; confidante of Lewinsky
Kathleen Willey	Volunteer worker in the White House
Lucianne Goldberg	Conservative literary agent; friend of Linda Tripp

Gennifer Flowers Former girlfriend of Clinton

Vince Foster Former Deputy White House Counsel; a suicide

Richard Mellon Scaife Clinton opponent

Robert Fiske Starr's predecessor as Independent Counsel

James Carville Political consultant; Clinton defender

Robert Bennett Clinton's lead lawyer in the Jones case

David Kendall Clinton's lead lawyer in the Starr investigation

Henry Hyde Chairman of the House Judiciary Committee; chief prosecutor of Clinton in the Senate trial

Tom DeLay House Republican whip

Charles Ruff White House Counsel; the President's lead lawyer in the impeachment and trial

Chronology

May 8, 1991	Paula Jones encounters Governor Clinton in a hotel room in Arkansas
November 3, 1992	Clinton is elected President
May 6, 1994	Jones sues Clinton for sexual harassment, asking for $700,000 in damages
August 9, 1994	Kenneth Starr is appointed Independent Counsel to investigate Whitewater real estate deal
July 1995	Monica Lewinsky becomes a White House intern
November 15, 1995	Clinton begins a sexual relationship with Lewinsky
April 5, 1996	Lewinsky is transferred to the Pentagon
November 5, 1996	Clinton is reelected President
March 29, 1997	Clinton's last sexual encounter with Lewinsky
May 27, 1997	The Supreme Court rules that the Jones suit can go forward
November 1997	Lewinsky enlists Vernon Jordan's aid in her New York job search
December 5, 1997	Lewinsky's name appears on the witness list in the Jones case
December 28, 1997	Betty Currie picks up gifts from Lewinsky, hides them under her bed
January 7, 1998	Lewinsky signs an affidavit in the Jones case

January 13, 1998	Lewinsky accepts a job offer (later rescinded) from Revlon
January 16, 1998	Kenneth Starr is appointed to investigate the Lewinsky matter
January 17, 1998	Clinton is deposed in the Jones case
January 18, 1998	Clinton meets with Betty Currie to discuss his deposition
January 21, 1998	The *Washington Post* reveals the Clinton-Lewinsky affair and investigation
April 1, 1998	The district court dismisses the Jones suit
July 28, 1998	Lewinsky agrees to cooperate with the Independent Counsel
August 17, 1998	Clinton testifies before the grand jury via closed-circuit television, then addresses nation
September 9, 1998	The Starr Report is submitted to Congress
September 21, 1998	Clinton's grand jury testimony is broadcast
October 8, 1998	The House of Representatives votes to conduct an impeachment inquiry
November 3, 1998	Mid-term congressional elections; Democrats do better than expected
November 9–10, 19, 1998	Hearings are held before the House Judiciary Committee
November 19, 1998	Jones suit is settled for $850,000
November 27, 1998	Clinton answers eighty-one questions propounded to him by the House Judiciary Committee
December 1, 8–10, 1998	Further hearings are held before the Judiciary Committee
December 11–12, 1998	The Judiciary Committee approves four articles of impeachment
December 19, 1998	The House of Representatives approves two of the articles; President Clinton is impeached

January 7, 1999   The trial of President Clinton by the Senate
                         begins

February 6, 1999   Videotaped witness testimony is presented to the
                         Senate

February 12, 1999   The trial ends; the President is acquitted

Introduction

The year-long political, legal, constitutional, and cultural struggle that began on January 21, 1998, when the world learned that Independent Counsel Kenneth Starr was investigating charges that President Clinton had committed perjury and other crimes of obstruction of justice (primarily subornation of perjury and witness tampering) in an effort to conceal a sexual affair with a young White House worker named Monica Lewinsky, is the most riveting chapter of recent American history. The investigation culminated on December 19, 1998, in the impeachment of President Clinton by the House of Representatives for perjury before a grand jury and for obstruction of justice.[1] It was only the second impeachment of a U.S. President. The first was the impeachment of Andrew Johnson 130 years earlier, although in 1974 Richard Nixon would have been impeached and convicted had he not resigned after the House Judiciary Committee recommended his impeachment to the full House. On January 7, 1999, the Senate trial of President Clinton began.[2] Truncated and anticlimactic—indeed, a parody of legal jus-

[1]The vote to impeach him for perjury before the grand jury was 228 to 206, with one member of the House not voting. The vote to impeach him for obstruction of justice was 221 to 212, with two members not voting.

[2]Although the trial nominally lasted more than a month, there was only one real day of trial—February 6, when the prosecution and defense presented the relevant portions of the videotaped depositions of the three witnesses (Monica Lewinsky, Vernon Jordan, and Sidney Blumenthal) whom the Senate had authorized the House managers (i.e., prosecutors) to call. (The transcript of the February 6 session is published at 145 Cong. Rec. S1290 [Feb. 6, 1999].) There is a semantic problem here. The term "trial" is used in the impeachment context to refer to the entire proceeding in the Senate, embracing both pretrial proceedings (preliminary motions and pretrial discovery) and the evidentiary hearing, which corresponds to a conventional trial.

tice—the trial ended on February 12 with the President's acquittal.[3] With this, the end of the main legal phase of the struggle that began on January 21 of last year, the record of events analyzed in this book was complete, though the aftershocks (such as Juanita Broaddrick's rape charge and Lewinsky's television interview and book) continue.

Three features of what at first seemed a political crisis of the first magnitude, but that now seems better described as a political drama or even a comedy (for other than the participants), hold a particular interest for me. The first is its intersection with issues, particularly of law and morality, that have long engaged my academic interest and attention.[4] The second is its sheer multifaceted complexity—factual, legal, political, and moral—which cries out for the sort of synoptic, compendious treatment that I have attempted in several previous books on cross-disciplinary subjects, such as sex and aging.[5] Not everyone was paying careful attention to the Clinton impeachment drama who should have been, and as a result there is a danger that the history of it will pass rapidly into myth.[6] The third feature that intrigues me is related to the second: the drama has so many "angles," and such an undercurrent of emotionality, that maintaining balance and perspective is an enormous challenge to one's powers of judicious reflection.

Judicious—not judicial. The framers of the Constitution carefully excluded the judiciary (all but the Chief Justice, who presides at the Senate trial of an impeached President) from the adjudication of impeachments. We other judges are confined to the observer role. And the ethical

---

[3]The vote to convict was 45 to 55 on the perjury article, and 50 to 50 on the obstruction of justice article. A two-thirds (67–33) vote was required for conviction. A motion to censure the President was rejected on procedural grounds.

[4]See my books *The Problems of Jurisprudence* (1990), *Overcoming Law* (1995), and *The Problematics of Moral and Legal Theory* (1999).

[5]See my books *Sex and Reason* (1992) and *Aging and Old Age* (1995).

[6]Before it was over, serious confusion was evident in the minds of members of the public. Illustrative is a letter to the editors of the *New York Times* shortly before the Senate trial ended attacking the *Times*'s "outdated proposal for a censure-plus-admission endgame. The charge of perjury seems to have fallen apart for lack of evidence, and while the House ayatollahs are trying to keep the obstruction charge alive, I have not seen any specific instances in which Mr. Clinton obstructed justice in a legal sense. So what would you have President Clinton admit to? Sex with Monica S. Lewinsky and lying about it? He has on numerous occasions admitted to that." *New York Times,* Feb. 3, 1999, p. A22. We shall see that the charge of perjury is solid, that the President in several instances obstructed justice in a legal sense, and that he has never admitted lying about his relationship with Lewinsky.

rules of the federal judiciary forbid public comment on pending cases, including, I assume, an impeachment—but I do not discuss any pending cases. One cannot, however, write about the Clinton impeachment and related matters without touching on politically sensitive issues, and in particular without criticizing President Clinton's conduct and that of members of Congress. This might be thought a decisive objection to a federal judge's writing about this subject even if the judge writes qua academic rather than qua judge. The principle that underlies the hypothetical objection, a principle I support as well as recognize as binding upon me, is that judges are not to be politically active. But criticism of the President's conduct, and that of other political actors in the drama, crosses party lines, indeed is nearly universal. I have striven to avoid any hint of partisanship in my analysis, and I hope that to the extent I have succeeded this will neutralize the objection.

Apart from its sheer narrative intricacy, Clinton's ordeal presents a number of distinct but interrelated issues that have to be sorted out and related to facts that are contested and incompletely known,[7] and so in need of being weighed and sifted. There are issues of law, including criminal and constitutional law, the law of evidence, and the substantive and procedural principles that should guide impeachment and impeachment trials. There are issues of jurisprudence, concerning the appropriate roles of historical scholarship and pragmatic reasoning in answering questions of law and policy, the difference between popular and legal justice, and (a related point) the meaning and appropriateness of characterizing impeachment proceedings as "legal." There are issues of morality, both private and public, and of political theory, political history, political science, and the specialized branch of history and political science known as Presidential studies. There are issues that evoke the theory of conflict, or strategy, and numerous perplexing issues of political and cultural sociology, including the peculiar sociology of the "moralistic Right" and of the "academic Left." (These are crude, even offensive, categorizations, but I shall defend them.)

I am unapologetic not only about my decision to write about the struggle to impeach and remove Clinton, despite its partisan overtones

---

[7] I have not tried to go beyond the public record of the facts. I am not a journalist or a detective or even an habitué of the World Wide Web. I have not conducted interviews, or rested conclusions on any of the rumors that continue to swirl around the controversy, although, while trying to avoid speculation, I have not hesitated to draw the kind of inferences that judges and jurors are permitted to draw from a public record.

and its origins in a sexual relationship widely regarded as tawdry, but also about attempting to write a scholarly book so soon after the event. After? During, really; I began writing in October 1998, when the crisis was very much *in medias res* and the end could not be foreseen, and I finished on February 16, 1999, four days after the Senate trial ended.[8] To write so close to the event is to write without the perspective that temporal distance enables, without a complete picture of the facts, and without being able to do more than guess at the long-term consequences. Thus it is to write without the possibility of being definitive. But it is also to write with better prospects of achieving freshness and immediacy than if I waited until history had applied its varnish. There is such a thing as distinguished contemporaneous history (oxymoronic as the term sounds), though I don't expect to be compared with Tacitus or Thucydides, or even Suetonius. To write close to the event is also to write with a *relative* freedom from hindsight bias,[9] though the qualification is important. This book is not a diary, and the judgments in it are informed by knowledge of how the story ends,[10] although not by knowledge of how it will come eventually to be judged by history.

Hindsight bias is a serious problem in historiography. Once a historical episode is declared "closed" (so far as any historical episode can be so described), there is a tendency to see the events that led up to, constituted, and resolved it as inevitable, if not indeed as the product of design. Outcome exerts an irresistible hydraulic pressure on interpretation. Blunders that had happy results for the blunderer are redescribed as brilliant tactical moves, while moves that were intelligent *ex*

---

[8]That was the day before I sent my final draft to the publisher. I have made only minor changes since.

[9]On which see, for example, Baruch Fischoff, "Hindsight ≠ Foresight: The Effect of Outcome Knowledge on Judgment under Uncertainty," 1 *Journal of Experimental Psychology: Human Perception and Performance* 288 (1975).

[10]If it *has* ended—a matter of definition. President Clinton and other participants in the ordeal remain in some jeopardy of being prosecuted for crimes; Clinton may be disciplined by the district judge in the Paula Jones case (the judge on April 12, 1999, found Clinton in civil contempt of court for lying in his deposition, Jones v. Clinton, 1999 WL 202909 [W.D. Ark.], but has not yet determined how much he must pay as a sanction for the contempt) and by the Arkansas bar; and if the political element in the story is emphasized, the story may not end until the elections of 2000. That is why I said earlier only that the "main legal phase" of the ordeal ended on February 12 with the President's acquittal by the Senate. Incidentally, although the independent counsel law expires by its own terms on June 30, 1999, it permits an independent counsel to complete any pending investigation. 28 U.S.C. § 599.

ante—were the best that could be devised on the basis of the information available at the time—are redescribed as avoidable blunders. The tendencies that hindsight bias foments were famously denounced by Tolstoy in *War and Peace*. For him, the basic law of history was the law of unintended consequences.[11] I think there's a lot to Tolstoy's theory of history and that the Clinton-Lewinsky investigation and the ensuing ordeal of the Presidency provide supporting evidence, but that while this is easy to see at present it may become obscured with the passage of time. But no doubt many of the judgments made in this book will some day have to be revised. And a case study, when the case is as multifaceted as this one is, is bound to lack the depth that monographic treatment of each facet would enable. But this particular case study can also be viewed as an empirical test of claims concerning law and philosophy that I have advanced in previous books.[12] Among these are claims for the superiority of pragmatic to formalistic, philosophical, and historical approaches to issues of law and public policy and against the utility of constitutional theory and moral theory in dealing with such issues. A case study is a study (analysis) as well as a case (description). I have tried to do justice to both halves.

The story of Clinton's ordeal is exhilirating as drama but sobering as a commentary on powerful and prestigious American institutions. The story that I shall be telling is a story of the failure of the judiciary, the political establishment, the Congress, the legal profession, and the academic community to cope with a novel challenge. It is also a story of personal failure by Clinton and others. But the institutional failures are the more interesting. We shall see that institutions that look strong may actually be brittle and therefore break when hit from an unexpected angle. This happened with American universities when they were faced with an unanticipated revolt of students in the late 1960s and early 1970s. President Clinton's extraordinary behavior—an explosive mixture of lust and mendacity—sprang an equal surprise on an overlapping set of institutions (universities being implicated in both upheavals), and they couldn't cope either. But because the nation was prosperous and

---

[11]Interestingly, there is evidence that hindsight bias can be reduced or even eliminated by pointing out the role of chance in human affairs and hence the unpredictable character of many events, David Wasserman, Richard O. Lempert, and Reid Hastie, "Hindsight and Causality," 17 *Personality and Social Psychology Bulletin* 30 (1991)—the very features that Tolstoy emphasized.

[12]See the references in note 4 above.

at peace throughout the ordeal, and has a resilience greater than that of any of its institutional components, it was able to weather the storm with what appears to be (although it is too soon to tell, really) minimal damage to the social fabric. Those who consider the stock market an accurate barometer of the nation's social health will say with zero damage.

This book is not a narrative of the ordeal, but Chapter 1 is a narrative, essential to what follows, of the President's conduct in and arising from his affair with Lewinsky. To the extent that the facts are contested, I have indicated both what I think the most probable version is and what its legal significance would be in an ordinary criminal proceeding (for example, if Clinton were the president of a university rather than of the United States). What if any crimes were committed? Are they the types of crime that, given the circumstances—but abstracting not only from Clinton's position as President of the United States but also from the investigative methods of the Independent Counsel—prosecutors prosecute and juries convict for?

Those methods are not discusssed in Chapter 1, but are the focus of Chapter 2, where I review how the Independent Counsel and his allies (including Paula Jones's lawyers and backers), and the President's lawyers and other defenders, developed and as it were marketed their respective versions of the facts. The critical questions here are whether the Independent Counsel committed legal or ethical violations in conducting what amounted to a "sting" operation against the President of the United States, whether the defenders misbehaved as well, and whether any of the misbehavior, prosecutorial or defensive, even if as bad as depicted by the opposing side, has any bearing on whether Clinton would have been prosecuted successfully for criminal conduct were he not President.

The first two chapters should dispel several persistent misunderstandings about the legal significance of Clinton's conduct, such as that no ordinary person would be prosecuted or if prosecuted convicted for what he did, that his only provable misconduct was giving misleading answers to questions about his relationship with Lewinsky, and that a determination of criminal liability requires balancing the defendant's misconduct against any misconduct on the part of the prosecutor. The reader should emerge from these chapters with a clear idea of the legal liabilities of a non-President who committed the acts that the President committed in the aftermath of his affair with Monica Lewinsky. So far as the public record discloses,[13] these acts were indeed crimes, though not as many as the Independent Counsel and the House of Representatives believed if attention is confined to those acts that could be proved criminal beyond a reasonable doubt. It is also possible to regard the Independent Counsel's investigation, though basically ethical so far as appears at this writing,[14] as overkill, given the intrinsic triviality not only of the President's extramarital escapades but also of the Paula Jones litigation, the original scene of the President's criminal violations. Her case was weak, and in any event the courts should not have proceeded with it until the end of Clinton's term of office.

For the hypothetical non-President, the arena for determining guilt and admeasuring punishment would be a federal criminal prosecution for having committed perjury and related crimes of obstructing justice in a federal civil litigation and before a federal grand jury. For President Clinton, once the Independent Counsel decided not to prosecute him criminally before giving the House of Representatives a shot at impeaching him—it is an unsettled question whether a President *can* be prosecuted while in office[15]—the arena was an impeachment proceeding. The impeachment of a federal officer is authorized only for "high Crimes and Misdemeanors," a term the Constitution does not define. The principal issues bearing on the impeachment of President Clinton are whether commission of a crime is either a necessary or a sufficient condition for the impeachment and conviction of a President;[16] whether

---

[13]This is an important qualification. Should the President ever be prosecuted in the ordinary way for the criminal conduct discussed in this book, the judgment of guilty or not guilty will be based on the specific charges brought and on the specific witnesses called and documents admitted in the trial, and not on the record on which the impeachment and Senate trial, and all the legal assessments in this book, are based. Nothing in the book should be taken to prejudge any future criminal or civil proceedings arising out of the matters discussed in it.

[14]This is a particularly important qualification, because the Independent Counsel's investigation of the President is itself, at this writing, under investigation by the Department of Justice for possible ethical and legal misconduct.

[15]See Chapter 3, where I also discuss the fascinating question of whether the President, if prosecuted, can pardon himself (perhaps even in advance of being prosecuted).

[16]The "impeachment" of a President is, technically, the determination by the House of Representatives that the President should be tried by the Senate for violation of the articles of impeachment voted by the House. Only if the Senate convicts the President is he removed from office. "Articles of impeachment" issued by the House thus correspond to an indictment in a criminal case, and the House to the grand jury, though we

the meaning of the Constitution's provisions on impeachment should be regarded as a historical question, to be answered by using the methods of historical inquiry; what weight political and pragmatic considerations should have in an impeachment of the President; and what the procedural rules should be, notably whether the burden of proof required to convict should indeed be the criminal burden of proof beyond a reasonable doubt and whether the House and the Senate should adopt, *in advance of* impeachment, detailed rules designed to bring impeachment proceedings into greater conformity with the requirements of due process of law.

I consider the history and propriety of "political impeachment," that is, the use of the impeachment process to vent purely political disagreement with the President. I also consider the interrelated issues of the trend toward "postelectoral politics" and of Democratic charges that the impeachment of President Clinton was marred by partisanship—even that it was invalid because the impeachment was voted by a lame-duck Congress. Although political impeachment, I conclude, is indeed improper, the impeachment of President Clinton cannot be written off as a political impeachment merely because the vote to impeach was largely on party lines. There was partisanship on both sides of the aisle.

Nor is impeachment proper, as many argued, only when the President misuses the powers of his office (although to some extent he did). Private acts can have grave public consequences—and with fewer redeeming features than public acts, for example of wartime Presidents, that violate positive law but may in doing so advance national interests. But because I conclude that the impeachment power is not limited either to actual crimes or to some narrow set of public acts enumerated by historical precedent, I have to return to the President's conduct and to attempt (in Chapter 4) to evaluate it in broader terms than those of criminal justice. In particular, the moral dimension of his conduct has to be examined. Here the critical distinction is between *private* and *public* morality. Some things that a President does may be immoral yet lack any public dimension, and those probably are not appropriate grounds for impeachment. Others, however, come within the scope of "public morality," the set of moral duties that is attached to an office

---

shall see in Chapter 3 that these analogies must not be pressed too hard. The word "impeachment" is often used to describe the entire process, including the conviction, and I shall employ this usage when there is no danger of ambiguity.

or to an activity that is undertaken voluntarily. In emphasizing these duties I invert the tradition, associated with Machiavelli, that emphasizes that the scruples of everyday life may be inappropriate in a political leader. Political leadership may add moral duties to those incumbent on a private individual rather than diluting the private duties.

The set of moral duties attached to the U.S. Presidency is broad. It includes both *executive* moral duties (moral duties that relate directly to the performance of a President's tasks) and *exemplary* moral duties, that is, moral duties arising from the symbolic dimension of the Presidency. Some of a President's moral duties of either type are so important that their violation might be grounds for impeachment and removal even if he committed no crime. The Lewinsky affair and its aftermath involve the exemplary much more than the executive duties of the Presidency, and the exemplary duties are entwined with the duties of private morality. Only toward the end, with the cruise-missile attack on Iraq during the week that culminated in Clinton's impeachment, did the ordeal begin to degrade his effectiveness as the federal government's chief executive.

President Clinton committed serious breaches of private morality. But they were not the ones to which he confessed: having an "inappropriate" intimate relationship with Lewinsky and misleading his family, friends, subordinate officials, and—placed last in his contrition litany—the American people by denying the existence of the relationship until a DNA test of the semen stains on one of Monica Lewinsky's dresses forced his hand. It is not clear whom the relationship wronged. And Clinton misled very few people—though we shall see that the liar whose lies are not believed may, paradoxically, be a more serious violator of the moral code than the credible liar.

The serious breaches of private morality were Clinton's violations of federal criminal law, which were felonious, numerous, and nontechnical. How far they should be considered serious breaches of *public* morality as well depends on one's conception of the Presidency. An older view, first clearly articulated and defended by Aristotle, exemplified in American history by the character and career of George Washington, and very damaging to President Clinton, conceives of the President as a moral leader and the symbol of our noblest aspirations. Holders of this conception of the Presidency are bound to attach great weight to the fulfillment of what I am calling the President's exemplary moral duties. A newer view—call it "postcharismatic politics"—is that the

American people have attained a level of political maturity at which widespread disillusionment with the moral and intellectual qualities of our political leaders will not cause the sky to fall. The fewer and less demanding the exemplary or "role model" duties assigned to the President, the less plausible it is to base impeachment on a violation of such duties, though when the full range and consequences of President Clinton's conduct are considered it becomes arguable that he disgraced and undermined the Presidency to a degree that warranted his removal from office.

Having considered the President's conduct both in detail and as a whole, as well as the appropriate scope and form of an impeachment proceeding, I ask in Chapter 5 whether he should have been impeached, as he was, and convicted, as he was not. These questions are difficult to answer because of the inescapable vagueness of the standard for impeachment and the importance of imponderable factors in applying the standard. On the one hand, President Clinton engaged in a pattern of criminal behavior and obsessive public lying the tendency of which was to disparage, undermine, and even subvert the judicial system of the United States, the American ideology of the rule of law, and the role and office of the President. On the other hand, the actual impact that his conduct has had or will have on the rule of law and other valued social goods is unknowable and possibly slight. And a decision for or against impeachment rightly involves pragmatic considerations to a degree that would be inappropriate in ordinary judicial proceedings. Those considerations are imponderables too. They include the effect of impeachment on the power of the Presidency and hence on the balance of power among the different branches of the federal government and between federal and state government; if the effect is to shift power from the President to Congress (by no means a certainty) or the states, whether it is a large or a small shift; and whether it is a good or a bad thing to make the Presidency somewhat stronger or somewhat weaker relative to other parts of government and perhaps relative to the private sector as well.

Chapter 5 also picks up and continues the discussion in Chapter 3 of procedural issues relating to Presidential impeachment. I consider the constitutional and prudential issues that would have been created by either a joint congressional resolution of censure or a Senate resolution of censure, as an alternative to conviction and removal from office. I consider whether it would have been proper for the Senate to abort the trial of the President by adjourning it right after it began, as a number of Democratic Senators (and the White House) wanted the Senate to do, or to combine a judgment of acquittal with a finding that the President had engaged in the misconduct alleged in the articles of impeachment, as a number of Republican Senators wanted the Senate to do.

A remarkable feature of the Clinton-Lewinsky saga, and the focus of Chapter 6, has been its polarizing effect; it touched off a *Kulturkampf*. There is a parallel (reminding one of Marx's dictum that every great event or character in history appears twice, the first time as tragedy and the second as farce)[17] to the Dreyfus case. Alfred Dreyfus, it became clear not long after his conviction and imprisonment, was innocent. But though himself conservative and patriotic, albeit Jewish, he had become so potent a symbol of everything the Right hated that it had to deny his innocence. The conduct of the Right in the Dreyfus Affair was in turn so odious to the Left that the affair became for the Left as potent a symbol as it was for the Right. On the basis of the facts developed by Starr's investigation and honed and winnowed in the House and Senate proceedings it appears that Clinton is as guilty of serious criminal conduct as Dreyfus was innocent. But Clinton's opponents on the Right were so odious to the Left that many on the Left, including a number of prominent intellectuals, denied (or evaded the issue of) his guilt, while Clinton himself, though a centrist rather than a leftist—indeed, though arguably the consolidator of the "Reagan Revolution"—became for many on the Right the preeminent symbol of all they hate.[18] *Why* Clinton had this polarizing effect is an important question in its own

---

[17]He had in mind Napoleon and Louis Napoleon.

[18]The assertions in the text concerning "Right" and "Left" must be qualified by acknowledgment that in contemporary American politics these terms identify tendencies rather than well-defined groups. A more nuanced classification, but needlessly cumbersome for my purposes, would distinguish among an extreme Right (including a number of "Clinton haters" and the most conservative Republican politicians), "right leaners" (like William Bennett and James Q. Wilson), centrists (like Clinton himself), "left leaners" or "left liberals" (like John Rawls, Ronald Dworkin, Bruce Ackerman, and many journalists and Democratic politicians), and a "hard Left" (the *Nation* magazine, extreme multiculturalists, Patrick Caddell, Marxists, and the remnants of the "old Left"). The representatives of the academic Left whom we shall encounter in Chapters 6 and 7 are mainly "left leaners" or "left liberals." Another distinction, this one within the Right, is between moralistic conservatives and libertarians. The rightists whom we shall encounter in those chapters are of the former, not the latter, ilk.

right. The key to the answer, I argue, is that the exposure of Clinton's private life made him a symbol not merely of a political position (it is difficult to identify him with a political position), but of a way of life, and an attitude toward personal responsibility, revolting to much of the Right and congenial to, even defining of, much of the contemporary American Left.[19] The debate quickly became frenzied and irrational. The rapidity and extremity of the polarization are illuminated by a recent literature in signaling and social-norm theory that shows how "norm entrepreneurs" can induce people to take sides on issues of little intrinsic moment to them.

In Chapter 7 I try to extract the lessons of the ordeal, apart from those evident from previous chapters. One is the inability of some public intellectuals to resist being caught up in the irrational Manichaeism of the popular and political reactions to Clinton and his troubles. Representative figures of the academic Left have been notable for the partisanship, precipitance, and moral insensitivity of their commentary on *l'affaire* Clinton. Representatives of the academic Right have been notable for their misreading of public opinion, their pessimism, and their hyperbole. The center has done better, and the much-maligned media pretty well. The episode has engendered doubts as to how many academic specialists in such fields as history, moral and political philosophy, and even law are competent to offer useful and disinterested advice on novel issues of public policy. It has engendered doubts about the utility of so-called public intellectuals. It has confirmed suspicions (mine at any rate) that normative moral theory, and cognate forms of legal and political theory, have little to contribute to the public life of the nation.[20] A number of legal professionals, both as participants and as observers, have behaved rather ignominiously as well.

Another lesson to be drawn from the ordeal is the remarkable degree to which political strife stirred up by an issue without clear precedent resembles war as elucidated by military theorists and historians (above all Clausewitz) and by novelists like Stendhal and Tolstoy. Clinton's struggle to save his Presidency was marked by intense emotion, by sudden and drastic reversals of fortune, by betrayals, concealments, and

---

[19]This is not to suggest that he is an apt symbol—that he is "typical" of the people who have embraced him. Nor is it to suggest that everyone who thinks of himself or herself as a "man of the Left" (as we used to say) identifies with or supports the President; I give some counterexamples in Chapter 6.

[20]As I argued at length in *Problematics*, note 4 above.

mis- and disinformation, by gross blunders induced by radical uncertainty that redounded to the advantage of the blunderers, by espionage ("leaks"), mood swings, and the dominance of chance, and by difficulty in checking one's headlong advance in time to avoid a devastating counterattack. The ordeal is unique in its particulars, but it has a structure that the study of warfare in the Clausewitzian tradition illuminates. Reflection on the commonalities between political and other forms of struggle may help us toward a more general understanding of human conflict and enable the country to avoid a repetition of some of the mistakes made by people who became involved in the Clinton-Lewinsky mess or its politico-legal aftermath.

An important lesson is the inability of a Supreme Court none of whose members has substantial political experience to deal adequately with cases that have a heavy political charge. In retrospect the Court's decisions upholding the constitutionality of the independent counsel law and allowing Paula Jones's suit against the President to go forward before he left office appear as naive, unintended, unpragmatic, and gratuitous body blows to the Presidency. Had either decision gone the other way—or even if the decisions had been written more narrowly (for example, if the Court had left open the question whether the independent counsel law can constitutionally be applied to the President, or had instructed the judge in the Paula Jones case to defer as long as possible any inquiry into the President's sex life)—Clinton's affair with Monica Lewinsky, an affair intrinsically (that is, as long as it was secret) devoid of any significance to anyone except Lewinsky, would have remained a secret from the public. The public would not have been the worse for not knowing about it. There would have been no impeachment inquiry, no impeachment, no concerns about the motives behind the President's military actions against terrorists and rogue states in the summer and fall of 1998, no spectacle of the United States Senate playacting at adjudication. The Supreme Court's decisions created a situation that led the President and his defenders into the pattern of cornered-rat behavior that engendered a constitutional storm and that may have embittered American politics, weakened the Presidency, distracted the federal government from essential business, and undermined the rule of law.

I say "may have" because only time will tell whether and to what extent any of these fell consequences will come to pass. It is not even certain whether the rule of law has been damaged or actually strengthened by Clinton's lies, denials, evasions, and pettifogging defenses. And some of the immediate consequences, at least, have not been bad at all. The operation of government has become more transparent; leading elements of the U.S. government, in particular the White House and both houses of Congress, have been seen for what they are. The rawness of political competition has been revealed. Layers of hypocrisy have been stripped away. Plaster saints have been shattered. The general public has been made a little more conversant with issues of legality, ethics, and politics, and thus more civic minded, though because the public's attention span for public issues is limited, the educative effects of the episode may soon dissipate. The complexity of the legal issues, moreover, has resulted in a certain amount of confusion, for example about how perjury is proved and the relevance to criminal liability of irregularities in the prosecution, that I shall try to dispel.

A good effect that probably will be lasting is the encouragement of franker public discussion of sex. The residuum of sexual puritanism in the United States is dysfunctional in a society in which contraceptive advances and the emancipation of women from their traditional role have destroyed the social foundations of traditional sexual morality. Among the more absurd assertions made in the public debate over the crisis are the Right's charge that the revelation of Clinton's affair with Lewinsky has weakened parental control over the sexual behavior of their children and the Left's charge that the Starr Report is voyeuristic and pornographic. People who say these things (and mean them, as perhaps few do) don't understand the family and sexual culture of late-twentieth-century America.

Above all, the ordeal has exposed institutional weaknesses in time for the nation to try to correct them before serious damage is done. They include the incapacity of the academic community, including some of its brightest lights in law, history, moral philosophy, and political theory, to contribute helpfully to a governmental crisis; the limited light that the study of history can shed on contemporary events; the emotionality and hypocrisy of the intellectual class and the mediocrity of the political class; Congress's inability to conduct a Presidential impeachment inquiry that the public will accept as procedurally fair; the hypertrophy of American law (the use of sexual harassment law, and the independent counsel law, to harass officials); the poor performance of many of the princes of the trial bar; and, as I have already stressed, the ineptitude of an unpragmatic Supreme Court locked in a backward-looking jurisprudence, a Court whose decisions all unwittingly incubated a political crisis.

Not all these weaknesses can be cured; perhaps none can be, except to let the independent counsel law expire. It is obvious, for example, that the House and Senate need better rules for the governance of impeachment proceedings; it is unlikely that either house has a sufficient sense of urgency to undertake such a project. But it is good to know where we are weak, because offsetting adjustments in the institutional framework or even individual mindsets, or other defensive measures, may be feasible. In any event, the timing has been fortunate. The effect of the Court's decisions in undermining the Presidency has become visible at a time when the nation can get along for a few years with a somewhat weakened Presidency. And the federal government has been distracted at a time when divided government; complacency-breeding peace, prosperity, and improvements in social indicators; a salutary recognition that the federal government has only limited power to solve difficult problems; and the President's lame-duck status have all made the prospects for active government dim at best. Were this a time of crisis, the Clinton-Lewinsky scandal might have been stillborn—unreported or ignored. (And it is unlikely that Clinton would have been elected or reelected President at a time of national crisis.) It is not a time of crisis. The nation seems to be running nicely on autopilot just now; a symptom is the total indifference of the stock market, and the economy more broadly, both national and international, to the "crisis" of Clinton's Presidency. Nineteen ninety-eight was a good year for staging an edifying political drama.

CHAPTER 1

The President's Conduct

The Facts

Monica Lewinsky, age twenty-one, fresh out of college, and attractive, aggressive, monied, and sexually experienced, became an unpaid White House intern in July 1995.[1] She and the President soon began flirting, though at first from a distance because as an intern she had no opportunity to get close to him. But in November, in consequence of a government shutdown caused by a budget standoff between the President and the Republican-controlled Congress, interns were assigned to work in the West Wing, where the Oval Office is located. Lewinsky had by this time turned twenty-two and been hired into a regular though low-level job in the White House. But the paperwork for the new job had not been completed, and so technically she was still an intern.

---

[1]My account is based partly on the Starr Report (technically, the Independent Counsel's "referral" to the House of Representatives), but more on the five volumes (some 8,000 pages, many in a condensed format that requires the aid of a magnifying glass to read) that the House Judiciary Committee published of excerpts, edited by the Committee, from the even more voluminous supporting evidence (much of it grand jury testimony) that Starr had submitted to it. See *Referral from Independent Counsel Kenneth W. Starr,* H. Doc. No. 310, 105th Cong., 2d Sess. (Sept. 11, 1998) (the "Starr Report"); *Appendices to the Referral to the U.S. House of Representatives,* H. Doc. No. 311, 105th Cong., 2d Sess. (Sept. 18, 1998); *Supplementary Materials to the Referral to the U.S. House of Representatives,* H. Doc. No. 316, 105th Cong., 2d Sess. (Sept. 28, 1998). The rebuttals to the Starr Report issued by the President's lawyers focused on legal issues and on the conduct of the investigation. They made relatively little effort to rebut the strictly factual allegations in the report, although they did quarrel—and with some justification, as we shall see—with a number of the inferences that the Independent Counsel and the House drew from those allegations.

The President and Lewinsky met one evening in the West Wing during the November shutdown, acknowledged a mutual attraction, and, in a moment of privacy in one of the offices in the rabbit warren that is the West Wing, Clinton asked whether he could kiss her and with no hesitation she consented. Later that night they had their first sexual encounter. These encounters (ten in number), which continued at a diminishing rate for the next sixteen months, followed a set pattern both as to time and place[2] and as to the sexual acts. She would perform fellatio on him and he would fondle her breasts and genitalia, frequently inducing orgasm; sometimes he would be talking on the phone (in three instances to Congressmen about government business) while she was fellating him. She wanted to have vaginal intercourse with him but he refused; indeed, he did not even ejaculate until the last two of their encounters.

Eight of the encounters (all of which were furtively staged in the President's study, hallway, or bathroom, rooms adjacent to the Oval Office and affording a degree of privacy) occurred between November 1995 and the following April. That month Evelyn Lieberman, a Deputy Chief of Staff to the President, had Lewinsky transferred against her will to a job in the Defense Department as confidential assistant (that is, secretary) to the Department's public affairs officer. Several of Clinton's White House aides appear to double as Presidential "minders" responsible for keeping the President away from attractive young women.[3] In May 1994, Clinton had been sued by Paula Jones, an employee of the Arkansas state government when Clinton was Governor

---

[2]As one Secret Service agent testified, referring to the period after Lewinsky was transferred from the White House to the Pentagon, "there was a pattern there . . . When Monica would come in when I was working, it was always like on a Saturday morning or a Sunday morning around 9:00 or 10:00 in the morning. Nobody else would be around in the West Wing except for the President and Betty [Betty Currie, the President's secretary]. Once Monica came in, even though the President was over in the residence, we know [sic] he would be coming over to the oval once Monica came in. It was just like clockwork." *Supplementary Materials,* note 1 above, vol. 1, p. 463. Many of the private meetings between the President and Lewinsky involved no sexual activity.

[3]Monica Lewinsky and Linda Tripp called them "protectors." See, for example, id., vol. 3, p. 4169. Cf. David Maraniss, *The Clinton Enigma: A Four-and-a-Half-Minute Speech Reveals This President's Entire Life* 60–61 (1998). Despite its garish subtitle, this is a responsible book by the author of a sympathetic though not uncritical biography of Clinton before he ran for President, *First in His Class: A Biography of Bill Clinton* (1995), on which *A Four-and-a-Half-Minute Speech* draws heavily.

of Arkansas, for sexual harassment, and the suit was still pending in 1996, which was also the year in which Clinton was running for re-election. The minders had noticed Lewinsky hanging around outside the Oval Office. Whether they suspected what was going on between the President and Lewinsky, or merely wanted to minimize the possibility of rumors or hanky-panky during the campaign and against the background of the Paula Jones litigation and the history of Clinton's adulteries, is unclear, although the former is the more plausible inference.[4] In any event, Lewinsky had to go. An additional reason was that her work was unsatisfactory because she was spending so much time away from her desk, roaming the West Wing (her office was in the East Wing). She was the classic "clutch" or "hall surfer," more interested in seeing and being seen with "principals," such as the President and the Vice President, than in doing her job. The Secret Service agents who guard the President were pretty certain that he was sexually involved with Lewinsky. Some of them also believed, though with less confidence, that he had had similar liaisons with other women who worked in or visited the White House.

With Lewinsky off the premises, it was difficult for her and the President to get together. When employed in the White House she had used the pretext, suggested by Clinton, of bringing him documents in order to explain her frequent presence in the Oval Office. That was no longer possible. And in May, by which time Lewinsky had fallen in love with the President ("he was sunshine," she explained to the grand jury),[5] he told her that he was ending their relationship. Whether he had gotten tired of her, was afraid that she was indiscreet, or, as he told her, felt guilty about having an extramarital relationship, is impossible to determine. The relationship was not broken off completely. The President and Lewinsky engaged in phone sex (a form of mutual masturbation)[6] from time to time, and exchanged gifts. And she made occasional visits to his office. She would be ushered into his office by the President's secretary, Betty Currie, who tried to conceal these visits, as well as the President's phone calls to Lewinsky, from the minders.

---

[4]See, for example, the interview and testimony of White House employee Jennifer Palmieri, in *Supplementary Materials,* note 1 above, vol. 3, pp. 3183–3200.

[5]*Appendices,* note 1 above, vol. 1, p. 968.

[6]One of the many gifts that Lewinsky gave Clinton was Nicholson Baker's *Vox* (1992), a graphic novel about phone sex.

There were no sexual encounters in 1996 after Lewinsky was transferred to the Pentagon. The last two occurred in 1997 (the second in March). In May of that year, just a few days before the Supreme Court ruled that the Paula Jones suit could proceed,[7] the President again told Lewinsky that their sexual relationship was at an end. Lewinsky accepted this. But she did not break off all contact with the President. She had been pestering him for a job in the White House ever since the November election; she disliked her job in the Pentagon and feared that her transfer from the White House would look bad on her resumé— would be interpreted as punishment or demotion even though the Pentagon job carried a higher salary. And so her efforts to get reemployed by the White House did not abate with the end of the sexual phase of her relationship with the President. Indeed, she became extraordinarily persistent, bombarding Betty Currie with phone calls in an effort to get through to the President. He repeatedly promised to help her obtain a White House job, but did little toward this end; in all probability he didn't want her anywhere near him.

Eventually Lewinsky realized that she would never get a White House job. She decided to leave Washington for New York, where her mother had moved, and she enlisted Clinton in her job search. He no doubt wanted her out of Washington and in a job in which she would be happy and keep her mouth shut about their relationship. In short order she received an offer of a job with the U.S. Ambassador to the United Nations, Bill Richardson. The offer was made on November 3, 1997. It is likely though not certain that Clinton was instrumental in the making of the offer. He also coached her over the phone for her interview with Richardson.

Lewinsky had already decided, however, that she would prefer to work in the private sector, and so she didn't accept Richardson's offer.[8] She had heard that Vernon Jordan, a prominent Washington lawyer who was a close friend of Clinton, was very good at getting people jobs; and through Betty Currie, a friend of Jordan's, Lewinsky had obtained an interview with him in the first week of November. Jordan was sure that Clinton had told Currie to ask him to help get Lewinsky a job in New York. After meeting with Lewinsky, Jordan told Clinton that he was trying to help her, and Clinton was pleased. Jordan made a few

[7]The President's lawyers had asked the Court to suspend the suit until he left office.
[8]Eventually, on January 5, 1998, she rejected it.

calls on Lewinsky's behalf to business associates in New York, but he was traveling a lot that month and his efforts on her behalf were quite limited.

Meanwhile, discovery was proceeding in the Paula Jones case. On December 5, 1997, her lawyers submitted a list of persons whom they wanted to depose—and Lewinsky's name was on it. The district judge who was presiding in the Jones case, Susan Webber Wright, had authorized Jones's lawyers to inquire into sexual relationships between Clinton and his subordinates in either state or federal government. The lawyers had learned about the President's dalliance with Lewinsky from a Lewinsky confidante, Linda Tripp.

On December 17, Clinton told Lewinsky in a phone conversation that her name was on the list of persons to be deposed by Jones's lawyers. She was upset. Clinton suggested that she might be able to avoid being deposed by filing an affidavit. He also repeated their "cover story"—she could say that when she visited the White House it was to see Betty Currie and that when she was in his office it was to deliver documents. It was implicit that the affidavit would deny a sexual relationship. A truthful affidavit would not have staved off a deposition. On the contrary, it would have spurred Paula Jones's lawyers to depose Lewinsky in an effort to find out whether she had received benefits in exchange for having sex with the President. Jones was claiming to have suffered job detriments as punishment for having spurned the President's advances; had Lewinsky been rewarded for accepting those advances, this would be further evidence of quid pro quo sexual harassment and thus would bolster Jones's case.

On December 19, Paula Jones's lawyers subpoenaed Lewinsky to appear for a deposition in late January. The subpoena directed her to bring with her any gifts that she had received from the President. She had received and retained almost twenty gifts from the President (all of small monetary value), ranging from a hatpin to a book of poetry. Now upset almost to the point of hysteria, she called Vernon Jordan and told him about the subpoena.[9] He told her to come to his office, and there he asked her point-blank whether she had had a sexual relationship with the President. She said no, but she didn't think Jordan believed her

---

[9]She did not tell him one of the things that worried her most about the subpoena— that it specified, among the gifts sought, hatpins. This showed that Paula Jones's lawyers had inside information and were not merely shooting in the dark.

denial. Apparently she was trying to signal him discreetly that she had been the President's girlfriend, so that Jordan would understand that he should exert himself on her behalf. Jordan said she needed a lawyer, and referred her to one—to whom she repeated, this time presumably convincingly, her denial that she had had a sexual relationship with the President. The lawyer drafted her affidavit accordingly.

Lewinsky also spoke to President Clinton. She raised with him the possibility of hiding the gifts or giving them to Betty Currie to hold. The President, according to her testimony, was noncommittal; according to his testimony, he told her that she would have to turn over to the Jones lawyers whatever she had in her possession that the subpoena called for.

This conversation took place on the morning of December 28, 1997. In the course of this meeting the President gave Lewinsky several Christmas presents. That afternoon, according to Lewinsky's testimony, Betty Currie phoned her and said she understood that Lewinsky had something to give her. Lewinsky said she did. Currie then drove to Lewinsky's apartment, picked up a box full of the President's gifts to Lewinsky (some of them, however, Lewinsky surreptitiously retained), and took it home and put it under her bed. Currie testified that it was Lewinsky, not she, who placed the phone call and suggested that Currie take custody of the gifts.

Lewinsky had breakfast with Jordan on December 31. She testified that at this breakfast Jordan told her to destroy any drafts of notes that she had sent the President; and when she got home, she did so. He denied to the grand jury that they had had breakfast or discussed the notes. He recanted this testimony when he was deposed during the Senate trial of the President. He now remembered that they had indeed had breakfast on December 31 and had discussed the notes, but he insisted that he had not told her to destroy them.

Lewinsky shared with the President her uncertainty about what her affidavit should say about why she had been transferred to the Pentagon. He suggested that she say that people in the White House office in which she had worked (the Office of Legislative Affairs) had gotten the Pentagon job, or helped get it, for her; actually, it had been arranged on the initiative of Evelyn Lieberman in order to separate Lewinsky from the President.

After editing the draft affidavit that her lawyer had prepared, Lewinsky signed the affidavit and showed the signed affidavit to Jordan. It is unclear why she did this, but she has denied that her signing an affidavit helpful to the President was part of the compensation for Jordan's getting her a job. She wanted the President, too, to read the draft of her affidavit, but he declined, saying he had seen fifteen such affidavits. It is unclear what he meant by that; he has refused to explain.

The day after Lewinsky showed Jordan her signed affidavit, he went into action. A member of the board of directors of Revlon, Inc., and a friend of the chairman of Revlon's executive committee, Ronald Perelman,[10] Jordan called Perelman and recommended that Revlon hire Lewinsky; earlier he had spoken about her to a relatively junior executive of Perelman's company. On January 9, 1998, two days after Jordan's call to Perelman, Revlon offered Lewinsky a job. When, four days later, she accepted the offer (withdrawn as soon as the scandal broke) and told Jordan, he relayed the news to the President, who expressed satisfaction.

One week later Lewinsky's lawyer mailed a copy of her affidavit, together with a motion to quash the subpoena, to the district court and to Paula Jones's lawyers. Clinton was deposed by those lawyers the next day, January 17, in the presence of Judge Wright. Much of the deposition concerned Lewinsky. The source of the lawyers' knowledge of Clinton's affair with Lewinsky was her former friend (and present enemy) Linda Tripp, who like Lewinsky had formerly worked in the White House and been transferred to the Pentagon and, also like Lewinsky, was on the witness list in the Jones case.

Tripp had worked in the Bush White House, and had been held over when Clinton took office in 1993. In the summer of 1996, disgusted (she claims) with what she considered to be a variety of shabby practices by the Clinton White House, "I made a decision to set the record straight, just to share what I had seen."[11] She got in touch with a conservative literary agent, in fact a Clinton hater, Lucianne Goldberg.[12] Goldberg wanted Tripp to write a book, an exposé of the Clinton White House. Tripp toyed with the idea but quickly dropped it. She was afraid

---

[10]Perelman is effectively the owner of Revlon, since he is the controlling shareholder of the holding company that owns it.

[11]*Supplementary Materials,* note 1 above, vol. 3, p. 4238.

[12]See Ryan Lizza, "Freepers Creepers," *New Republic,* Nov. 23, 1998, p. 18; Elisabeth Bumiller, "The Agent: Tripp Friend Says She's Proud of Her Role," *New York Times* (national ed.), Feb. 13, 1999, p. A10 (Goldberg is "a self-described Clinton hater"). I discuss the phenomenon of "Clinton hating" in the next chapter and also in Chapter 6.

that publishing such a book would cost her her job and that the book would not earn her enough money to compensate her for that cost. This was before Lewinsky told Tripp, in the fall of 1996, about her relationship with the President.

One of the things that Tripp had "seen" in the White House may have been critical to her eventual decision to tape record her phone conversations with Lewinsky. In March 1997, Michael Isikoff, a reporter for *Newsweek,* asked Tripp about an incident in 1993 involving a friend or former friend of hers, a White House volunteer named Kathleen Willey, who had told Isikoff that she had been "groped" by the President and that Tripp had been a witness. Tripp told Isikoff that she had run into Willey shortly after the latter had come out of the Oval Office and that Willey was "disheveled. Her face was red and her lipstick was off. She was flustered, happy and joyful." Tripp said that Willey had told her that "the president had taken her from the Oval Office to his private office, a small adjoining hideaway, and kissed and fondled her." Thus it "was not a case of sexual harassment." Tripp's statements to Isikoff were accurately reported in *Newsweek.*[13] She also told him, and this he did not report, that rather than wasting his time with the Kathleen Willey story he should be investigating a relationship between the President and a White House intern. Tripp did not tell Isikoff the intern's name.

Tripp claims that Isikoff had promised not to reveal her own name in his article, but he did—along with a comment by the President's lawyer in the Jones case, Robert Bennett, that Tripp was "not to be believed." For by this time Paula Jones's lawyers had subpoenaed Willey, and the White House was denying that the President had ever had an erotic encounter with her, whether of a harassing or, as Tripp had told Isikoff, of a purely consensual nature.

Shortly after being interviewed by Isikoff, Tripp began taking detailed notes of her conversations with Lewinsky. She began tape recording the conversations in October at the suggestion of Lucianne Goldberg, with whom she had reestablished contact. Tripp testified before the grand jury that her motive in taping her conversations with Lewinsky was to protect herself in the Jones case. After the *Newsweek* article appeared in August 1997, it was certain that Paula Jones's lawyers would sub-

---

[13]See Michael Isikoff, "A Twist in Jones v. Clinton: Her Lawyers Subpoena Another Woman," *Newsweek,* Aug. 11, 1997, pp. 30, 31.

poena Tripp, and they might ask her what she knew about Lewinsky. Tripp's lawyer had warned her that she might be asked about other women, besides Willey, with whom the President had been intimate—and that designation included Lewinsky. If Tripp was asked about Lewinsky and lied, she might be prosecuted for perjury, while if she told the truth she might be disbelieved—after all, Bennett had claimed to disbelieve her statement about Kathleen Willey. In that event, too, she would be at risk of being prosecuted for perjury, because Lewinsky and the President were bound to deny the relationship under oath and were likely to be believed. Indeed, Lewinsky urged Tripp to deny any knowledge of the relationship should she be asked about it at a deposition, assuring her that there would be two other denials under oath—Lewinsky's and the President's.

Tripp thus claims that it was in self-defense that she began taping her phone conversations with Lewinsky. This probably is not the whole truth. She had urged Isikoff to investigate the President's relationship with an intern. She admitted to the grand jury that she desired the relationship to become known; this was part of a broader desire to expose what she considered the seamy goings-on, sexual and otherwise, in the Clinton White House. She had confided in Goldberg, whom she knew to be a Clinton hater. Some of her testimony to the grand jury suggests that she is one herself—that she believes that Clinton or his aides may have been involved in the so-called murders that the Clinton haters like to hint about.

With the encouragement of Goldberg and of Jones's lawyers and backers,[14] Tripp got in touch with the Independent Counsel's office early in January 1998. She told his staff everything she knew about Lewinsky's affair with the President, and gave them the tapes. Meanwhile, Paula Jones's lawyers had learned about the affair, and Tripp's role, from Goldberg. Tripp agreed to be interviewed by them in lieu of being deposed, on January 16, the day before Clinton's deposition. And so the lawyers were primed to question Clinton about Lewinsky at his deposition the next day. Clinton seems to have been caught off guard by some of their questions. He had been unaware until then that Jones's lawyers knew so much about his affair with Lewinsky, although he knew they suspected something because they had subpoenaed her.

[14]See Don Van Natta, Jr., and Jill Abramson, "Quietly, a Team of Lawyers Kept Paula Jones's Case Alive," *New York Times* (national ed.), Jan. 24, 1999, pp. 1, 21.

Asked whether he had ever been alone with Lewinsky, Clinton said that he did not remember (the videotape of the deposition shows him furrowing his brow in an apparent effort to jog his recollection) but that he might have been alone with her briefly on a few occasions when she delivered documents to him. He denied that he had had sexual relations with her, even though the term "sexual relations" was broadly defined for purposes of the deposition: "a person engages in 'sexual relations' when the person knowingly engages in or causes . . . contact with the genitalia, anus, groin, breast, inner thigh, or buttocks of any person with an intent to arouse or gratify the sexual desire of any person . . . 'Contact' means intentional touching, either directly or through clothing." That is, "sexual relations" was defined to include what used to be called "heavy petting." Clinton studied the definition, and indicated that he understood it, before denying that he had had sexual relations with Lewinsky. He was not questioned about specific sexual acts, however, such as fellatio.

The day after his deposition, a Sunday, a shaken President Clinton summoned Betty Currie to his office. They had a conversation in which he appears to have been asking her to back up the testimony that he had given at his deposition. According to Currie's testimony before the grand jury, he said such things as "We were never really alone," "You could see and hear everything," "Monica came on to me, and I never touched her, right?" and "She wanted to have sex with me, and I can't do that."[15] The first two statements were plainly false, and the third and fourth could not have been questions because they were asking for information that Currie was in no position to give.[16] He had a similar conversation with her a few days later; it is unclear whether this was before or after it became public knowledge that Independent Counsel Kenneth Starr was investigating Clinton's relationship with Lewinsky.

For the past three and a half years Starr had been investigating President Clinton's possible involvement in criminal activities growing out of the Whitewater real estate development in which Clinton and his wife had been investors in the early 1980s. The day before Clinton's deposition in the Paula Jones case, Starr obtained from the Special Division of the U.S. Court of Appeals for the District of Columbia Circuit

[15]*Supplementary Materials,* note 1 above, vol. 1, p. 559.

[16]As she acknowledged with reference to the third statement: "And 'Come on to me,' I considered that more of a statement as opposed to a question." Id., vol. 1, p. 682.

authorization to expand his investigation to embrace possible obstruction of justice in the Paula Jones case.[17] Starr had learned from Linda Tripp not only about the relationship between Clinton and Lewinsky but also that Vernon Jordan had been working to secure a job for Lewinsky with Revlon. That rang a bell. Jordan had previously obtained a lucrative consulting contract with Revlon for Webster Hubbell, the disgraced former Associate Attorney General who Starr believed was withholding knowledge of criminal conduct by the Clintons in the Whitewater matter. It seemed that Jordan might be trying to buy Lewinsky's silence in a similar fashion;[18] Lewinsky herself had in a taped conversation with Linda Tripp expressed concern that someone might draw such a parallel. And Lewinsky had given Tripp, who in turn had handed over to the Independent Counsel's office, a three-page memorandum of "talking points" to guide Tripp in giving dishonest testimony if deposed in the Paula Jones case. The talking points seemed too sophisticated to have been drafted by Lewinsky without legal assistance, and the Independent Counsel suspected that the assistance had come directly or indirectly from the White House.

Lewinsky had both signed a false affidavit, thus committing perjury when the affidavit was filed,[19] and attempted to suborn Tripp to commit perjury.[20] The conversations that Tripp had taped proved the former; the tapes and the "talking points" memo proved the latter. The fact that the tapes may have been made in violation of state law would not have defeated a federal prosecution; and perjury and other obstructions of justice committed in a federal proceeding, as the Jones case was, are federal crimes. So Lewinsky was highly vulnerable to prosecution. Lawyers from the Independent Counsel's office confronted her on January 16 with their knowledge of her crimes and offered her immunity from

---

[17]The Special Division is a panel of three federal judges that appoints, and has some oversight duties with respect to, independent counsels.

[18]"The timing, sources, and extent of the payments [to Hubbell, including those from Revlon] make the belief that they were hush money reasonable." United States v. Hubbell, 167 F.3d 552, 563 (D.C. Cir. 1999) (per curiam). In 1994, while under criminal investigation, Hubbell had received $450,000 in consulting fees, and it has never been made clear what if anything he did to earn those fees.

[19]The filing occurred on January 17, 1998, when the affidavit, which she had signed on January 7, was received by the district court, having been mailed on the sixteenth.

[20]Among other things, she had offered Tripp an interest in a condominium in Australia that Lewinsky owned if Tripp would deny that Lewinsky had told her about a relationship with the President.

prosecution if she would cooperate with them and specifically if she would agree to record conversations with Clinton and Jordan. She refused.

So matters stood when, on January 21, 1998, the world learned about the Tripp tapes and the Independent Counsel's expanded investigation. The essentials of the scandal as I have narrated them were fully and on the whole accurately revealed by the media within a few days. Nevertheless, President Clinton emphatically, repeatedly, and unequivocally denied, both publicly to the nation on television and privately to his assistants, to his friends (such as Jordan), and to the members of the Cabinet, that he had had any form of sexual or otherwise improper contact with Lewinsky, whom he described to one of his assistants, Sidney Blumenthal, as a reputed "stalker." It is plausible, though not proven, that Blumenthal—who, when his grand jury testimony was published, was exposed as having publicly misrepresented the questions he had been asked by the prosecutors, in an effort to convince the public that the Independent Counsel's investigation was a puritanical witch hunt[21]—fed the media stories that Lewinsky was a stalker, deranged, "not playing with a full deck," and, in short, unworthy of belief.

The period of total denial lasted until August 17, 1998, and included, besides the efforts to trash Lewinsky, a chorus of emphatic public denials of the Lewinsky affair and attacks on Starr by Presidential aides, lawyers, and political supporters. During this period, Starr's team conducted a meticulous investigation. The principal investigative tool was a Washington, D.C., grand jury that Starr was already using to investigate aspects of the Whitewater matter, such as the mysterious disappearance and later reappearance of pertinent documents.[22] The President's lawyers tried to derail, or failing that delay, Starr's investigation

[21]James Bennet, "The Aide: Managers Pursue Adviser's Talks with Clintons," *New York Times,* Feb. 3, 1999, p. A15. For example, Blumenthal "recalled" having been asked, "Does the President's religion include sexual intercourse?" and having been "forced to answer questions about conversations, as part of my job, with The New York Times, CNN, CBS, Time magazine, U.S. News, The New York Daily News, The Chicago Tribune, The New York Observer, and there may have been a few others." He had not been asked these questions. His grand jury testimony appears in *Supplementary Materials,* note 1 above, vol. 1, pp. 159–206. He was upbraided for his misrepresentations by the foreperson of the grand jury during a subsequent appearance. Id. at 206.

[22]Later, Starr convened a second grand jury to investigate the Clinton-Lewinsky matter, but I will ignore that detail.

of the Lewinsky matter by making expansive claims of executive and attorney-client privilege with respect to witnesses summoned before the grand jury. They also proposed a new privilege which would prevent Secret Service officers from testifying about conduct by the President that they observed in the course of performing their duties. The President's claims of privilege were quickly and in some instances abruptly rejected by the courts.[23]

On July 28, 1998, Lewinsky, advised by new and more experienced counsel, signed an immunity agreement with the Independent Counsel's office. The office then interrogated her at length, both inside and outside the grand jury, to establish the details of her story. The story was corroborated by the mass of evidence that the Independent Counsel had already extracted from her e-mails, from the Tripp tapes, from White House telephone records, from grand jury appearances by Betty Currie and by friends and relatives to whom Lewinsky had revealed her relationship with the President, from testimony by Secret Service agents which established the frequency of Lewinsky's private visits to the Oval Office, and, most decisively, from DNA testing of one of Lewinsky's dresses, on which traces of semen were obtained that, beyond any reasonable doubt, had come from the President. Although Betty Currie testified that Lewinsky had called her about the return of the gifts, rather than, as Lewinsky had testified, Currie's calling Lewinsky, she acknowledged that Lewinsky might have the more accurate recollection of the incident. Also during this period (a hiatus between the media explosion in January and the media explosion that followed the President's speech to the nation on August 17, 1998,[24] a few hours after he testified before the grand jury), the district court dismissed Paula Jones's suit on the ground that there was no evidence that she had suffered sufficient injury to have a valid claim of harassment.[25] She appealed.

After protracted negotiations, the President agreed to testify before the grand jury over closed-circuit television from the White House. In his testimony[26] he acknowledged (unavoidably, in view of the results of the DNA test, which had not yet been announced but which he must have assumed he would "flunk") having had an "inappropriate"

---

[23]For a summary of this litigation, see *Appendices*, note 1 above, vol. 1, pp. 183–200.
[24]For the text of this famous four-and-a-half-minute speech, see id., vol. 2, p. 2523.
[25]Jones v. Clinton, 990 F. Supp. 657 (E.D. Ark. 1998).
[26]*Appendices*, note 1 above, vol. 1, p. 453.

relationship with Lewinsky involving "intimate contact" of a sexual nature, though he claimed that the first sexual encounter had occurred in 1996 and that there had been only one encounter, not two encounters, in 1997. He refused to go into the details of his sexual relationship with Lewinsky, but implicitly acknowledged that she had fellated him. He was emphatic, however, that he had not testified falsely in his deposition in the Paula Jones case when he had denied having sexual relations with Lewinsky. Fellatio, he claimed, is not a form of "sexual relations" within the meaning given the term for purposes of the deposition because the person fellated causes contact with the lips of the fellator rather than with any of the body parts listed in the definition. He acknowledged that fondling Lewinsky would constitute sexual relations within that meaning. And so by denying that he had had "sexual relations with her," he implicitly but unmistakably denied having fondled her.

He denied having lied when he testified at the deposition that he had not been "alone" with Lewinsky except on a few occasions when she was delivering documents. They were not really "alone," he testified, because there had always been other people in the vicinity. But he conceded that no one except himself and Lewinsky had actually been present at their sexual encounters.

He denied having helped her with job-hunting in order to dissuade her from testifying truthfully in the Paula Jones case, or having done anything else to encourage her to lie. He denied that in telling her that if the gifts were subpoenaed she would have to hand over whatever she had, he had been hinting that she should get rid of them. He denied having suggested to Betty Currie that she recover from Lewinsky the gifts that he had given her or having tried to shape any testimony that Currie might be asked to give either in the Paula Jones case or in a grand jury proceeding. He testified that in talking to Currie after his deposition he had just been trying to refresh his recollection of the details of his affair with Lewinsky and anyway that he hadn't known that Currie might be called as a witness or even that there was a grand jury investigation. He admitted trying to conceal his sexual affair with Lewinsky from all and sundry but denied that his motivation had been either the Jones suit or the Independent Counsel's investigation. And he denied having told any actual falsehoods to his aides, although according to their testimony he told them he had not had sex in any form, specifically including oral sex, with Lewinsky.

After testifying before the grand jury, President Clinton and his lawyers and supporters, while now publicly conceding that the President had had an "inappropriate relationship" with Lewinsky and had made misleading statements, continued to insist that he had not actually lied in the Paula Jones deposition; and now they added that he had not lied in his grand jury appearance either. He repeated these denials under oath on November 27, 1998, in response to eighty-one questions put to him by the House Judiciary Committee. Most of his answers were evasive or nonresponsive rather than outright falsehoods. But he testified falsely when he denied recalling any conversation with Lewinsky about her status as a witness in the Paula Jones case; when he denied discussing with Currie the recovery of the gifts from Lewinsky; when he denied having lied in testifying in his deposition in the Paula Jones case that he hadn't recalled giving any gifts to Lewinsky; and when he denied having lied in testifying that Lewinsky had given him gifts only once or twice—she had given him some thirty gifts. He came within a millimeter of lying when he said that he had been telling the truth when he told the grand jury that he had "never told anybody to lie" about his relationship with Lewinsky. He had suggested lies to both Lewinsky and Currie, as well as to aides who he knew would be talking to the media or testifying before the grand jury; but he hadn't actually *told* them to lie.

Just days after his grand jury testimony—at a time when calls for his impeachment were mounting in the wake of his acknowledgment of his affair with Lewinsky and the poor impression made on media pundits and the Congress by the four-and-half-minute television address in which he acknowledged the affair and that he had misled people about it—President Clinton ordered a cruise-missile attack on suspected terrorist sites in Afghanistan and the Sudan. Although there was some suspicion that he had ordered the attack to distract public attention from the swelling scandal, the suspicion was largely dispelled by assurances from defense officials. When four months later, on the eve of the debate over impeachment in the House of Representatives, the President suddenly ordered a massive cruise-missile attack on Iraq, a larger wave of suspicion broke. Again the defense officials assured the nation that their recommendation that the President order the attack was unrelated to a concern with the President's political fortunes, and undoubtedly this was true, since the defense community had wanted to attack Iraq for years. But in the past the President had hesitated to endorse such recommendations. It is impossible to determine on the basis of what is known at present whether the President's decision to accept the recommendation of his military and national security advisors to bomb Iraq was influenced by a desire to head off the looming vote for impeachment. The President assured the nation that it had not been; but by December 18, 1998, when he offered this assurance, his credibility lay in tatters.

I have now sketched the facts that are essential to resolving the issues that are the subject of this book. Left out are a myriad of details, many of them fascinating from a human-interest standpoint. The evidentiary record compiled in a legal proceeding always contains details that however interesting have no relevance to the legal issues. And while my interest in the circumstances of and surrounding the Clinton-Lewinsky investigation extends beyond the legal issues, most of the details that I have omitted are irrelevant to the moral, political, and cultural issues as well. Public understanding of the ordeal touched off by the revelation of the affair has been retarded by a surfeit of extraneous detail. The facts that matter are few and simple, the ones I narrate in this chapter plus a few in subsequent chapters.

My sketch depends critically on the credibility of Monica Lewinsky; and so it is necessary to consider how credible she is. As Clinton's defenders pointed out, Lewinsky had lied under oath in the affidavit she submitted in the Paula Jones case; had told lies to Linda Tripp, for example about the complicity of Lewinsky's mother in Lewinsky's plan to lie to protect the President; had admitted to Tripp that she had been lying all her life; and had told tall tales, such as that she had had lunch with Mrs. Clinton on Martha's Vineyard or had had a sexual encounter with the President in which she had taken off all her clothes. Moreover, Lewinsky was never subjected to the fires of cross-examination.

Not much weight, however, can be given to her lies or to the fact that she wasn't cross-examined. Everyone lies in everyday life; and many people lie under oath, especially about sex—that was one of the cornerstones of the President's defense. The question is whether Lewinsky told the truth about the matters on which she was interrogated under oath by lawyers from the Independent Counsel's office, by grand jurors, and eventually by the House prosecutors when they deposed her on February 1 during the President's trial before the Senate. With regard to those matters, the voluminous statements, both oral and written, that she made over the course of more than fifteen months, from the first conversations taped by Linda Tripp in October 1997 to her final interrogation by lawyers from the Independent Counsel's office in September 1998 and her Senate deposition of February 1, 1999, are consistent to a high degree (no one is entirely consistent), plausible in both the main narrative and the details, and abundantly corroborated by other witnesses, by documents, by White House phone logs, by the history and character of the President, and by nonverbal evidence such as the dress. The picture that emerges from this huge record is of a woman who is intelligent,[27] who has a retentive memory, and who has very little "woman-scorned" hostility toward the President. Although she has long taken antidepressant drugs such as Prozac, there is no evidence of a psychiatric disorder that might cause her to confabulate. Nor can much significance be attached to the fact that she once falsified her college transcript to impress her father; and as far as submitting a perjurious affidavit is concerned, she was encouraged to do that by the President of the United States. Most important, only two of her assertions that bear on central issues have been denied. The President, as I have noted, denied that he had fondled her. The denial is utterly implausible, implying as it does that in all of their encounters he merely sat (or stood) passively while she fellated him. He had a powerful incentive to lie about this, moreover, since to admit that he had fondled Lewinsky would be to confess that he had lied in his deposition in the Paula Jones case. Lewinsky, protected from prosecution by a blanket immunity conditioned only on her telling the truth, had no incentive to lie.

The second denial is Currie's that she initiated the recovery of the gifts. On this point, too, Lewinsky's is the more credible testimony. Currie, like the President, had an incentive to lie because to acknowledge that she was acting as the President's agent to recover the gifts might implicate her in his obstruction of justice. Her testimony before the grand jury, unlike Lewinsky's, seems, whenever it got near sensitive questions, nervous, evasive, forgetful (perhaps feignedly so), uncertain,

---

[27]There has been a tendency to underestimate Lewinsky's intelligence because she had mediocre grades at a rather obscure, though actually well regarded, college (Lewis and Clark, in Portland, Oregon). The evidentiary record reveals a woman who is savvy and articulate, with a good feel for legal and political issues; it appears that she really did draft the "talking points" herself, although she borrowed some material from her affidavit, which (as is customary) her lawyer had drafted.

and at times downright unbelievable, for example when she denied suspecting that there was a physical relationship between the President and Lewinsky. Her acknowledgment of the possibility that Lewinsky had a superior recollection of the incident concerning the gifts sounds like an effort to avoid prosecution for perjury; no doubt her lawyer warned her, as Lewinsky's lawyer had warned *her* in December 1997 when it looked as if Lewinsky would be deposed, that it is perilous to make a positive denial under oath. Telephone company records reveal that Currie called Lewinsky on the afternoon of December 28 from her cell phone, just as Lewinsky testified; there is no record of a call that day from Lewinsky to Currie, as Currie testified there was.[28] And it is unlikely that if the return of the gifts was Lewinsky's idea, she would have summoned Currie (a much older woman) to pick them up rather than have delivered them herself to Currie's home. Or that Currie would have accepted custody of the gifts, no questions asked, if the request had come from Lewinsky rather than from the President or one of the President's aides. And if Lewinsky's purpose had been merely to avoid complying with the subpoena, it would have made more sense for her to throw the gifts away than to entrust them to the President's secretary. It is true that in her conversation with the President on the morning of Currie's call and visit, Lewinsky herself had suggested the possibility of handing over the gifts to Currie for safekeeping. But what is likely is not that she followed up this suggestion by summoning Currie to her apartment, but that Clinton took up the suggestion and told Currie to call Lewinsky.

Clinton's lawyers argued that it was implausible that he would shower Lewinsky with gifts the morning of the twenty-eighth yet endeavor that same afternoon to get them out of Lewinsky's hands. Implausible that *Clinton* would act foolishly and recklessly? The history of his behavior in the ordeal of his Presidency argues the contrary. And would it have been *so* foolish? He may have given her the gifts to keep her happy and "on board," confident that she would not produce them in response to the subpoena. But it was a risky move (and thus quite in character for Clinton), and it would be natural for him to think better of what he had done and decide, as Lewinsky had suggested, that the

---

[28]The telephone company's records reveal that the cell phone call was made later than Lewinsky testified, but it would not be surprising if Lewinsky had misremembered the exact time of the call.

gifts would be safer in Currie's hands.[29] For then Lewinsky could truthfully, if misleadingly, respond to the subpoena's demand for gifts that she didn't have any to produce. Since Lewinsky and Currie were friends, Lewinsky could be confident of being able to reclaim the gifts after she completed her role in the Paula Jones litigation. Clinton must have known that Lewinsky might have refused an order to discard them. And who would give such an order? For him to do so or tell someone else to do so would be excessively reckless even by his standards.

Clinton's lawyers urged the Senate to call no witnesses. Had the Senate agreed there would have been no possibility of cross-examining Lewinsky. Probably the President's lawyers did not think they could undermine her credibility or that of any of the other witnesses on whom the Independent Counsel had relied. Given the President's emphatic denial of key factual allegations in the bill of impeachment and his obvious desire for vindication and exoneration, it is unlikely that he would have agreed to forgo the opportunity for cross-examination had his lawyers thought that cross-examination would bolster the President's story.

The Senate allowed three witnesses to be deposed, and though one of them was Monica Lewinsky and her testimony was consistent with her grand jury testimony and thus very damaging to the President's defense, his lawyers did not cross-examine her. Nor did they attempt to call any witnesses of their own, such as Betty Currie, whose grand jury testimony had contradicted Lewinsky's on the matter of who had been responsible for the secreting of the President's gifts to Lewinsky. It is true that by the time the Senate got around to witnesses, the President's strategy was that of running out the clock. But at no time were his lawyers eager to present or cross-examine witnesses.

The Violations of Law

Having fixed the essential facts, so far as that is possible to do on the basis of the public record, I want to consider now whether they establish criminal or other unlawful activity on the part of the President. The inquiry may seem premature. I have not discussed whether the commission of a crime is either a necessary or a sufficient condition for impeachment, and in fact, as we shall see in Chapter 3, it is neither. But

---

[29]No doubt by this time he rued not having taken an earlier suggestion of hers—to settle the Paula Jones case.

the law's decision to punish a particular type of conduct, whether criminally or civilly, is some evidence of the transgressive character of that conduct. Anyway my interest in the Clinton-Lewinsky mess is not limited to issues of impeachability. And we shall see in Chapter 4 that whether the President committed any crimes also bears on the morality of his decision neither to resign his office nor to come clean about his conduct with Lewinsky.

ADULTERY, SODOMY, AND HARASSMENT

We can begin with the sexual relationship itself. Adultery is a misdemeanor under the law of the District of Columbia,[30] as it is in about a third of the states. But it is very rarely prosecuted. And it is uncertain whether fellatio would be classified as sexual intercourse within the meaning of the adultery law.[31] Being securely contraceptive, relatively unlikely to transmit a sexually transmitted disease,[32] and (for most men and women) less emotionally intimate than vaginal intercourse, it is less threatening to a marriage.[33] In any event, no one thinks that violating a statute forbidding consensual sex between adults is a high crime or misdemeanor. Such statutes are dead letters, more embarrassing to the legislatures unable to muster the political will to repeal them than to the violators.

There is no basis for accusing the President of sexual harassment of a subordinate. The initial media publicity about the affair played heavily on the theme of the President's having taken advantage of a star-struck intern only a few years older than his daughter. This picture cannot be squared with Lewinsky's own words. We learn from them not only that when she met the President she was already sexually experienced and indeed had recently broken off an affair with another

[30]D.C. Code Ann. § 22–301.

[31]The definition of adultery in the D.C. Code is limited to intercourse, but "intercourse" is not defined. Some states expressly define intercourse to include oral sex. See, for example, Pa. Consolidated Stat. § 3101; cf. Allen v. State, 316 S.E.2d 500 (Ga. App. 1984).

[32]See, for example, Tomas J. Philipson and Richard A. Posner, *Private Choices and Public Health: The AIDS Epidemic in an Economic Perspective* 22 (1993).

[33]Before 1994, fellatio would almost certainly have been classified as intercourse, because a statute of the District of Columbia repealed that year made it a felony "to place one's sexual organ in the mouth . . . of another." D.C. Code Ann. § 22–3502. And this means that, but for the repeal, President Clinton would have been guilty of a sexual felony.

married man, but also that she is well to do, socially sophisticated, self-assertive to the point of brazenness, and not in the least overawed by the President or the Presidency.[34]

Even if one rejects, as common sense requires us to do, Clinton's claim to have been completely passive in their sexual encounters, there is no indication that he ever used the powers of his office to obtain sexual favors from her; that he ever promised her anything if she had sex with him or threatened her with any consequences if she did not; that he ever pestered her for sex; that he did anything to break down her resistance to fellating him (there was no resistance); or even that he seduced her. She wanted to have sex with him at least as much as he wanted to have sex with her, and probably more. It is telling that she had to plead with him to be allowed to cause him to ejaculate and that he rejected her entreaties to engage in vaginal intercourse; their relationship involved virtually a reversal of the traditional sex roles. The charge that there was "an element of exploitation based on age and status"[35] cannot be sustained.

OBSTRUCTION OF JUSTICE

The only crime plausibly attributable to the President growing out of his affair with Lewinsky is obstruction of justice. I must make clear what this term means in federal law. The public debate over the President's behavior distinguished between "obstruction of justice" and "perjury." The House of Representatives reflected the distinction in the ar-

---

[34]She once said to Clinton on the phone, "I love you, butthead," and apparently he didn't react. When she told this to Linda Tripp, Tripp remarked: "the one thing I'm sure he's aware of is that you don't think of him as who he is. I think that has come across loud and clear . . . the entire time. So I don't think he'd be so appalled [at being called 'butthead']." *Supplementary Materials*, note 1 above, vol. 2, pp. 2627–2628. Tripp told the grand jury that Lewinsky never "treated [Clinton] the way any one of us sitting in this room would treat the President . . . She spoke to him abolutely no differently than she would speak to me or anyone." Id., vol. 3, p. 4173. Lewinsky's summary description of Clinton, made in an August 11, 1998, interview by the Independent Counsel's staff, is worth quoting: Lewinsky "describes the President as 'a sweet little boy,' affectionate, kind, warm, selfish, self-centered, self-righteous, [an] incredible person who does what is in the best interest of the country. The President has a 'Saturday night personality,' where he gives in to his sexual desires and a 'Sunday personality,' where he is remorseful and goes to church . . . The President has said such . . . things as, 'My life is empty.'" *Appendices*, note 1 above, vol. 1, p. 1539.

[35]William J. Bennett, *The Death of Outrage: Bill Clinton and the Assault on American Ideals* 24 (1998).

ticles of impeachment that it adopted; one of the articles charged perjury and the other charged obstruction of justice. Until the Senate trial, it was the conventional wisdom that while Clinton almost certainly had committed perjury before the grand jury (as well as in his Paula Jones deposition, but that perjury was not charged, directly at any rate, in either article of impeachment), there was much less evidence that he had committed obstruction of justice. More Senators voted to acquit him of perjury than of obstruction of justice. They thought perjury the less serious offense and the more difficult one to prove. Both points are mistaken.

The House prosecutors were at fault here. Because they bought into the idea that the offenses of perjury and obstruction of justice are distinct, and because "obstruction of justice" sounds worse than perjury, they put most of their effort into the uphill fight to prove obstruction of justice (excluding perjury) and allowed the impression to be formed that they lacked confidence in what was actually the stronger of the two articles of impeachment: the perjury article.

"Obstruction of justice" is an umbrella term for a variety of specific statutory crimes involving corrupting or otherwise interfering improperly with the course of legal justice. It *includes* perjury[36] when committed in either a civil or a criminal proceeding; it excludes perjury in other settings, for example before a congressional committee unless the committee is inquiring into possible violations of law—which, however, the House Judiciary Committee, in the impeachment inquiry, was. Obstruction of justice also includes killing witnesses, judges, or jurors, or wounding, threatening, bribing, retaliating against, or otherwise intimidating or tampering with them; destroying evidence; making misrepresentations in an application for bail; and a variety of related offenses. A chapter of the federal criminal code entitled "Obstruction of Justice" contains separate sections criminalizing sixteen of these specific offenses, plus some offenses that are not really obstruction of justice,[37]

---

[36]United States v. Norris, 300 U.S. 564, 574 (1937). For example, the federal sentencing guidelines provide for an "obstruction of justice" penalty enhancement when a criminal defendant lies on the stand. U.S.S.G. § 3C1.1 and Application Note 4. It thus is incorrect that "prosecutors almost never pursue a perjury charge once a defendant who has proclaimed his innocence on the stand is found guilty." Jeffrey Rosen, "The Perjury Trap," *New Yorker*, Aug. 10, 1998, pp. 28, 29. An obstruction of justice punishment add-on is common in federal criminal trials in which the defendant testifies that he is innocent but is found guilty.

[37]U.S. Code, tit. 18, ch. 73. See Lisa R. Rafferty and Julie Teperow, "Obstruction of

such as making a false application for a passport even if one is not fleeing justice. But it omits perjury. Perjury is the subject of its own chapter[38] and is not limited to lies told under oath in legal proceedings. Also omitted from the obstruction of justice chapter is extortion, another common method of obstructing justice.

So, in federal law at any rate, and that is the law relevant to Clinton's conduct, "obstruction of justice" is a generic term for a variety of offenses scattered throughout the federal criminal code; the technical designation of a subset of these offenses; and the name of one of the specific offenses.[39] The first usage is the most illuminating in reference to the charges against President Clinton, and is the one that I shall generally employ. On this construal, to ask whether the President was guilty of obstruction of justice is to ask whether he committed any of the specific offenses that constitute forms of obstruction of justice when the purpose is to thwart a legal proceeding.

IMPROPERLY INFLUENCING WITNESSES

The President's alleged obstructions of justice fall into two classes: improperly influencing other witnesses, mainly in the Paula Jones case; and committing perjury in his deposition in that case, in his testimony before the grand jury, and in his answers to the questions put to him by the House Judiciary Committee. The evidence of his guilt is weaker with respect to crimes in the first class (improperly influencing witnesses) than crimes in the second class (perjury), and let me begin with the former.

One issue is whether Clinton tried to buy Lewinsky's cooperation in the Paula Jones suit with a job. Clinton had dual motives (putting aside, as rather implausible, the possibility of motives of affection or altruism) for keeping Lewinsky from spilling the beans and for enlisting Betty

---

Justice," 35 *American Criminal Law Review* 989 (1998). To complete the confusion, one of the offenses codified in the obstruction of justice chapter, 18 U.S.C. § 1503, which is captioned "Influencing or Injuring Officer or Juror Generally," contains a catchall provision that punishes anyone who "corruptly . . . influences, obstructs, or impedes, or endeavors to influence, obstruct, or impede, the due administration of justice"— which covers pretty much the entire waterfront (possibly excepting perjury!). For a thorough discussion of the federal criminal laws that President Clinton may have violated, see *Appendices,* note 1 above, vol. 1, pp. 266–375.

[38]U.S. Code, tit. 18, ch. 79.

[39]The catchall provision, note 37 above.

Currie's, Vernon Jordan's, and probably Bill Richardson's help in doing so. One motive was to avert the personal and political disaster that revelation of his relationship with Lewinsky might precipitate; the other was to prevail against Paula Jones and later, after the Independent Counsel became involved, against him. It is impossible, on the basis of the facts as they are known today, to determine with any confidence how large a role the latter motive played in his conversations with Lewinsky and others concerning a job for her.

All these conversations, with the possible but uncertain exception of the second one with Currie, took place before Clinton knew, and probably before he even suspected, that the Independent Counsel was or would become involved. Until then the only legal proceeding he would have been concerned about was the Paula Jones suit. Since that suit concerned an incident that had occurred in 1991, before Clinton became President, and since Jones's evidence was weak and her injury probably nil (and hence her damages, even if she won, unlikely to be great), and since an entirely consensual affair with Lewinsky would bear only tangentially on the merits of the suit,[40] it seems unlikely that a desire to ward off an adverse judgment in that suit played a big role in Clinton's efforts to keep his relationship with Lewinsky secret. The personal and political consequences of exposure probably seemed far more ominous than the consequences for his struggle with Paula Jones—as events were to prove. What is more, while Lewinsky threatened to tell her parents about her relationship with Clinton unless she got a good job (in fact, she had already told her mother, and believed that her father had guessed), she never threatened, or so much as hinted, that she might turn on Clinton in the Jones case. She had always expressed the greatest disdain for Paula Jones. Her cooperation in denying the relationship was reasonably assured. She was emphatic about this in her Senate deposition.

Consider Jordan's efforts, apparently instigated by Clinton, to get Lewinsky a job in New York. Clinton had motives unrelated to the Jones case for wanting her happily ensconced in a job in a different city, where she wouldn't be pestering him for a White House job and generally getting in his hair and causing trouble.[41] She had written him a

---

[40]But it would bear; it would be "material," as we shall see shortly.

[41]She once threw a tantrum in front of Secret Service officers when she learned from

letter threatening to tell her parents about their relationship if she didn't get a good job. This is called blackmail. She was dangerous and a pest. These were more than sufficient reasons to want her to land a good job in New York. It is true that Jordan's efforts to find her such a job accelerated after he learned that she was caught up in pretrial discovery in the Jones suit. It is true that the President monitored these efforts intensively. Besides the timing and the monitoring, there is the coincidence (if it was merely a coincidence) that Jordan had previously recommended to Revlon another Clinton friend who might testify against the President (Webster Hubbell), and the oddity that Jordan referred Lewinsky to a criminal lawyer to assist her in preparing an affidavit in a civil case—as if Jordan suspected that perjury was in the offing and so Lewinsky needed the protection of a criminal lawyer. And some of Jordan's grand jury and Senate testimony was implausible.[42] All these things make it plausible that the President's desire to keep her "on board" in the Jones case played a role in his efforts to get her a job, but it is not, on the basis of what is known today, provable.

And so with Clinton's efforts to influence Currie's "recollection" of his relationship with Lewinsky. When, on the day after his deposition, Clinton none too subtly endeavored to align Currie's version of the facts with his own—in fact inviting her to lie to protect him—he may just have been anticipating the media frenzy that in fact ensued within days, rather than anticipating that Currie might be a witness either in the Paula Jones case or before a grand jury investigating him. The alter-

---

one of them that the President was meeting with another woman, whom Lewinsky believed to be a girlfriend of the President, in the Oval Office.

[42]Recall his testimony about the breakfast with Lewinsky on December 31, 1997—first denying that it had taken place, and months later "recalling" it in great detail. Here is another example of implausible testimony by Jordan: he testified before the grand jury that calling Ronald Perelman on Lewinsky's behalf after he learned that she had been served with a subpoena in the Paula Jones case did not set off "alarm bells" in his mind, even though the consulting contract that Revlon had given Webster Hubbell at Jordan's behest was already, as Jordan appears to have acknowledged, "a major public issue." *Supplementary Materials*, note 1 above, vol. 2, p. 1788. Indeed, given this history and Jordan's position as a director of Revlon, it is exceedingly odd that he would have tried to get Lewinsky a job at Revlon after learning that she had been pulled into the Jones case. As an experienced lawyer, he should have known that the danger of embarrassing Revlon, as well as getting himself in trouble, was acute. This was a serious misstep on Jordan's part; but we shall see that almost all the lawyers involved in the Clinton-Lewinsky investigation and the Paula Jones litigation, from Clinton and the Justices of the Supreme Court on down, committed blunders.

native possibility, once again, is that both thoughts coexisted in his mind. At his deposition he had made repeated references to Betty Currie as being Monica Lewinsky's friend, the person she visited at the White House, the person who asked him to bring back gifts for Lewinsky from Martha's Vineyard, the person who had put Vernon Jordan in touch with Lewinsky, the person who could corroborate his testimony about Lewinsky. At one point he had even replied to questions by Jones's lawyers by saying, "Those are questions you'd have to ask her."[43] He was fairly asking them to depose her, and though the witness list in the Jones case was closed, it could always be reopened by the judge for good cause. In fact, shortly after the President's deposition, Jones's lawyers did issue a subpoena to Currie to testify, though it was never enforced, because Judge Wright decided, as we'll see, to exclude from the Jones litigation all evidence bearing on Clinton's affair with Lewinsky.

And so when Clinton talked to Betty Currie on the day after his deposition, he may have regarded her as a prospective witness in the Jones case whose testimony he wished to influence. If so, he was guilty of witness tampering. If the conversation was repeated after Clinton learned that the Independent Counsel was investigating the possibility that he had perjured himself at his deposition, this would be evidence that he wanted to influence her as a prospective grand jury witness as well. But the timing of the second conversation is uncertain; and he may just have wanted to make sure she remembered their previous conversation in the event that the press, or someone who might talk to the press, got hold of her. Once again, then, dual intentions are possible, maybe even likely. But once again the presence of the improper intention—the intention of inducing a prospective witness to testify falsely—cannot be regarded as proven fact.

It can be argued, however, that the absence of such proof is irrelevant; that it is enough that the President knew, as he must have, that getting Currie "on board" would influence her testimony were she to be called as a witness, even if he didn't intend to bring about that result. I may, in other words, be using "intention" in too narrow a sense. Deliberately to do an act that one knows will have a certain result is often in the criminal law enough to establish the requisite intention to bring about that result. Intention and desire are not synonyms. If you plant a bomb

[43]Videotaped Oral Deposition of William Jefferson Clinton in Jones v. Clinton, Civil Action No. LR–C–94–290, E.D. Ark., Jan. 17, 1998, p. 66.

in a plane desiring only to kill the passenger whose heir you are, you are guilty of first-degree murder (deliberate, premeditated) of the other passengers who die in the crash as well, even though you didn't desire their death.

There is precedent for drawing this distinction in obstruction of justice cases too.[44] But applied in such cases the distinction is sufficiently esoteric, and its soundness sufficiently open to debate, to dissuade me from trying to fasten it around the neck of the President of the United States. A President ought not to be convicted of "high Crimes and Misdemeanors" on the basis of debatable interpretations of the criminal law. Furthermore, it is uncertain whether President Clinton thought Currie would be called as a witness in either the Jones case or the Independent Counsel's investigation.

I am even more dubious about the argument that the President lied to his assistants intending them to repeat the lies before the grand jury. He did lie to them, and that may have been his motive. But he had plenty of other reasons to lie. Nor would their repeating his denials to the grand jury be any warrant of the truth of those denials, as Clinton, an intelligent man and a lawyer, would have realized. Were Clinton to be prosecuted for perjury, the fact that he had made statements out of court that were consistent with the statements alleged to be perjurious would be inadmissible hearsay.[45]

---

[44]United States v. Neiswender, 590 F.2d 1269 (4th Cir. 1979). For the general principle, see Planned Parenthood of Wisconsin v. Doyle, 162 F.3d 463, 469 (7th Cir. 1998); Wayne R. LaFave and Austin W. Scott, *Substantive Criminal Law,* vol. 1, § 3.5(a)–(c), pp. 304–311 (1986). The *Neiswender* approach has been followed in a number of cases in different federal courts of appeals, but it has also been criticized; on both points, see Joseph V. De Marco, Note, "A Funny Thing Happened on the Way to the Courthouse: Mens Rea, Document Destruction, and the Federal Obstruction of Justice Statute," 67 *New York University Law Review* 570 (1992).

[45]The general rule that prior consistent statements are inadmissible to bolster a witness's testimony does have an exception for statements offered to rebut charges that the witness fabricated his testimony or was improperly influenced or had an improper motive in giving it. But the exception is inapplicable here. On the rule and the exception, see Tome v. United States, 513 U.S. 150 (1995); Fed. R. Evid. 801(c), (d)(1)(B). There was no argument that the President's grand jury testimony was a recent fabrication, or reflected improper influence or a motive not previously present; that would be the kind of argument that might be refuted by showing that he had taken a consistent position all along. In contrast, to the extent that the President's defenders suggested that Monica Lewinsky may have fabricated some of her testimony against the President in order to "buy" immunity from prosecution by the Independent Counsel, her many consistent

Less ambiguity attends Clinton's suggestion to Lewinsky that she provide the Jones lawyers with an affidavit. She didn't want to be deposed, and he pointed out that she might be able to get out of being deposed by giving an affidavit. On its face, the suggestion concerned the form rather than the content of her testimony. But it was implicit that the affidavit would be false; and since it is much easier to lie convincingly in an affidavit (normally drafted by one's lawyer) than in a deposition, where one is in effect being cross-examined, Clinton's suggestion was almost certainly intended to facilitate Lewinsky's giving false testimony.

But it seems incurably ambiguous whether, when he told her that in response to the subpoena she would have to turn over anything called for in it that she had in her possession, he was inviting her to get rid of the gifts or merely stating a legal truism. *If* that's what he said. Her testimony was that in response to her suggestion that she get rid of the gifts, he said he would think about it. That would not be obstruction of justice in itself, though it would be further evidence that he was instrumental in getting her, later that day, to hand over the gifts to Currie.

Until Lewinsky was deposed at the Senate trial, it appeared pretty certain that the President, in his phone conversation with Lewinsky on December 17, had suggested to her that she include in her affidavit in the Jones case the phony "you were delivering documents to me" cover story. If so, this would be a clear case of suborning perjury.[46] But in her Senate testimony Lewinsky denied having understood the President's remark about delivering documents to be "in connection with the affidavit."[47] She explained that it was a long conversation that touched on other topics besides the affidavit. This testimony is not conclusive on the question of the President's intent in referring to the cover story. But it would make it difficult to prove beyond a reasonable doubt that he was suggesting to her that she use the story in her affidavit.

On another occasion, however, he was explicit in suggesting that she could say in her affidavit that the Office of Legislative Affairs had arranged for her job in the Pentagon.[48] This was suborning perjury. The

---

statements to friends, relatives, and therapists made long before the investigation would be admissible to bolster her testimony.

[46] 18 U.S.C. § 1622.

[47] 145 Cong. Rec. S3105 (Feb. 6, 1999). The House impeachment manager who was questioning her neglected to ask what the President's mention of the cover story was in connection with, if not her affidavit.

[48] "I was concerned . . that if, you know, if I at some point had to kind of—under oath,

lie that he was inviting her to tell under oath was material and therefore perjurious because a truthful explanation for why she had been transferred would furnish a clue that she had indeed been involved sexually with the President. And likewise when, as is almost certainly the case, the President suggested to Betty Currie that she recover the gifts that he had given Lewinsky, he was tampering with a witness (Lewinsky).[49] That these obstructions were of a civil rather than of a criminal proceeding, indeed of a civil proceeding later dismissed, and that, as Lewinsky testified before the grand jury, no one ever *asked* her to lie or to conceal evidence, is immaterial. Obstruction of justice can be committed with a wink and a nod.

PERJURY

It is clear that Clinton perjured himself in the Paula Jones deposition, even though, as Clinton's defenders emphasized, the crime of perjury is narrowly defined in federal law. A false statement under oath is not enough. The statement must be deliberately false, that is, a lie; it must be material to some issue in the proceeding in which it is made; and it must be false rather than merely misleading. The purpose of the last requirement, which the Supreme Court announced in the *Bronston* case,[50] and which is the least intuitive, is to avoid insoluble uncertainties about the declarant's intentions and understanding by putting on the questioner, if he wants to lay a predicate for a charge of perjury, the burden of asking unequivocal questions. Jones's lawyers did not conduct a skillful examination of Clinton; in particular, they failed to ask him about specific sex acts and to follow up his often meandering and evasive answers with questions designed to pin him down. As a result,

---

answer these questions and in the course of answering a question I mentioned people at the White House who didn't like me, that somehow I would end up getting—they'd get me in trouble. And so he [the President] when I told him the questions about my job at the Pentagon, he said, 'Well, you could always say that the people in Legislative Affairs got it for you or helped you get it.' " *Appendices,* note 1 above, vol. 1, p. 1012 (grand jury testimony of Monica Lewinsky). In her February 1 Senate testimony, Lewinsky said, "He [the President] didn't discuss the content of my affidavit with me at all, ever," 145 Cong. Rec. S3106 (Feb. 6, 1999), but in context the reference to "ever" appears to be limited to the phone conversation of December 17.

[49] 18 U.S.C. § 1512(b)(2)(A) (withholding evidence). He was also violating the catchall obstruction of justice statute, 18 U.S.C. § 1503 (see note 37 above), and perhaps conspiring with both Lewinsky and Currie to obstruct justice.

[50] Bronston v. United States, 409 U.S. 352 (1973).

many of his answers, though probably lies, would not expose him to prosecution for perjury.

The requirement of materiality serves two purposes. One is to carve out lies that are harmless; the law generally leaves harmless acts alone even when done with an improper motive. The second reason, one that is particularly important in a sex case, is to protect reasonable interests in personal privacy. In many legal settings, including both depositions and grand jury investigations, the rules of relevance are extremely lax, which enables the questioner to inquire about activities that are at once intensely private and entirely marginal to the purpose of the inquiry. If the witness refuses to answer on grounds of privacy, his refusal is likely to be understood as an acknowledgment that he has indeed engaged in whatever disreputable private activity he is being questioned about. The grand jury and deposition transcripts published by the House Judiciary Committee are replete with such questions. Several of Clinton's answers to questions put to him in his grand jury appearance, as we shall see, appear to fall within this informal "privilege" to lie under oath about immaterial matters in order to protect one's personal privacy. But obviously the fact that a witness is asked about his sex life does not confer a license to lie, on the theory that sex is private and questions about sex therefore immaterial per se. Sexual activity is material to many legal claims, both old and new, ranging from actions for divorce and disputes over custody and prosecutions for rape, incest, sodomy, child molestation, and the production of pornographic films to actions for sexual harassment, palimony, defamation, the knowing transmission of a sexually transmitted disease, and paternity.

Several of the false statements in Clinton's deposition were clearly perjurious. The first was his denial of having ever been alone with Monica Lewinsky except possibly on a few occasions, each no more than a few minutes in duration, when she brought him documents. The only link between this denial and the truth is that the delivery of documents was a pretext that Clinton and Lewinsky sometimes used to conceal the purpose of her visits to his office. Since there was no actual delivery of documents (certainly on most occasions, though on a few she may have jokingly handed him a file folder into which she had slipped some papers), his answer could not be thought even the literal truth. Nor is it conceivable that he had forgotten their sexual encounters or had forgotten that some of her visits had lasted for much more than a few minutes; a number of them had lasted for more than an hour. These are not the sort of things that people forget unless their memory is impaired; Clinton has by all accounts an excellent memory.

The President also clearly and materially lied when he said that he had never had an erotic encounter with Kathleen Willey, that Monica Lewinsky had given him only one or two gifts, that he had no recollection of ever having given her any gifts (he had given her about twenty, some only three weeks before), that his only discussion with Lewinsky about her being subpoenaed in the Jones case had been a joking reference to the fact that the Jones lawyers would probably try to subpoena every woman he had ever talked to, that he hadn't known she had received an offer of a job with Bill Richardson's office, that no one other than his lawyers had told him about Lewinsky's being subpoenaed in the Jones case (both Vernon Jordan and Lewinsky herself had told him), and that when Lewinsky visited the White House it was to see Betty Currie.

In his testimony before the grand jury, Clinton repeated many of the lies he had told at his deposition. He also lied when he testified that he had testified truthfully at the deposition and when he denied having improperly influenced other witnesses; we have just seen that he did. He lied when he said he had been literally truthful in the denials he made to his aides of a sexual relationship with Lewinsky; for he had flatly stated to at least one of them that he had not had oral sex with her. He denied having suggested to Currie that she retrieve his gifts to Lewinsky: another lie, almost certainly. He lied when he said that his conversation with Currie on January 18, the day after he was deposed, had been intended to refresh his recollection about his affair with Lewinsky; the rattling off of a series of lies to Currie could not have had any such purpose.

He lied when he said that he had never been "alone" with Lewinsky because there had always been other people in the vicinity, notably Betty Currie at her desk outside the Oval Office, stewards in a nearby pantry, Secret Service agents prowling about seemingly everywhere. It is not a defense to perjury that the declarant assigns private meanings to words,[51] provided he knows they're private; were it a defense, there

---

[51]Though not a Catholic, let alone a Catholic in a society in which Catholics are persecuted, Clinton is a master of the Catholic doctrine of equivocation—"guiltlessly getting a falsehood across," Leo Katz, *Ill-Gotten Gains: Evasion, Blackmail, Fraud, and Kindred Puzzles of the Law* 29 (1996), as by swearing to a magistrate inquiring into one's religious practices "that one has not done something, though one really has done it, by

could never be a successful prosecution for perjury. It would be ridiculous to suggest that Jones's lawyers, before asking Clinton whether he had ever been alone with Monica Lewinsky, should have defined the word "alone." There is no possibility that he misunderstood the question[52] and no even remotely plausible interpretation of his answer that would make it other than a deliberate falsehood. A jury well disposed to Clinton might decide, or pretend to decide, that he really does understand even common English words differently from everyone else, and let him off; to be guilty of perjury, you must *know* that you are testifying falsely. But no *reasonable* jury could believe that Clinton's problem is an imperfect command of English.

And likewise with his answer to the question whether he had had sexual relations with Lewinsky. For the passive participant in a sexual act not to be engaged in sexual relations would imply that when Lewinsky was fellating the President she was engaged in sexual relations but he was not. It would imply that the rapist engages in sexual relations but his victim does not. It would imply that in the typical furtive restroom encounter in which one male fellates the other (who indeed is often passive), the fellator would be engaged in sexual relations and the person fellated would not be, even though in many states he would be guilty of sodomy. Clinton had been accused by Jones of asking her to fellate him; it was unlikely that her lawyers had devised a definition of sexual relations under which he would not have been engaged in sexual relations with her had she accepted the alleged invitation and fellated him.

Furthermore, although the definition of sexual relations used in the deposition was clumsy, it did not exclude the passive partner in fellatio. Even if Clinton was completely passive, he "cause[d] . . . contact with the genitalia . . . of any person with an intent to arouse or gratify the sexual desire of any person." The "any person" was himself, and he caused Lewinsky to make contact with his genitalia, for purposes of arousal or gratification of his sexual desire, by inviting her to do so. Clinton claimed to have studied the definition carefully, is intelligent

---

inwardly understanding that one did not do it on a certain day, or before one was born." Blaise Pascal, *The Provincial Letters* 140 (A. J. Krailsheimer ed. 1967). Despite Professor Katz's suggestion to the contrary ("guiltlessly"), we are about to see that equivocation is not a defense to a charge of perjury.

[52]On the significance of this qualification, see United States v. DeZarn, 157 F.3d 1042, 1049–1050 (6th Cir. 1998).

enough to have understood it, and is given to literalism when answering hostile or embarrassing questions. In hindsight it is apparent that rather than attempt a global definition of "sexual relations," the lawyers should have asked Clinton about specific sex acts. They knew from Linda Tripp that Lewinsky had fellated him; they could have asked him, "Did Lewinsky's lips ever touch your penis?" But their failure to be more concrete would not be fatal to a prosecution for perjury, for "where it can be shown from the context of the question and the state of the testifier's knowledge at the time that the testifier clearly knew what the question meant," an ambiguity in the question will not let the defendant off the hook.[53] In any event, the questions were not ambiguous, and though they might have confused a witness slower-witted than Clinton, he has never complained that they confused him.

Finally, Clinton was not physically passive in his sexual encounters with Lewinsky. When asked at his grand jury appearance whether he had been passive, he refused to answer, instead just repeating that he had not had sexual relations with Lewinsky. The inescapable inference from this testimony, given the definition of sexual relations in the Paula Jones deposition, was that Clinton had indeed been completely passive in his sexual encounters with Lewinsky, as if she were a prostitute. The implausibility of his story would have become plain to the dullest intelligence had he stated outright that while she was fellating him he was not touching her in an erotic manner. Obviously he fondled parts of Lewinsky's body named in the definition and did so with erotic intent. (If his intent wasn't erotic, what was it?) And once again it is not credible that he merely forgot having done so,[54] that all he remembered was being fellated. He lied not only about what he did, but also about what he remembered.

Clinton's defenders overread the Supreme Court's decision in the *Bronston* case to hold that any answer that could be tortuously interpreted to be literally truthful cannot be perjurious. *Bronston* does not go that far. It involved a nonresponsive and misleading, rather than a false, answer. The defendant was asked, "Do you have" any Swiss bank

---

[53]Id. at 1049.

[54]His lawyers, in their submission to the House Judiciary Committee, hopefully quoted the following passage from Griswold v. Hazard, 141 U.S. 260, 280 (1891): "The difference in the recollection of gentlemen, in respect to transactions in which they took part, often happens, without any reason to suspect that any of them would intentionally deviate from the line of absolute truth."

accounts? He answered no. The follow-up question was, "Have you ever?" To that he answered, "The company had an account there for about six months."[55] The truth was that he had had Swiss bank accounts for five years, but did not have any at the time of the trial, and so his first answer was correct. Had he said "no" to the follow-up question, he would have been guilty of perjury. Instead he gave an answer (a truthful one) to a question that had not been asked, whether not he but his company had ever had a Swiss bank account. The answer was misleading, but it was not false. The answers given by President Clinton were literally false as well as misleading.

Bronston does not license equivocation.[56] "An answer that is responsive and false on its face does not come within *Bronston*'s literal truth analysis simply because the defendant can postulate unstated premises of the question that would make his answer literally true."[57] The *DeZarn* case recognizes another pertinent exception to the "literal truth" defense to a perjury charge.[58] The defendant was charged with perjury in answering questions put to him about illegal political fundraising activities. He had been asked whether there had been fundraising at a party that he had attended in 1991, and he had answered that he hadn't seen or been aware of any. In fact the party about which he was being asked had been held in 1990, not 1991, and so he argued that his answers were true, since he had attended a party in 1991 at which there had been no fundraising. The court rejected the argument, and upheld DeZarn's conviction, on the ground that there was ample evidence that when he answered "no" to the investigator's questions he knew that the investigator was asking him about the 1990 party. That the questions had been imprecise, because of the erroneous date, did not let the defendant off the hook. If this decision is sound, and there is no reason to doubt that it is, the President's defense to the perjury charges evaporates—assuming his lies were material.

The district judge presiding in the Paula Jones case thought they were, because she permitted the questions that elicited them to be asked over the vigorous objection of Clinton's lawyer. She was right; the lies were material to Paula Jones's case, though only just. Jones had been an

[55]Bronston v. United States, note 50 above, at 354.
[56]See note 51 above.
[57]United States v. Abroms, 947 F.2d 1241, 1245 (5th Cir. 1991).
[58]United States v. DeZarn, note 52 above.

employee of the Arkansas state government when Clinton was governor of the state, and her suit accused him of having solicited her for fellatio by exposing himself to her. He denied the accusation. Whom to believe? Lewinsky was a federal government worker when Clinton was President, and she fellated him. His willingness to be fellated by a subordinate made Jones's charge more credible. There was an important difference between the two incidents: Clinton had not asked Lewinsky to fellate him the first time; she had taken the initiative. But it is plausible that Clinton was more cautious as President than he had been as governor. He was under greater scrutiny by the media and the Republicans; he had less privacy; and, partly because of the Jones suit itself and the revelations in his first Presidential campaign about a sexual relationship between him and Gennifer Flowers, he had a "record" that would make it difficult for him to deny future charges of sexual harassment convincingly.

Judge Wright later decided to exclude evidence about the President's relationship with Lewinsky from the Jones case. The judge's decision has been widely understood to be a ruling that the relationship, and hence the President's deposition, and hence the lies in that deposition, were immaterial to that case. This understanding is incorrect on two grounds. First, materiality is assessed as of the time the lie was uttered, and not with the wisdom of hindsight. All that must be shown is that the lie had the potential to impede the interrogator's investigation.[59] Hence "a false statement can be material even if ultimately the conclusion of the tribunal would have been the same."[60] This principle is not inconsistent with the law's policy of excusing harmless lies. The lie that seems (though it isn't) pertinent to the investigation is likely to send the investigator on a wild goose chase. Justice is obstructed not only when a miscarriage of justice results but also when the course of justice is unreasonably delayed or burdened.[61] Had Clinton told the truth at his deposition, or simply refused to answer questions about Lewinsky, the Paula Jones case would almost certainly have been resolved, either by settlement or by the entry of a default judgment, before November 1998, when it was finally settled.

---

[59]Id. at 1051–1052; Kathryn Kavanagh Baran and Rebecca I. Ruby, "Perjury," 35 *American Criminal Law Review* 1035, 1052 (1998), and cases cited there.

[60]United States v. DeZarn, note 52 above, at 1051.

[61]See, for example, United States v. Wells, 154 F.3d 412, 414 (7th Cir. 1998).

Second, Judge Wright's ruling was critically influenced by the fact that the Independent Counsel had moved to suspend further pretrial discovery in the Jones case because he was afraid that it would interfere with his investigation. The case for suspension was compelling, but an indefinite suspension would have meant an indefinite delay in the resolution of the Jones litigation, which was already four years old and concerned an incident almost seven years in the past. Weighing the materiality of the Clinton-Lewinsky relationship against the interest in expediting the Jones case, Judge Wright decided to exclude evidence of that relationship (and hence any occasion for further discovery, as by deposing Monica Lewinsky or Betty Currie or further deposing the President) so that she could proceed with the resolution of the case. This was a ruling not that the relationship was immaterial but that it was inessential. Judge Wright acknowledged that the evidence concerning the relationship "might be relevant to the issues in this case" (and no more was required to establish materiality); the evidence merely "was not essential to the core issues."[62]

A number of the President's lies before the grand jury were incontestably material to the grand jury's investigation into whether he had perjured himself in his deposition in the Paula Jones case and whether he and others had committed other obstructions of justice in that case. The absence of any issue of materiality, or of any possible argument of confusion that might have made some of his false statements at the deposition nondeliberate, made the charge of perjury before the grand jury even stronger than the charge of perjury at the deposition in the Paula Jones case. In addition, since the grand jury was investigating crimes, both Clinton's and other people's, the argument that "no one is ever punished for perjury in a civil case" was inapplicable.[63] It happened also to be unsound. The rejection by the House of Representatives of the proposed article of impeachment that charged Clinton with perjury

---

[62]Jones v. Clinton, 993 F. Supp. 1217, 1219 (E.D. Ark. 1998). See also her later ruling, reported at 1999 WL 202909 (April 12, 1999), n. 7.

[63]Another, esoteric distinction between perjury in the Jones case and perjury before the grand jury is that the "two witness" rule of ordinary perjury cases—the rule that the falsity of a defendant's testimony cannot be proved beyond a reasonable doubt by the uncorroborated testimony of one person—is inapplicable to perjury before a grand jury. 18 U.S.C. § 1623(e); United States v. DeZarn, note 52 above, at 1052. The distinction is not critical, because Lewinsky's testimony was amply corroborated. Also, the rule is applicable only to the issue of falsity, not to the issue of deliberateness. Id. at 1053.

in his deposition should not be considered an exoneration of the President. The rejection either was an exercise of prosecutorial discretion in the accused's favor or bespoke doubt that perjury by the President in a civil deposition is an *impeachable* offense.

Not all the President's lies to the grand jury were clearly material to the investigation. He denied (probably to avoid admitting that he had had sex with an intern) having had sexual encounters with Lewinsky before 1996. This must have been a lie because it is well-nigh inconceivable that he would have forgotten the year of their first encounter, especially since it occurred during the government shutdown, one of the most dramatic events of his first term. He denied the last encounter, in March 1997, and this was probably a lie as well rather than a genuine lapse of memory, a lie designed to shift the termination of the relationship as far back in time as possible so as to make his pretense of forgetfulness about it more plausible. But the question the grand jury was investigating—whether Clinton had perjured himself in the Paula Jones case or otherwise obstructed justice—did not depend on the number of encounters that he had had with Monica Lewinsky or on when they had begun and ended. He testified that his relationship with Lewinsky began in Platonic friendship and molted into a sexual relationship, whereas the sequence was the opposite. This lie, doubtless intended to make him seem less predatory, more "romantic," in his adulterous activities, was not material either.

But there is more. In response to the questions put to him by the House Judiciary Committee in an effort to determine exactly what issues were in dispute, Clinton repeated (again under oath) a number of the lies in his deposition and grand jury testimony. The repetition was clearly deliberate, and clearly material to the Committee's impeachment inquiry. Perjury before and false statements to Congress are federal crimes.[64]

CLINTON'S OFFENSES: A SUMMARY

On January 25, 1999, during the President's trial in the Senate, a number of Republican Senators asked the President to respond to ten questions. He refused. False answers would have been unbelievable; true answers would either have been confessions of criminal guilt or led on to further questions the answers to which would have revealed the truth

[64]See 18 U.S.C. §§ 1621, 1001.

about certain (though not all) of the crimes with which Clinton was charged. I paraphrase the questions:[65]

1. Was everything you testified to in the Jones deposition true?
2. When you told Betty Currie that "Monica came on to me, and I never touched her, right?" (and the other things you told her on January 18, 1998), did you think you were speaking the truth?
3. How do you explain Monica Lewinsky's failure to take your "advice" to give Paula Jones's lawyers the gifts you had given her if they asked for them?
4. Did your aides testify truthfully when they said you denied having had any sexual relationship of any sort with Lewinsky (and that she was known as a "stalker") and were your statements to them truthful?
5. Why did Dick Morris conduct a poll on whether the American people would forgive you for committing crimes?
6. Was Monica Lewinsky lying when she testified (and told her friends) that you had fondled her?
7. Did you tell Lewinsky that she could say in her affidavit in the Jones case that when she visited the Oval Office area in the White House she was visiting Betty Currie or delivering papers?
8. Did you violate Judge Wright's gag order when you talked to Betty Currie on January 18, the day after your Jones deposition?[66]
9. What did you mean when you told Lewinsky that you didn't have to look at her affidavit (when she offered to show it to you before submitting it in the Jones case) because you had already seen fifteen others?
10. When did you first learn that Lewinsky had not turned over the gifts you had given her to the Jones lawyers, that Currie had them?

The President's silence in the face of these questions is eloquent. It is true that in an ordinary criminal trial, the jury is not permitted to infer guilt from the defendant's refusal to testify. But the reason is not that

[65]For the full text, see "The President's Trial," *New York Times* (national ed.), Jan. 26, 1999, p. A16.

[66]At the end of the deposition, Judge Wright had ordered all persons present "not to say anything whatsoever about the questions they were asked, the substance of the deposition," or about "any details" of it. Videotaped Oral Deposition, note 43 above, p. 213.

the inference would be unsound; it is to back up the constitutional right not to be forced to testify against oneself. The President's silence—not only his refusal to answer the House managers' questions but also his refusal to testify (as requested by a number of Senators) at his Senate trial—is most plausibly explained by a fear on the part of himself and his lawyers that whatever he said would tend to confirm rather than to refute the charges against him.

To summarize, it is clear beyond a reasonable doubt, on the basis of the public record as it exists today, that President Clinton obstructed justice, in violation of federal criminal law, by (1) perjuring himself repeatedly in his deposition in the Paula Jones case, in his testimony before the grand jury, and in his responses to the questions put to him by the House Judiciary Committee;[67] (2) tampering with witness Lewinsky by encouraging her to file a false affidavit in lieu of having to be deposed, and to secrete the gifts that she had received from him; and (3) suborning perjury by suggesting to Lewinsky that she include in her affidavit a false explanation for the reason that she had been transferred from the White House to the Pentagon. He may also have tampered with potential witness Currie, conspired to bribe Lewinsky with a job that would secure her favorable testimony, and suborned perjury by Lewinsky by suggesting that she include in her Paula Jones affidavit the "delivering documents" cover story; but these offenses cannot be proved with the degree of confidence required for a criminal conviction.

Even if, as I do not for a moment believe, none of President Clinton's lies under oath amounted to perjury in the strict technical sense, they were false and misleading statements designed to derail legal proceedings, and so they were additional acts of obstruction of justice—as well as additional overt acts of a conspiracy to obstruct justice involving Clinton, Lewinsky, Currie, and possibly Jordan and others as well, such as Blumenthal. An imaginative prosecutor could no doubt add counts of wire fraud, criminal contempt, the making of false statements to the government, and aiding and abetting a crime.

It is interesting to speculate on what punishment a person might receive who committed the series of crimes that I have sketched. The

---

[67]As the *New York Times*, which opposed impeachment, put it: "We believe the evidence presents an ironclad case that he [President Clinton] lied, by plan and repetitiously, while under oath in a civil suit and before a grand jury." Editorial, "For Us, Not Him: Vote No on Impeachment," *New York Times* (national ed.), Dec. 16, 1998, p. A30. The *Times* never retreated from this judgment. Judge Wright, in her April 12 ruling, specifically found that Clinton had lied in his deposition.

maximum punishment for one count of perjury or subornation of perjury is five years in prison,[68] and for one count of witness tampering ten years.[69] The calculation of the actual sentence would be a complex process governed by the federal sentencing guidelines. A conservative estimate of the outcome (ignoring perjury in Clinton's answers to the questions put to him by the House Judiciary Committee and certain other peripheral offenses) would be a prison sentence of thirty to thirty-seven months.[70]

Apart from criminal sanctions for Clinton's campaign of lies and other obstructions, there are potential civil sanctions; his lies were civil as well as criminal wrongs. Judge Wright has decided to impose monetary sanctions on Clinton for his misconduct in the Jones case. And the state of Arkansas could disbar him for conduct unbecoming a member of the bar.

The Starr Report claims that President Clinton "unlawfully" invoked executive privilege in an effort to conceal his criminal activity from the Independent Counsel.[71] I do not think that this claim can be sustained.[72]

---

[68]18 U.S.C. §§ 1621, 1622.

[69]18 U.S.C. § 1512(b)(2)(A).

[70]This assumes conviction of (a) perjury and related offenses (such as witness tampering) in the Paula Jones case and (b) perjury before the grand jury. The base offense level for both (a) and (b) is 12. For (a), 2 points would be added for a leadership role in a criminal activity involving more than one (but fewer than five) persons and 2 more for abuse of a position of trust, yielding an adjusted offense level of 16. For (b), 3 points would be added for substantial interference with justice and 2 for abuse of a position of trust (since Clinton used his position as President to bolster his credibility and extract concessions that facilitated perjury, such as being allowed to have lawyers attend him during his testimony to the grand jury), yielding an adjusted offense level of 17. The level of the more serious offense is then adjusted upward by 2 more units to reflect the other, less serious "unit" of crime (what I have designated as (a)). The sentencing range for a first-time offender whose offense level is 19 is then read off from the sentencing table in the guidelines manual; and that range is thirty to thirty-seven months. *United States Sentencing Commission, Guidelines Manual* 310 (Nov. 1, 1998); for the other relevant provisions of the guidelines, see id., §§ 1B1.1, 2J1.2, 2J1.3(a), (b)(2), 3B1.1(c), 3B1.3, 3D1.4. Where in the sentencing range to fix the sentence would be in the discretion of the sentencing judge, who might also depart upward from the range in recognition of the protracted and repetitive character of the defendant's criminal activity.

[71]*Referral,* note 1 above, at 206.

[72]Clinton's lawyers were correct to point out (in their 184-page submission to the House Judiciary Comittee) that the Starr Report, id. at 207–208, quoted Clinton out of context in support of its charge that he falsely denied having discussed executive privilege with his lawyers.

At worst, Clinton's lawyers, presumably acting with his knowledge and approval, at times went overboard, invoking executive privilege frivolously and thereby inviting the sort of financial sanctions that courts impose on litigants and lawyers who make claims or defenses that have no colorable basis in law. What is certain, but is not a ground for impeachment, is that Clinton's lawyers matched the Independent Counsel's hardball tactics with their own hardball tactics. What they gained by these tactics is a little obscure, though I'll offer a hypothesis in Chapter 7. What they lost was the right to claim the moral high ground in the contest between the opposing teams of lawyers; and their stonewalling and evasions reinforced the impression that Clinton had a lot to conceal.

The Accuracy of the Articles of Impeachment

We have still to consider whether the misconduct discussed in this chapter is a proper basis for impeachment (which is a question for Chapters 3 through 5), and whether Clinton, had he been prosecuted in the ordinary way, would have been able to defend himself by reference to the tactics used by the prosecutors and their allies (see Chapter 2). But it is not too soon to consider whether the charges made in the articles of impeachment voted by the House of Representatives were accurate. Their accuracy is relevant not only to the question whether the House acted responsibly, but also to the abortive proposal, discussed in Chapter 5, for the Senate to find Clinton guilty of the offenses with which the House had charged him, en route to acquitting him of *impeachable* offenses.

The first of the two articles accused President Clinton of perjury before the grand jury concerning (1) the nature of his relationship with Lewinsky, (2) the truthfulness of his deposition in the Paula Jones case, (3) "allow[ing]" his lawyer at the deposition to make a false and misleading statement to the judge, and (4) "his corrupt efforts to influence the testimony of witnesses and to impede the discovery of evidence in" the Jones case. The evidence obtained by the Independent Counsel strongly supports these accusations, with the possible exception of the third, the only one I haven't discussed.

During President Clinton's deposition in the Paula Jones case, his lawyer, Robert Bennett, had told the judge that Lewinsky had said in her affidavit "that there is absolutely no sex of any kind in any manner, shape or form, with President Clinton,"[73] and Clinton, though it is apparent from the videotape of the deposition that he was listening carefully to what Bennett was saying—and he could hardly fail to miss Bennett's emphatic repetition of the central lie of his and Lewinsky's testimony—had not corrected him. The impression conveyed was that Bennett was speaking for him. Testifying before the grand jury, Clinton denied both that he had been listening to Bennett[74] and that what Bennett said was false and misleading.[75] Neither statement is plausible; it is merely because they are more equivocal than the other statements that the House singled out that there is greater doubt whether they are perjurious. The argument of the President's lawyers that only Clinton knows what was going through his mind when Bennett was speaking, though true, implies that no one can be convicted of a crime that requires proof of the state of mind of the defendant—which in fact most criminal statutes do require. Arguments like these damage the rule of law.

The other article of impeachment that the House adopted (Article III of the four articles proposed to the House by its Judiciary Committee) charged the President with improperly influencing witnesses (that is, suborning perjury and witness tampering) in seven different ways. The first, that Clinton encouraged Lewinsky to file a false affidavit in the Jones case, is well supported, though with respect to the embellishments that Clinton may have suggested to her—that when she visited the White House it was to see Betty Currie, that when she was in the Oval Office it was to deliver documents, and that the White House Office of Legislative Affairs had gotten her the job in the Pentagon—only the last was clearly intended for inclusion in the affidavit.

The second specific charge in Article III—that the President encour-

---

[73]Videotaped Oral Deposition, note 43 above, p. 54; also in *Appendices,* note 1 above, vol. 1, p. 471.

[74]"I don't believe I ever even focused on what Mr. Bennett said in the exact words he did until I started reading this transcript [the transcript of his deposition in the Jones case] carefully for this hearing. That moment, that whole argument just passed me by." Id., vol. 1, p. 481.

[75]"It depends on what the meaning of the word 'is' is." Id., vol. 1, p. 510. "At the time of the deposition, it had been—that was well beyond any point of improper contact between me and Ms. Lewinsky. So that anyone generally speaking in the present tense, saying there is not an improper relationship, would be telling the truth if that person said there was not, in the present tense; the present tense encompassing many months." Id., vol. 1, pp. 512–513.

aged Lewinsky to testify falsely if she was deposed in the Paula Jones case—is not well supported. Lewinsky needed no encouragement; and it was not testifying falsely at a deposition, but filing a false affidavit in order to get out of being deposed, that was the President's suggestion. Also insufficiently substantiated are Article III's charges that the President helped get Lewinsky a job in New York in order to keep her from testifying truthfully about their relationship, sought to shape Betty Currie's "recollection" of his relationship with Lewinsky in order to influence Currie's testimony in grand jury or other proceedings, and lied to his associates in order to induce them to mislead the grand jury by repeating the lies in their testimony. These things may be true; they just are not solidly grounded in the record. That leaves, in Article III, Clinton's pregnant silence when Bennett was telling the judge at the Paula Jones deposition about Lewinsky's affidavit, and Clinton's orchestration of the retrieval by Betty Currie of his gifts to Lewinsky. The latter charge is solid, but not the former. For Clinton's silence when Bennett was vouching for Lewinsky's affidavit to count as an obstruction of justice would imply that whenever a litigant failed to correct the false testimony of a witness, or a false statement in argument by his lawyer, the litigant would be guilty of obstruction of justice. Since a lawyer in opening or closing argument is likely to repeat the gist of his client's testimony, every case of perjured testimony by a party to a lawsuit would also be a case of obstruction of justice.

Articles I and IV, which the House did not adopt, are nevertheless factually well supported. They charge that President Clinton perjured himself in his deposition, and in his answers to the House Judiciary Committee's questions, respectively.

CHAPTER 2

Prosecution and Defense

The process by which crimes and other legal wrongs are investigated, prosecuted, judged, and punished or otherwise remediated is surrounded by a dense foliage of rules and customs. The best known are the rules of criminal procedure set forth in the Bill of Rights and other provisions of the federal Constitution, but there are many others; and the informal, extralegal customs that constrain the law-enforcement process are almost as important. For example, law-enforcement officials are not supposed to hate criminals. It is all right for the public to hate them, but the people charged with apprehending, convicting, and punishing them should not. The impersonality, the unemotionality, of law enforcement is a notable advance over justice as revenge, which preceded the modern notion of criminal justice and founders on (among other things) the lack of emotional distance between law enforcer (the avenger) and the criminal.[1]

Another important custom is the responsible exercise of prosecutorial discretion to protect the population against the felt injustice of the law when it is enforced to the hilt (one of Shakespeare's themes in *Measure for Measure*). The criminal codes of the United States contain thousands of separate prohibitions. Many are either totally obscure (such as the prohibitions against using the coat of arms of Switzerland in advertising[2] or using "Smokey the Bear" as a trade name without the authori-

---

[1]See Richard A. Posner, *Law and Literature,* ch. 2 (enlarged and revised ed. 1998), esp. pp. 53–54.
[2]18 U.S.C. § 708.

zation of the Department of the Interior[3]), or so broadly drafted, either out of ineptitude or in an effort to stop up any loopholes, that they sweep within their minatory scope much conduct that is of little or no danger to the community. Partly through limiting appropriations to prosecutors' offices, legislatures force prosecutors to make choices among whom to prosecute, and for what crimes; and we hope they will make these choices in a just, restrained, and sensible manner.

The rules and customs that constrain law enforcement are paralleled by ones that constrain the defense of the criminal suspect, of which punishing for obstruction of justice is an example; another example is the ethical constraints on defense lawyers.

The Conduct of Starr's Investigation and His Link to the Jones Suit

The rules and customs that surround the process of law enforcement—let me call them "procedure" for short—are distinct from the key substantive concept that guides law enforcement, that of guilt in fact. Especially when guilt is clear, a standard defense strategy is to attack the procedure by which guilt has been determined and to urge that defects in the procedure should cancel the defendant's guilt. The ordinary law (I postpone consideration of impeachment law, which is far from ordinary) is rightly reluctant to countenance such a response. To turn the trial of a suspected criminal into a trial of the law-enforcement process complicates and protracts the trial and distracts and confuses the tribunal. It produces acquittals that excuse a greater wrong to punish a lesser one. Better that the defendant and the enforcer should be tried separately and punished separately than that they should be tried together and the enforcer punished by annulling the defendant's punishment. The two-stage process is simpler and less confusing and does not undermine deterrence by excusing the criminal on account of the wrongs done by the enforcer. American criminal procedure has long been criticized as being too concerned with assuring a "sporting" contest between prosecutor and defense and too little with getting at the truth.[4] The Supreme Court has been right to swing over to the position

---

[3]18 U.S.C. § 711. Another nice example is stepping on a shrub on the grounds of the Library of Congress. 2 U.S.C. § 167c.

[4]This criticism is powerfully argued in William T. Pizzi, *Trials without Truth: Why*

that convictions should not be voided as a means of punishing prose-cutorial misconduct that does not create a substantial risk of an erro-neous conviction.[5]

Occasionally, it is true, the criminal *is* allowed to benefit from such misconduct. The best-known example is the exclusionary rule in search and seizure cases. Evidence obtained in violation of the prohibition in the Fourth Amendment of the U.S. Constitution against unreasonable searches and seizures is excluded from the defendant's trial even when it establishes his guilt conclusively and without it he cannot be con-victed. But this is an exception (and an exception increasingly riddled with its own exceptions) to the general rule, which is not to let the criminal go free merely because the police or the prosecutors have mis-behaved, unless the misbehavior undermines the court's confidence that the defendant is actually guilty. The exception is inapplicable to Linda Tripp's taping of conversations with Lewinsky. Even if the taping both violated state law and was indispensable to Starr's obtaining authori-zation to enlarge his investigation, evidence or leads to evidence ob-tained in violation of state law are not excludable in federal proceed-ings. And even if the taping had violated federal law, the fact that it was done by a private citizen rather than by a law-enforcement officer would take it out of range of the exclusionary rule, which is limited to unlawful *governmental* seizures of evidence.[6] This is not to deny that Tripp's behavior was morally questionable. She repeatedly assured Lew-

---

Our System of Criminal Trials Has Become an Expensive Failure and What We Need to Do to Rebuild It (1999).

[5]United States v. Hasting, 461 U.S. 499 (1983); Bank of Nova Scotia v. United States, 487 U.S. 250, 254–257 (1988). For a strong statement of this position in the context of a prosecution for obstruction of justice, see United States v. Neiswender, 590 F.2d 1269, 1271–1272 (4th Cir. 1979). Of particular relevance, given the analogy between the role of the House of Representatives in impeachment and that of the grand jury in ordinary prosecutions, the Supreme Court has held that prosecutorial misconduct before the grand jury is pretty much harmless per se. Conviction at trial requires more proof than indictment, and so shows that the defendant would have been indicted in an error-free grand jury proceeding. United States v. Mechanik, 475 U.S. 66 (1986). See also United States v. Williams, 504 U.S. 36 (1992).

[6]United States v. Jacobsen, 466 U.S. 109 (1984). The fact that Linda Tripp was em-ployed by the federal government is irrelevant; she was not employed in a law-enforce-ment capacity. The federal wiretapping statute does prohibit the use of evidence obtained in violation of the statute, even if it was obtained by a private person (18 U.S.C. § 2515), but Tripp's recordings of her telephone conversations with Lewinsky did not violate the statute. See 18 U.S.C. § 2511(2)(d).

insky, in the very phone conversations that she was taping, that she was Lewinsky's good friend, that her feelings toward Lewinsky were almost maternal, and that Lewinsky should trust her. She invited trust and then betrayed it. I leave the reader to decide, on the basis of the circumstances surrounding her decision to tape (see Chapter 1), whether she had adequate justification for this prima facie breach of moral duty.

We have now to consider whether there were other irregularities (besides the unlawful taping) in the process by which Clinton was brought to the verge of impeachment,[7] and, if so, whether, either singly or together, they were so grave that if Clinton were not President and were being prosecuted in the ordinary way, we would think it either unlawful or unjust that he should be punished. These issues turn out to be inseparable from the fact that Clinton has become a polarizing figure in American politics and culture. The why of this, and its broader significance, are for later; what is important here is the phenomenon itself. Some Presidents are popular, and though there is opposition it is not passionate. Eisenhower is a good example, and Lyndon Johnson in his first term. Some Presidents are unpopular, and while they have some support it is not passionate either; examples are Jimmy Carter and Lyndon Johnson in his second term. Some Presidents are mildly popular and have passionate detractors; that was the situation of Nixon during his first term. Other Presidents, however, such as Lincoln, Franklin Roosevelt, and Reagan, generate strong passions among both supporters and opponents. Until September 1998, Clinton was in the approximate position of Nixon in his first term; popular (more popular than Nixon), but without a large core of passionate supporters, and an object of fierce antipathy to a core of opponents. In that month, when the push to impeach him first crested, a number of previously tepid supporters of the President became passionate in his support, for reasons, however, that are not directly relevant to this chapter.

The true "Clinton haters" are only the fringe of the considerable opposition to him, but a fringe that bled into and in the eyes of many contaminated the investigation and prosecution of his suspected crimes. The fringe has beliefs best described as paranoid fantasies, such as that

---

[7] Whether there were irregularities in the impeachment process itself, that is, the process in Congress, I consider briefly at the end of this chapter and at greater length in the next chapter.

Vince Foster, the Deputy White House Counsel who committed suicide early in Clinton's first term, was murdered because he knew too much about the Clintons' complicity in Whitewater crimes; that Clinton when Governor of Arkansas had operated an international drug-trafficking ring from a secret airport in the state; that Clinton is or was a cocaine addict and as a result has had to have surgery on his nose (cocaine destroys the septum); and that his supporters regularly murder anyone who might reveal his illegalities to the world. In or near the fringe is the wealthy philanthropist Richard Mellon Scaife, who has financed investigations into whether Vince Foster was murdered. (That Foster was murdered is the core, the defining, belief of Clinton haters.) A bridge between the fringe and the rational opposition to Clinton has been constructed by the editorial-page writers of the *Wall Street Journal*, who believe that Clinton condones and may even encourage threats of violence against anyone who might give evidence against him, such as Kathleen Willey.[8]

The Independent Counsel's investigation of Clinton's affair with Monica Lewinsky took off from the Paula Jones suit. When a person such as Jones who does not have a lot of money yet is not indigent and so does not qualify for legal aid has a legal claim, she cannot as a practical matter sue unless she can persuade a lawyer to handle her suit on a contingent-fee basis, which means that he'll get a percentage of the judgment (usually 33 to 40 percent) if she wins and nothing if she loses. Paula Jones's claim was not likely to be attractive in purely monetary terms to a lawyer good enough to litigate effectively against the President of the United States. Sexual harassment litigation is usually an uphill battle,[9] and Jones had no evidence to support her claim besides her own say-so. An Arkansas jury (perhaps any jury) would be quite likely to believe the President's denial—or at least would have been until

[8]See Editorial, "Don't You Get the Message?" *Wall Street Journal*, Oct. 26, 1998, p. A22. The editorial draws in part from a book by Clinton hater Ambrose Evans-Pritchard, *The Secret Life of Bill Clinton: The Unreported Stories* (1997). The book hints broadly that Clinton has been responsible for a number of murders, including that of Vince Foster, and for drug-running. The author labels Starr a "Pontius Pilate" for determining, after an exhaustive investigation, that Foster indeed committed suicide. Id. at 113.

[9]See Bonnie S. Dansky and Dean G. Kilpatrick, "Effects of Sexual Harassment," in *Sexual Harassment: Theory, Research, and Treatment* 152, 157–159 (W. O. Donohue ed. 1997).

the Lewinsky affair became public knowledge (another indicator of the affair's materiality to Jones's suit).

Also, Jones's claim had legal infirmities that threatened to derail it before it could get to a jury—that did derail it, when Judge Wright dismissed the suit before trial.[10] Jones, it is true, appealed the dismissal, and the case was settled before the court of appeals could rule on the appeal. But Judge Wright's opinion makes a persuasive case that Jones had not been sufficiently harmed by the alleged incident with Clinton to be permitted to maintain her suit. So even if she had been permitted to go to trial, and had won, she probably would not have won much because nothing very bad had happened to her. I say "probably" only because a jury might have awarded Jones punitive as well as compensatory damages; but punitive damages are rarely more than a slight multiple of the compensatory damages. Her case became an $850,000 case (the amount of the settlement) because it became a threat to the President's continuation in office as a result of the Lewinsky matter, and this could not have been foreseen when the suit was filed back in 1994.

Most "colorable" (plausible, nonfrivolous) legal claims are not pressed, for the sorts of practical reasons that I have been discussing. Paula Jones's claim might well have been one of them, had it not been for the desire of Clinton's opponents to use the suit to score political points off him. Her suit was sponsored and financed from start to finish by political opponents of Clinton,[11] some, though not all, of whom belonged to the oppositional fringe that I am calling the "Clinton haters." And this made it possible for Clinton to charge, for example in his grand jury testimony and in the address to the nation that followed, that the Independent Counsel's investigation of his affair with Lewinsky had grown out of a politically motivated lawsuit. It had—and for the further reason that it was a Clinton hater, Lucianne Goldberg, who instigated Linda Tripp's program of taping telephone conversations with Monica Lewinsky, encouraged Tripp to go to the Independent Counsel with the tapes, and put Tripp in touch with Paula Jones's lawyers, who, armed with what Tripp told them, were able to interrogate

---

[10]Jones v. Clinton, 990 F. Supp. 657 (E.D. Ark. 1998).

[11]See Ed Vulliamy, "The Clinton Gambit: How the President's Men Prised Paula's Mini-Skirted Life Apart," *Observer*, April 5, 1998, p. 11; Kim Masters, "The Country Lawyer, Taking a Swing at Goliath," *Washington Post* (final ed.), June 24, 1994, p. B1; Don Van Natta, Jr., and Jill Abramson, "Quietly, a Team of Lawyers Kept Paula Jones's Case Alive," *New York Times* (national ed.), Jan. 24, 1999, p. 1.

Clinton in detail concerning his relationship with Lewinsky, thus precipitating his perjury.

The first independent counsel appointed to investigate Clinton (concerning Whitewater), Robert Fiske, was removed in favor of Kenneth Starr when the independent counsel law was reenacted. The panel of judges that appoints independent counsels under that law[12] was and is headed by a very conservative judge, David Sentelle, a close friend of a very conservative Senator from North Carolina, Lauch Faircloth (defeated for reelection in November 1998), who had publicly called for Fiske's removal.[13] The reason given by the panel for replacing Fiske was pretty feeble. It was that since he had been appointed by Clinton's Attorney General, Janet Reno, there was an "appearance" that he was not completely independent, though in fact there was no reason to suppose him a pal, let alone a tool, of either the Attorney General or the Clintons. He was a Republican, and could hardly be expected to go easy on Clinton out of "gratitude" for having been appointed an independent counsel by Clinton's Attorney General—who is, moreover, not close to the Clintons herself or ambitious for a higher or different office that Clinton might bestow on her. Fiske had been at work investigating Whitewater for eight months when he was removed in favor of Starr, which made removal and replacement a source of delay and of duplication of effort. The Clinton haters were hostile to Fiske because he was unreceptive to the notion that Vince Foster had been murdered. The panel of judges that replaced Fiske was, however, unanimous in doing so and there is no evidence that Clinton haters swayed Judge Sentelle or either of the other two judges on the panel.

Here I must pause to note that there is an unavoidable asymmetry in my discussion of Clinton's misconduct and my discussion of the alleged misconduct of his prosecutors/persecutors. The former has been exhaustively investigated; the latter has not, not yet anyway. Fuller investigation may bring worse skullduggery to light. But I am confined to the public record. Subject to that qualification, not much significance can be attached to the fact that Sentelle was seen lunching with Faircloth and Jesse Helms shortly before the replacement of Fiske by Starr, either.

---

[12]The Special Division. See Chapter 1.

[13]Ruth Marcus, "Kenneth W. Starr," *Washington Post,* Jan. 30, 1998, p. A1; Jane Mayer, "How Independent Is the Counsel?" *New Yorker,* April 22, 1996, pp. 58, 59.

Kenneth Starr, moreover, would hardly have been the choice of the Clinton haters. His reputation as a judge of the U.S. Court of Appeals for the District of Columbia Circuit during the Reagan Administration and as Solicitor General of the United States under Bush was that of a moderate, not a right-winger. It has been rumored that he was passed over for appointment to the Supreme Court during the Bush Administration because of opposition from the Right. He is, it is true, a seriously believing Christian, which may or may or may not have been known by members of the panel; and seriously believing Christians (also seriously believing Jews and Muslims) are more likely than other people to be outraged by sexual misconduct. But it was unforeseeable in 1994 that the investigation of Whitewater would molt into an inquiry into Clinton's extramarital escapades. And while Clinton was already widely believed to be an adulterer, there is no basis for thinking that Starr was so indignant about this that it would color his investigation.

Starr's appointment could, however, be questioned on grounds unrelated to his personal qualities and outlook. President Bush had run for reelection in 1992 and been beaten by Clinton; Starr, as Solicitor General, had been a high official of the Bush Administration. It would have been better, for appearance's sake, had the Special Division appointed, to investigate Clinton, a lawyer who did not have such a recent and senior connection to the President whom Clinton had defeated. Yet Archibald Cox, the first independent counsel ("special prosecutor," it was then called) to be appointed to investigate Nixon concerning Watergate, had been active in John Kennedy's 1960 Presidential election campaign against Nixon and had gone on to serve as Solicitor General during the Kennedy Administration. And Cox's conduct as special prosecutor is widely admired.

So far, there is a bit of ammunition for Clinton's defenders but nothing that would actually delegitimize Starr's investigation of the Lewinsky matter. But we must consider now the circumstances in which that investigation began. Apart from the roles played by Tripp, Goldberg, and Paula Jones's lawyers, all of them political foes of Clinton, we know that those lawyers consulted Richard Porter, a junior partner in the law firm of Kirkland and Ellis and an active Republican, on some issues related to the Paula Jones case.[14] Starr was also a partner in Kirkland

---

[14]In the interest of full disclosure of facts that might lead a reader to suspect bias on my part, I should mention that Richard Porter is a former student and law clerk of mine.

and Ellis. He continued to practice law with the firm until July 31, 1998, shortly before the completion of his investigation of the Clinton-Lewinsky affair. And so he was a partner of Porter's when the investigation began,[15] though Porter was in Kirkland's Chicago office and Starr in its Washington office. It is a large firm, and Starr has denied having had any contact with Porter concerning the Jones case.

We know that one of Paula Jones's lawyers had consulted Starr from time to time concerning issues of Presidential immunity, that Starr's office began its investigation of the Clinton-Lewinsky affair before he received authorization to expand the Whitewater investigation to take in the affair, that Starr had almost resigned as independent counsel to become the dean of a public policy school in California financed by Richard Mellon Scaife (as well as dean of the university's law school), and that Starr did not disclose his or Porter's involvement in the Paula Jones case when applying for that authorization. The law does not forbid an independent counsel to continue practicing law while serving as independent counsel. But it does forbid him, and anyone employed by or otherwise associated with his law firm, to "represent in any matter any person involved in any investigation or prosecution under [the independent counsel law]."[16] Jones was "involved" in the independent counsel's investigation in the practical sense that she had something to gain from it; the large settlement that she eventually received in her suit against the President was undoubtedly a product of the investigation and of the impeachment inquiry to which the investigation led. But it is uncertain whether Porter's, and unlikely that Starr's, contacts with her lawyers amounted to representation of her. There is no suggestion that Kirkland and Ellis was to receive a fee for whatever assistance

---

I have not discussed with him Clinton's affair with Lewinsky, or any of its sequelae, since before I began working on this book; and so far as any of our earlier conversations are concerned, I recall nothing in them that is not public knowledge. As I indicated in the Introduction, I have no inside knowledge of the Clinton-Lewinsky affair and its aftermath. For journalistic accounts of Porter's role, and of other links between Jones's lawyers and the Independent Counsel's office, see Van Natta and Abramson, note 11 above, and Michael Isikoff, "The Right Wing Web," *Newsweek,* Feb. 22, 1999, p. 32.

[15]And perhaps when it ended; for Starr's "resignation" from Kirkland and Ellis was in the form of an indefinite unpaid absence, which may not be the equivalent of resignation for purposes of the conflict of interest provision of the independent counsel law.

[16]28 U.S.C. § 594(j)(1)(A).

Porter rendered Paula Jones, but unless it was there would be no possibility of Starr's benefiting financially from Porter's involvement in the
Jones case.

And there is nothing unethical about a public prosecutor's obtaining
a "tip" about a possible crime from a party to private litigation or a
party's lawyer. A great many perfectly lawful, indeed unexceptionable
and indispensable, criminal prosecutions result from tips from criminal
accomplices, paid informers, competitors, disgruntled former spouses
and employees, and other private individuals who have axes to grind.
If these sources were deemed fatally tainted, the criminal justice system
would crumble. What may have made Starr reluctant to acknowledge
aid from Paula Jones's team was that such aid would have colored accusations that Clinton was the victim of a partisan witch hunt, since
Jones's lawyers and backers were intensely partisan.

Would the prosecutorial irregularities, if known, have derailed the
investigation of Clinton's affair with Lewinsky? They would not as a
matter of law have precluded the appointment of Starr to investigate
the Lewinsky affair. It is even arguable, though I think only weakly, that
the link through Vernon Jordan to Webster Hubbell and hence Whitewater, and through Linda Tripp to the White House travel office matter,
also under investigation by Starr,[17] was enough to empower Starr to
investigate the affair without a fresh authorization; Starr's office apparently did not know that Jordan had begun helping Lewinsky with
her job search before she was identified as a possible witness in the
Jones case. It is unlikely that full disclosure of Starr's links to the Jones
case would have led the Attorney General or the Special Division to
have appointed a different independent counsel to investigate the affair.
The affair did seem connected to the Whitewater investigation through
Vernon Jordan and Linda Tripp; and the Attorney General would have
been reluctant to subject the President to the indignity of being investigated by two independent counsels at once. And, to repeat, Starr had
not yet been labeled a right-wing zealot. Moreover, time was of the
essence. It was not until January 12, just days before President Clinton's

---

[17]Tripp had worked in the travel office when several of its employees were fired in
questionable circumstances, and had been interviewed by the Independent Counsel's
staff in connection with the matter.

scheduled deposition in the Jones case, that Starr's team learned, from Tripp, that Lewinsky was planning shortly to submit a perjurious affidavit and that the President might have encouraged her to do so. There was a chance—but only if the prosecutors moved very quickly—of catching suspected criminals in the act.

Even if a different independent counsel should have been appointed— and it is certainly arguable that by disqualifying Fiske on such flimsy grounds as it did the Special Division had raised the purity hurdle so high that Starr couldn't clear it either and would not have received the appointment if everything concerning his relationship to the Jones suit had been disclosed—it is merely speculation that the investigation would have followed a different course. There is no basis for the claim by Clinton's defenders (and others, notably the *New York Times* columnist Maureen Dowd) that the vigor with which Starr pursued the investigation into the affair was a consequence of his being a sex-obsessed puritan witch hunter, or a puritan of any kind; no basis either, as I have already suggested, for thinking him a fire-breathing right-wing prosecutorial pit bull. It is no doubt the case, given his religious beliefs, that he disapproves of extramarital sex. But it is a bit much to argue that anyone who disapproves of extramarital sex must be a puritan, let alone that he must be obsessed with sex—a repressed pervert incapable of maintaining a professionally detached attitude in investigating conduct that involves sex. Nothing is known about Starr's personal life that would support such a theory; nothing in his marathon testimony before the House Judiciary Committee on November 19, 1998, or in his television interview by Diane Sawyer shortly afterward, was suggestive of sexual obsession.

Even the gratuitous sexual details—and some of them were indeed gratuitous, as I'll explain shortly—in the Starr Report do not require a postulate of sexual obsession (or "mere" puritanism, or partisan zealotry) to explain. Starr and his team learned from Linda Tripp that it was likely that Clinton had obstructed justice, and they proceeded to use typical hardball prosecutorial methods to try to nail him for these crimes. They had been frustrated by Webster Hubbell's refusal (as they thought) to cooperate with them; now they saw what seemed to be the explanation, a kind of underground railroad running from the government in Washington to Revlon in New York along which Clinton and Vernon Jordan whisked potential witnesses against Clinton out of reach of investigators. Starr and his team may have jumped to conclusions too soon. As we saw in Chapter 1, the initiative for using Jordan to help Lewinsky get a job came from Lewinsky herself rather than from the White House and was unrelated, at least initially, to Lewinsky's being subpoenaed in the Paula Jones case. The "talking points" memo was also a false lead. And the investigation into the travel office petered out without any charges being filed against anyone. But it was a natural inference from what was known when Tripp first approached Starr that Clinton and Jordan were engaged in a pattern of obstructing justice in matters already under investigation by the Independent Counsel. Where there is smoke, there is usually fire.

Starr thus was duty-bound to bring the contents of Tripp's tapes to the attention of the Attorney General, and she was duty-bound to advise the Special Division to appoint someone to investigate the suspicious Presidential conduct that the tapes suggested, though it need not have been Starr. Another independent counsel might, in deference to the Presidency or to privacy, have proceeded more cautiously in the investigation of Clinton's and Lewinsky's conduct in the Jones case. But in view of Linda Tripp's tapes, which were bound to surface sooner or later, it is unlikely that a responsible independent counsel would simply have dropped the matter without any investigation, or have taken the President's unconvincing denials at face value and thus pretermitted the inquiry that led to the semen-stained dress. Most of the irregularities of which the Independent Counsel's office was accused had no effect on the course of the investigation, notably the aggressive tactics used in the initial encounter with Lewinsky, which produced no cooperation from her. In any event, it is irresponsible to suggest that it was the sexual angle that energized Starr's investigation, especially since Starr had no previous prosecutorial experience and therefore perforce relied heavily on the advice of the experienced prosecutors who worked for him on how to proceed. They have not been accused of being sex-obsessed puritans. Prosecuters are aggressive people; if they were not, our crime rate would be even higher than it is.

Conceivably Starr was upset by the campaign of vilification to which he was subjected by Clinton's defenders, who depicted him as a sex-obsessed religious nut, an extreme right-winger, and a Clinton hater. These were slanders with no credible basis. It is unknown whether the President played any part in this campaign; but he could have killed it with a word, just as later he shut up James Carville for a time, when the latter's vicious attack on Speaker Newt Gingrich appeared to have backfired.[18]

Consider, as possibly bearing on Starr's state of mind, the participation in this campaign of Abner Mikva, a former colleague of Starr's on the D.C. Circuit who had resigned as chief judge of that court to become White House Counsel, though he had left that position by the time the scandal broke. As soon as the media reported that Starr was investigating the Lewinsky affair, Mikva began telling reporters, "He's totally out of control. The man I served with is a different person." "He's become a bottom feeder." "I think the attorney general has to seriously consider removing Judge Starr from this investigation." "I think Judge Starr is behaving in an outrageous manner" and should not base an investigation on "gossipy talk between two young women." "I know nothing about the facts, but I think Judge Starr is sick."[19] Admitting to knowing nothing about the facts—and in January and early February of 1998, the period from which these quotations come, very little could have been known with confidence about the facts—Mikva was irresponsible in pronouncing Starr "sick" and "out of control." If anything was capable of infuriating Starr, it would be this barrage by Mikva, coming as it did from a former colleague mantled with the prestige of a former chief judge of a federal court of appeals. Clinton could easily have silenced, and even more easily have disavowed, his irresponsible defenders.[20] He did neither. He either encouraged or condoned a "low road" attack on Starr, spearheaded by Carville[21] but supported by re-

---

[18]Carville acknowledges that the White House is able to shut him up. James Carville, *... And the Horse He Rode in on: The People v. Kenneth Starr* 15 (1998).

[19]The sources of these quotations are, respectively, Tony Mauro, "Tapes Presented Starr Little Time, Complex Issues," *USA Today,* Jan. 30, 1998, p. 3A; David Hawpe, "Feeding off the Bottom," *Courier-Journal,* Feb. 1, 1998, p. 3D; David Willman and Cecilia Balli, "After Testifying, Starr Critic Vows He Won't Lighten Up," *Los Angeles Times,* Feb. 27, 1998, p. A28; David G. Savage, "In Public's View, Starr Is Falling," *Los Angeles Times,* Jan. 30, 1998, p. A16; Roger Simon and William Neikirk, "Cover-up Charges Embroil Clinton," *Chicago Tribune,* Jan. 22, 1998, pp. 1, 12.

[20]Not all of them; not Alan Dershowitz, for example. See Chapter 4.

[21]Carville has called Starr "an abusive, privacy-invading, sex-obsessed, right-wing, constitutionally insensitive, boring, obsequious, and miserable little man." Carville, note 18 above, at 10. Also a "media whore." Id. at 106. Carville quotes with approval Camille Paglia's description of Starr as "a simpering, shilly-shallying fascist milquetoast... who has a face like creamed corn and the brains to go with it." Id at 141. And he goes the Clinton haters one better by intimating that Richard Mellon Scaife, who suspects that Vince Foster was murdered, had himself murdered a man and staged it as a suicide. Id.

spectable Democrats such as Mikva, that may well have provoked a response in kind.

It is only speculation that Starr, whose demeanor is phlegmatic and who remained at least outwardly imperturbable throughout the ordeal (and it *was* his ordeal, as well as Clinton's), was furious, or that if he was this influenced his conduct of the investigation. It is, however, a much more plausible if less colorful speculation than that he is obsessed with sex. It is an especially plausible conjecture that his subordinates, feeling that their reputations as prosecutors were at stake, redoubled their efforts to "nail" Clinton. The harder they fought, the harder he and his supporters, some unscrupulous, fought back. The conflict escalated all the way to a Senate trial. It strikes me as unjust to blame the Independent Counsel's office for this spiral.

The Independent Counsel's investigation lasted from January 1998 to September, when Starr submitted his report to Congress. During this period he was criticized for, among other things, hauling "little people," such as White House stewards, Betty Currie, Secret Service agents, and Monica Lewinsky's mother and aunt, before the grand jury, thereby forcing them to spend in the aggregate hundreds of thousands of dollars in legal fees.[22] Some of these people may have committed felonies,[23] and so we needn't wring our hands over their incurring legal expenses. Others were not in any legal jeopardy—and this raises the question why anyone summoned before the grand jury who was not a target or even a subject[24] of the Independent Counsel's investigation bothered to hire

---

at 118–119. In the television interview on January 26, 1998, in which Mrs. Clinton described the charge that her husband had had an affair with Monica Lewinsky as the product of "a vast right-wing conspiracy," she described Carville as a "great human being." *Appendices to the Referral to the U.S. House of Representatives,* H. Doc. No. 311, 105th Cong., 2d Sess., vol. 2, p. 1973 (Sept. 18, 1998).

[22]Some of these witnesses, however, were represented by government lawyers at no expense; and how much of the fees charged by other lawyers will ever actually be paid, by the clients or by anyone, is unclear.

[23]Or it seemed they had: Monica Lewinsky had told Linda Tripp in their tape-recorded conversations that her mother had advised her to lie in her deposition, but Lewinsky may have been making this up. She testified that she had become suspicious of Linda Tripp and had begun to lie to her. But this testimony came after Lewinsky's mother testified before the grand jury. When the mother testified, Lewinsky had not yet begun cooperating with the Independent Counsel, and so Starr's team had no basis for believing that the mother was in the clear.

[24]A "subject" is someone who, though not a target of the grand jury's investigation, may have participated in some of the target's illegal behavior and may therefore be in

a lawyer. Some may have been frightened by the prospect of having to testify in secret before a grand jury. But more may have hoped that a lawyer would help them to testify in a way that did as little harm to the President and to their own reputations, and in some cases their careers, as possible. Most of the witnesses hired lawyers recommended by the White House Counsel's office, and some of the lawyers had joint defense agreements authorizing them to share notes with lawyers for other witnesses. Witnesses are not allowed to have a lawyer with them in the grand jury room when they testify, but they are free to tell their lawyer (or anyone else for that matter) what they have told the grand jury and to authorize the lawyer to share the information with the lawyers for other witnesses.

The hypothesis that witnesses who were neither targets nor subjects of the grand jury investigation may have hired lawyers not for their own legal protection but for the protection of the President is supported by the grand jury testimony of Alex Nagy, the head of the White House telephone service. He testified that the White House Counsel's office was angry with him for refusing to retain a lawyer when he was called to testify before Starr's grand jury. He knew he wasn't going to be prosecuted and so he saw no reason to bother with a lawyer.

Once the Starr Report was published, the purpose of all these interrogations became clear. The testimony of Betty Currie and Vernon Jordan, and of course of Lewinsky herself, was vital to determining whether the President had obstructed justice. The testimony of the other witnesses, not only Secret Service agents and White House staff but also Lewinsky's friends, aunt, and mother, was necessary to corroborate her testimony and thus to prove that the President had indeed obstructed justice in his deposition in the Paula Jones case and later in his own testimony before the grand jury. It is possible that if the President had told the truth in January, no one would have been called before the grand jury.

Starr's office has been accused of leaking some of the grand jury testimony, in violation of Rule 6(e) of the Federal Rules of Criminal Procedure, which forbids disclosure of matters before the grand jury unless necessary for law enforcement purposes. Some testimony got into the media long before the House Judiciary Committee published the tran-

---

jeopardy. Most of the witnesses before Starr's grand jury were neither targets nor subjects.

scripts of it. But since witnesses are free to disclose their own testimony to anyone they want and many of the witnesses before Starr's grand juries were exchanging information among themselves through their lawyers, it is hard to know which "leaks" came from the Independent Counsel's office. Even testimony adverse to Clinton may have been leaked by "friendly" witnesses, in order to reduce the shock value of Starr's anticipated report.

In any event, if there were leaks by the Independent Counsel's office, an issue at this writing under investigation, they were a part of the Independent Counsel's public relations battle (which he lost) with the White House's slander machine,[25] and so in retrospect they are inconsequential. But the waging of such warfare is not a proper law-enforcement purpose even when there is provocation. Since the primary reason for grand jury secrecy is to protect the efficacy of the grand jury as an investigative tool of prosecutors by encouraging witnesses to testify without fear of intimidation,[26] prosecutors who compromise that secrecy are shooting themselves in the foot. For this reason and because the Independent Counsel's office achieved nothing by its leaks (if it did leak, which has not yet been established), it is difficult to see how the President can complain, especially when his own lawyers were part of the campaign of slander directed against the Independent Counsel's office.

At worst, the disclosures of grand jury testimony were premature. Nothing forbade the Independent Counsel to forward transcripts of grand jury testimony to the House of Representatives. Having found "substantial and credible information . . . that may constitute grounds for an impeachment," he was required by the independent counsel law to so inform the House,[27] and most of that evidence was in those tran-

---

[25]Not, I think, too strong a term for the efforts of White House staff (such as Sidney Blumenthal, whose misrepresentations of his grand jury testimony, designed to "trash" the Independent Counsel's investigation, I mentioned in Chapter 1), Mrs. Clinton (with her accusation of a vast right-wing conspiracy and her testimonial for the character of James Carville), and other defenders of the President to blacken the reputations of the President's adversaries in his desperate, no-holds-barred struggle to retain his office.

[26]A secondary purpose, however, is to protect people who do not end up being indicted from embarrassment. This purpose, we shall see later, was compromised, not by the leaks so much as by the publication of the grand jury transcripts, with minimal redaction, by the House Judiciary Committee.

[27]28 U.S.C. § 595(c).

scripts. Nothing in law or custom forbade the House to publish excerpts from (or for that matter the entirety of) the transcripts. Without such publication, whatever action the House eventually took on Starr's referral would lack public acceptability, though we shall see that the House Judiciary Committee could have edited the transcripts with a heavier hand.

Televising grand jury testimony is certainly unusual and releasing the television tape for broadcasting worldwide is unheard of, but again the President cannot complain. He consented to having his testimony televised in lieu of his having to appear before the grand jury in person, and he knew that a tape was being made and would be made public sooner or later and probably sooner. And insofar as his principal goal throughout was to escape impeachment and conviction, he benefited from the broadcasting of his grand jury testimony, humiliating as it was. Clinton is well known for his charm and intellectual agility, and these qualities are far more discernible in a broadcast than in a transcript. In the transcript his grand jury testimony is evasive, equivocating, halting, uncertain, and deeply unconvincing. But when one watched it on television, the dominant sense was of a person in an impossible position doing his plucky best to elude his tormentors. I happened to be in Paris the day his testimony was broadcast, and I watched it on CNN, which brags that it reaches a billion people. I doubt that a billion people watched the President's testimony that day or later, but tens of millions did and they saw him fencing with faceless inquisitors over the details of his extramarital sex life. The reaction of many viewers was that the subjection of a President of the United States to this unprecedented humiliation rite in a "stadium" of millions was punishment enough and that impeachment and conviction would constitute a gratuitous anticlimax.

Starr has been criticized for calling Clinton before the grand jury in the first place. Targets of a grand jury investigation generally are not called as witnesses because they are sure to take the Fifth Amendment and refuse to testify. Clinton could have taken the Fifth, though at a political cost. He seems to have preferred, as criminal suspects sometimes do, to try to lie his way out of trouble.

It has been thought odd, and maybe improper, that a grand jury should be used as, in effect, an investigative arm of Congress. But Starr's grand jury (actually juries) were investigating other persons besides the President, and his testimony might be germane to their investigation;

and there was (and still is) a possibility that the President would be prosecuted for his crimes in the ordinary way.

Starr has also been criticized for his initial approach to Lewinsky, when his people threatened in effect to send both her and her mother to prison unless she cooperated with them. Had she made a self-incriminating statement and later been prosecuted, it is possible though unlikely that the statement would have been excluded from evidence as having been obtained by coercion. No such thing happened, and so these hardball tactics were at most what the law calls harmless error. Probably they were not error at all. Both Lewinsky and her mother were in criminal jeopardy, though the prosecutors grossly exaggerated when they told Lewinsky that she might be sent to prison for twenty-seven years;[28] twenty-seven months would have been closer to the mark, as we know from the hypothetical calculation of Clinton's "sentence" in Chapter 1. And even though she could have avoided prosecution for perjury by retrieving her false affidavit before it was filed in court,[29] she was already, irrevocably, guilty of attempting to suborn perjury (by Linda Tripp), witness tampering (Tripp again), and conspiracy (with her mother, as well as the President, if what she had said about her mother in the conversations recorded by Tripp was true) to commit perjury and otherwise obstruct justice. The prosecutors offered her a good deal—immunity, and for her mother as well as herself, in exchange for cooperation. It was the deal she accepted six months later.

Because Lewinsky could have retrieved her affidavit before it was filed, the Independent Counsel has been accused of having sprung a "perjury trap" on her by failing to advise her of that possibility. She was already, however, in deep jeopardy. Moreover, as used in the law, the term "perjury trap" refers to a completely different situation—the situation in which the government puts a witness before the grand jury (or in any other situation involving testimony under oath) for the purpose not of eliciting useful information but of enticing the witness to commit perjury.[30] It was not the Independent Counsel's idea to place

---

[28]This was the most coercive aspect of the encounter.

[29]The confrontation with Lewinsky took place on January 16, 1998; the perjurious affidavit had been mailed that day by her lawyer by overnight express, and was not received by the court until the next day. Until it was filed in the court, she was not guilty of perjury, at least under 18 U.S.C. § 1623. Dunn v. United States, 442 U.S. 100, 109–113 (1979).

[30]See, for example, United States v. Chen, 933 F.2d 793, 796–797 (9th Cir. 1991).

Monica Lewinsky's name on the witness list in the Paula Jones case, in the hope that she would commit perjury in that case.

When Starr's people first approached Lewinsky, she had a lawyer, and they knew it. The Justice Department's policies regarding criminal law enforcement, which are applicable to independent counsels as well as to lawyers employed by the Justice Department,[31] forbid prosecutors to approach directly a criminal suspect who they know has a lawyer. However, Lewinsky had hired a lawyer to help her prepare an affidavit in a civil case, not to represent her in criminal proceedings; she had no idea that such proceedings were looming. Because the lawyer was not representing her in the criminal proceeding in connection with which the Independent Counsel's office sought to question her, or indeed in any criminal proceeding, it is doubtful whether she was a "represented party" within the meaning of the policy against approaching a suspect who is represented.[32] The fact, moreover, that Jordan had picked Lewinsky's lawyer—and picked a criminal lawyer—created a possibility that the lawyer was a member of the conspiracy to obstruct justice; that possibility might have warranted bypassing the lawyer, too. Anyway the normal sanction imposed on prosecutors who bypass a suspect's lawyer is to exclude from evidence at the suspect's trial any statement that the suspect may have made to them, and Lewinsky neither made a statement nor was prosecuted for her crimes. And in any event a defendant (Clinton) cannot complain about the infringement of someone else's rights, in this case Lewinsky's.

The argument that the Independent Counsel's office sprung a "perjury trap" on Lewinsky blends into the broader argument that it conducted a "sting" operation against the President. The term refers to a scheme by prosecutors or police to induce a person to commit a crime for which he can be arrested and prosecuted. By being tricked into committing the crime in circumstances that have been rigged to ensure his being detected, the target of the sting delivers himself into the hands of justice.

[31]28 U.S.C. § 594(f)(1).

[32]See 28 C.F.R. § 77.3. The Justice Department has issued a number of policy statements concerning perjury and other forms of obstruction of justice. See U.S. Department of Justice, *United States Attorneys' Manual: Criminal Resource Manual* §§ 1720–1767 (1999) (http://www.usdoj.gov/usao/eousa/foia_reading_room/usam/); U.S. Department of Justice, *United States Attorneys' Manual,* vol. 1, § 9–69 (1998). There is, at this writing, no proof that the Independent Counsel contravened any of them in his investigation of the President.

The Independent Counsel could have warned the President about what awaited him at the Jones deposition on January 17. And it could have refrained from asking Lewinsky to record conversations with the President. It may have been trying to "set up" the President to commit and suborn perjury; and it may have been doing this in direct or indirect cooperation with Paula Jones's lawyers.

Sting operations are not unlawful. They are a common and often an indispensable method of catching the perpetrators of "victimless" crimes, broadly defined to include crimes in which the victim (Paula Jones, for example—the intended victim of Clinton's and Lewinsky's obstructions of justice) is unaware that she *is* a victim. They become unlawful only when they slide over into entrapment, which means inducing the commission of a crime that the criminal would never have committed had it not been for the abnormal inducements offered by the authorities (such as paying someone a million dollars to steal a bicycle). There was nothing like that here. But to conduct a sting operation against the President of the United States, in concert with the President's partisan enemies, is certainly questionable as a matter of sound enforcement policy. It is also a potent argument against the independent counsel law, without which such a scheme would be unthinkable. What it is not is a legal defense against prosecution.

The Starr Report and the Question of Privacy

The most vociferous criticisms of the Independent Counsel's investigation of Clinton have been leveled against the Starr Report itself, and they are three. The first is that the report should have contained an analysis of what conduct rises to the level of an impeachable offense. There is a certain logic to this demand. How could the Independent Counsel determine whether there was substantial and credible evidence of impeachable offenses without first deciding what an impeachable offense is? But as we shall see in subsequent chapters, no one knows what an impeachable offense is. Had the Independent Counsel tried to define it, he might have defined it more narrowly than the House of Representatives would think proper, and as a result leave out evidence that the House might consider important to its deliberations and invite the accusation that he was usurping the House's prerogative of defining impeachable offense. If he defined it broadly, again he might be accused of usurpation, and certainly of lacking objectivity. The course he chose, implicitly defining impeachable offense as arguably including obstruction of justice even in a basically private matter, was probably, in the circumstances, his best choice.

The second criticism of the report is that it is one-sided against the President. It is, but it cannot be faulted for that. It is one-sided because the evidence of Clinton's criminal activities is very strong. The report would not have been one-sided only if it had not been judgmental at all. Starr could just have dumped the raw grand jury transcripts, the transcripts of his staff's numerous interviews with (and a deposition of) Lewinsky, the DNA report, the e-mails, Linda Tripp's tape recordings, and so forth on the House Judiciary Committee. But Starr's charge, derived from the language of the independent counsel law, was to inform the House whether he had found substantial and credible evidence of impeachable offenses. A judgment that the evidence he had found was substantial and credible required the drawing of inferences from the raw data—required, that is, the kind of analysis that the report provided and that, given the state of the evidence, was bound to be one-sided. That did not make him an "advocate" for impeachment. Evidence cannot be warranted to be probative or believable unless it is analyzed. Moreover, Clinton's defenders argued that they wanted the impeachment inquiry wound up as quickly as possible; its completion would have been retarded by months had the task of sifting the raw data collected by the Independent Counsel devolved on the inexperienced staff of the House Judiciary Committee.

Remember that impeachment means, in effect, indictment, and so the House of Representatives corresponds to the grand jury. (The Senate corresponds to the petit jury, that is, the jury that decides the guilt or innocence of a person whom the grand jury has indicted.) Prosecutors do not just dump raw data in the laps of grand jurors. They analyze the data and advise the grand jury whether they think there is enough evidence to warrant indictment. Of course the House of Representatives has more resources for independent analysis than a grand jury. But those resources are actually quite limited, because the House is not in the business of conducting criminal investigations. In any event, the nation was impatient for a resolution of Clinton's "case"—it didn't want to wait months while the House of Representatives traipsed over ground already well trodden by the Independent Counsel. One can disagree with specific portions of the analysis in the Starr Report, as I do, and even note some tendentious omissions,[33] without supposing that Starr misbehaved in offering his conclusion that there was indeed substantial and credible evidence of impeachable offenses. We shall see in Chapter 4 that the report may actually have overlooked one such offense.

The most compelling criticism of the Starr Report is that there was no need to put so much sex into it. Some had to be put in because Clinton had denied both in his deposition in the Paula Jones case and in his grand jury testimony that he had ever touched Lewinsky erotically. His principal lawyer in the Independent Counsel's investigation, David Kendall, had made a public statement after the President gave his grand jury testimony that the testimony showed that the President had not committed perjury. The testimony showed the opposite. Starr was duty-bound to unmask these lies, not because it "matters" whether Clinton was an active or a passive participant in his sexual encounters with Monica Lewinsky but because he had lied about this to a grand jury and the lies were material to the grand jury's investigation and therefore criminal.

But Starr could have unmasked these lies simply by listing each of the ten sexual encounters by date, time, and place and as to their content stating that in each of them Lewinsky fellated the President while the President touched parts of her body enumerated in the definition of sexual relations in the Paula Jones deposition with the intention of arousing or gratifying Lewinsky's sexual desire. That would have been enough to show that the President had lied in denying that he had engaged in sexual relations with Lewinsky.[34] There was no need to add that he stuck a cigar in her vagina and then put it in his mouth and said

---

[33]The President's lawyers were rightly critical of the Starr Report's failure to quote Lewinsky's testimony that no one had told her to lie or offered her a job in exchange for her silence. The report could have pointed out that this may just have meant that no one had *explicitly* told her to lie or *formally* offered her a job in exchange for her silence, but her denials were important enough to deserve being quoted rather than just paraphrased, which is what the report did. And I noted in Chapter 1 that the report had quoted President Clinton out of context to make him seem to have lied about whether he had discussed executive privilege with his lawyers. But basically the report is one-sided because the facts are one-sided.

[34]Actually more than enough. We saw in Chapter 1 that Clinton engaged in "sexual relations" (as defined for purposes of the deposition) even if he was, like a rape victim, the completely passive object of Lewinsky's sex acts.

it tasted good, that after one of his encounters with Lewinsky he masturbated into the sink in his bathroom, or that they engaged in phone sex.[35] The inference arises that Starr's intention (or that of his subordinates but concurred in by him) in including these details, which were irrelevant to whether the President had committed any impeachable offenses, was to destroy Clinton. If this is correct—it may not be; it is just speculation; the prosecutors may have believed that every detail was necessary to bolster Lewinsky's credibility and nail down their case, given Clinton's extraordinary verbal agility—it was a natural response to the campaign of vilification that Clinton's supporters, necessarily with at least his tacit support, had mounted against Starr. But we expect better from our prosecutors; as I said at the beginning of this chapter, they are not to hate their quarry. And we shall see in Chapter 4 that revelations of intimate details about a President can damage the office of the Presidency, and perhaps, therefore, the nation as a whole.

It might be argued that once the central facts of Clinton's sexual relationship with Lewinsky had been made public—that she had fellated him and he had fondled her—the invasion of privacy was complete and the disclosure of additional details (the use of a cigar as a dildo, and the phone sex and other masturbation) marginal. But this argument would miss an important aspect of privacy. Privacy operates as a screen against information overloads and as an antidote to the cognitive quirk known as the salience or (more commonly) availability heuristic.[36] Rational thought requires selection from the immense, the overwhelming, masses of data that confront our senses and compete for the attention of our mind. We do *not* want to know everything about the thoughts and actions of other people, because the knowledge would obstruct interpretation and understanding. The details of Clinton's sexual proclivities are a distraction to anyone who wants to understand and eval-

---

[35]It is true that he testified misleadingly about phone sex in his grand jury testimony by saying only that some of his phone conversations with Lewinsky had involved "sexual banter." That is not what phone sex is, as any reader of *Vox* knows. But phone sex is not a form of "sexual relations" in any but the most contrived sense of the term as it was defined for purposes of the President's deposition in the Paula Jones case.

[36]See, for example, Amos Tversky and Daniel Kahneman, "Availability: A Heuristic for Judging Frequency and Probability," 5 *Cognitive Psychology* 207 (1973); Christine Jolls, Cass R. Sunstein, and Richard Thaler, "A Behavioral Approach to Law and Economics," 50 *Stanford Law Review* 1471, 1477, 1518–1522 (1998); Timur Kuran and Cass R. Sunstein, "Availability Cascades and Risk Regulation," 51 *Stanford Law Review* 769 (1999).

uate Clinton's Presidency or the role and function of the President in American government and society. They are a riveting distraction (that is the operation of the salience heuristic). In one of the gamier exchanges recorded on Linda Tripp's tapes and, though properly unmentioned in the Starr Report, included in the mass of evidence published by the House Judiciary Committee, Lewinsky and Tripp discuss the dimensions of Clinton's penis. Everyone knows that the President, like all but a very few unfortunate males, has such an organ. But a public discussion or description of it, like a photograph of it, brings what is properly background knowledge into the foreground, where it serves only to distract. Similarly, we might have guessed from what is revealed about Clinton elsewhere in the Starr Report that something like the cigar phallus, or phone sex, might well be part of his sexual repertoire. But once the guess is converted to a public fact, it acquires a salience that makes it more difficult for people to think straight about what is already a dauntingly complex moral and legal situation. And it also makes it more difficult for Clinton's family to avert their eyes, as it were, from his relationship with Lewinsky.

Other sexual details in the report, such as that Clinton several times talked on the phone to members of Congress while being fellated, were relevant to the Independent Counsel's investigation only if Clinton attempted to deny that Lewinsky fellated him, which he could not do after he flunked the DNA test on Lewinsky's dress, or if Starr thought that the disrespect to Congress that Clinton could be thought to have displayed in these incidents was relevant to a judgment on impeachment, which the report does not suggest. So this was another gratuitous swipe at the President, as was reporting Clinton's hint to Lewinsky that he might leave his wife when he completed his term of office[37] and his confession to having had innumerable adulterous affairs in the past.

I do not wish to fetishize privacy. Privacy is concealment, and often what is concealed is discreditable.[38] Sunshine is a disinfectant. If people could not conceal their adulteries from their spouses, adultery would be less common. But my concern here is with disclosures that go beyond

---

[37]This was especially gratuitous because the Starr Report omitted the statement by Monica Lewinsky's best friend, Catherine Allday Davis, that Clinton had told Lewinsky "that he loved, respected, and wished to spend the rest of his life with the First Lady." *Supplementary Materials to the Referral to the U.S. House of Representatives,* H. Doc. No. 316, 105th Cong., 2d Sess., vol. 1, p. 832 (Sept. 28, 1998).

[38]Richard A. Posner, *Overcoming Law* 531–536, 539 (1995).

the revelation of discreditable conduct and reveal details that distract, confound, and embarrass more than they inform or deter.[39] The Starr Report's *unnecessary* invasions of the President's privacy—invasions surely hurtful to his wife and daughter as well as to himself—are thus to be regretted. But this form of prosecutorial misconduct has no standing in criminal or civil law. You cannot defend against a criminal prosecution on the ground that the prosecutor has made public disclosure of more details of your private life than he had to do in order to carry out his prosecutorial duties.

In the cross-examination to which Starr was subjected when he appeared before the House Judiciary Committee, there were suggestions that the objectionable features of his report and of the entire investigation showed that the report was not worthy of being believed. This suggestion is inconsistent with the argument that he overinvestigated the case and ignores the actual evidence gathered by Starr's team and published by the Committee, as distinct from the report's summary of that evidence. The fact that there is so *much* evidence that the President committed crimes suggests, as is often the case with excess prosecutorial zeal, that the excesses of the Independent Counsel's investigation reflected his and his staff's confidence in the justice of their cause.

In an ordinary criminal trial, none of the alleged investigative or prosecutorial improprieties that I have been discussing at such length would even have been admissible as evidence or argument that the defendant should be acquitted. The purpose of a criminal trial—the main purpose anyway, and a purpose we lose sight of at our peril—is to get at the truth rather than to decide whether the prosecutors have been unsporting. In charging prosecutorial misconduct the President's defenders were waging a political rather than a legal battle for his exoneration. Naturally they waged it primarily in the media. They waged it with more partisan zeal, more stridency, more sophistries, and less respect for truth than the Independent Counsel.

The Question of Prosecutorial Discretion

We must consider whether a proper concept of prosecutorial discretion would have led a well-motivated prosecutor not to press charges against

---

[39]No doubt there is some incremental deterrence; imagine if all known adulterers were forced to supply the media with photographs of themselves engaged in adulterous activity.

someone who engaged in the misconduct that Clinton did. Clinton's defenders pointed out that prosecutions for perjury committed in a civil proceeding are rare, that the civil proceeding in question here (Paula Jones's suit) was dismissed, that the Lewinsky affair was only tangentially related to the issues in that proceeding, and that Clinton wouldn't have had any occasion to lie before a grand jury if his perjury in the Paula Jones litigation had been judged not worth investigating. They also argued that everybody lies about sex and that the investigation of Clinton not only was rooted in a politically motivated litigation (the Jones case) but also was enabled by the peculiarity that an independent counsel, unlike an ordinary prosecutor, operates essentially without the constraint of limited resources that would induce the ordinary prosecutor to drop so marginal and difficult to prove a criminal charge as perjury in a civil deposition. The ordinary prosecutor, moreover, either is an elected official or is (as in the case of federal prosecutors) appointed by an elected official. Politically sensitive, such a prosecutor usually avoids prosecuting people for esoteric crimes, as obstruction of justice arising out of a sexual affair might be thought to be. It is the combination of the political and budgetary constraints of prosecutors that makes our vague and broad criminal statutes tolerable; and their breadth and vagueness in turn stop up the loopholes through which serious criminals might otherwise escape justice. The form of the laws and the incentive structure of prosecutors constitute a system that the independent counsel law shatters.

The argument concludes that if Clinton were not President or otherwise within the compass of the independent counsel law, so that Linda Tripp would have been offering her tapes to an ordinary prosecutor, Clinton would not have been prosecuted. Prosecutions for perjury committed in a civil case are rare relative to the frequency of such perjury, though they are not so rare as Clinton's defenders claimed[40] and though their rarity is due, in part at least, to the fact that perjury is usually very difficult to prove because the offense is narrowly defined, as we saw in Chapter 1. In Clinton's case, it was easy to prove perjury provided that

---

[40]See *Appendices,* note 21 above, vol. 1, pp. 271–274; William Glaberson, "In Truth, Even Those Little Lies Are Prosecuted Once in a While," *New York Times* (late ed.), Nov. 17, 1998, p. A1; Henry Weinstein, "Starr's Perjury Tack a Road Less Traveled," *Los Angeles Times,* Feb. 15, 1998, p. A1. Remember the *DeZarn* case discussed in Chapter 1.

the resources for a thorough investigation were available, as they were.

Prosecutions for perjury committed in a civil case involving sex or domestic relations are especially rare. A search of judicial databases for decisions within this class since January 1, 1992, yields only two in which the defendant wasn't charged with other offenses as well.[41] Clinton did commit other, though closely related, offenses as well, but my search uncovered only four more sex or domestic relations cases involving perjury in which the defendant was also charged with other offenses, of which two were military prosecutions.[42]

The infrequency of sex-related perjury prosecutions may reflect a fear by prosecutors that juries agree with Clinton's defenders that lying even under oath about sex is less culpable than other perjury because "everybody lies about sex." Cutting the other way is the fact that prosecutors generally prefer to prosecute prominent rather than obscure people who commit crimes; prosecutions of the prominent are much more likely to generate publicity, which both promotes deterrence and advances the prosecutor's career. Were Clinton a prominent person but not the President, he would have been more likely to be prosecuted than the run-of-the-mill sex perjurer.

Maybe a prosecutor of this hypothetical non-Presidential Clinton would have thought it enough to alert the judge in the Paula Jones case to Clinton's misconduct. Judge Wright could have entered an order defaulting Clinton or administered some other civil sanction if she found he had lied at his deposition.[43] The matter would have stopped there, with no grand jury investigation to provide opportunity and temptation for additional perjury. But as I have tried to show, it is not at all certain that the matter would have stopped short of criminal prosecution. A lot would have depended simply on how busy the prosecutor was or how he felt about sexual harassment suits.

---

[41]State v. French, 509 N.W.2d 698 (S.D. 1993) (per curiam); Britt v. N.C. Sheriffs' Education & Training Standards Comm'n, 501 S.E.2d 75 (N.C. 1998).

[42]LaParle v. State, 957 P.2d 330 (Alaska App. 1998); State v. Dye, 1998 WL 666751 (Ohio App. Aug. 28, 1998); Schneider v. Tilley, 998 F. Supp. 1210 (D. Kan. 1998); United States v. Czekala, 38 M.J. 566 (Army Ct. of Military Rev. 1993). In two other sex-related cases the defendant received a sentencing enhancement for having committed perjury in the course of his trial or related proceedings. United States v. Nasiruddin, 1998 WL 539468 (4th Cir. Aug. 25, 1998) (per curiam); United States v. Rabin, 986 F. Supp. 887 (D. N.J. 1997).

[43]See, for example, Fed. R. Civ. P. 37(a)(3).

In the end, moreover, the House of Representatives decided not to base impeachment on Clinton's lies at his deposition. It decided to make his lies before the grand jury the focus of its perjury charge. Investigations of perjury are more common than actual prosecutions. To commit perjury during an investigation in order to avoid prosecution is a more serious offense, and one therefore more likely to be prosecuted, than committing perjury in a deposition.

Suppose that everything is as it was in the investigation of Clinton except that he was not the President of the United States but instead the president of a corporation, university, or foundation, or the mayor of a medium-sized city. These comparisons were used throughout the debate over impeaching Clinton to argue that since anyone in the list of counterpart chief executives who engaged in conduct similar to Clinton's would be booted out forthwith, so should Clinton be. The argument is unpersuasive, not only because the stakes are different but also because in the other examples the same body that appointed the executive and is his hierarchical superior is being asked to remove him. My point is different. I want to assume that a well-funded prosecutor, utilizing a grand jury, has gathered all the evidence that Starr had, and I want to ask whether on that assumption prosecution would be likely. A defendant in a sexual harassment case, desperate to avoid exposure of an extramarital affair, perjures himself repeatedly in his deposition in that case as well as suborning perjury by another witness and tampering with a third witness; and later, before a grand jury investigating these obstructions of justice to determine whether they warrant prosecution, he again perjures himself repeatedly. Such a lengthy string of crimes would invite prosecution, especially if the criminal was a prominent person already under investigation, by the same prosecutor, for other possible criminal activity (Whitewater and its many progeny, including the suspected payment of hush money to Webster Hubbell). The fact that the crimes originated in sex and in the natural impulse to conceal an extramarital relationship would not argue compellingly for an exercise of discretion in favor of the criminal, as can be seen by assuming that Clinton murdered Lewinsky to shut her up. Our hypothetical non-President Clinton is a person who flouts the law in too brazen a fashion for his transgressions to be easily overlooked. Failure to prosecute would send a signal that the legal system smiles at obstructing justice.

I concluded in Chapter 1 that the President committed criminal obstructions of justice. I have added here that despite the unusual and to an extent irregular aspects of the process by which he was apprehended, if—as is quite likely—he were prosecuted in an ordinary court, he would be unable to invoke the irregularities of the process as grounds for dismissal or acquittal of the charges. Of course it is a separate question, but one for later in this book, whether he should have been impeached for any of these crimes.

There is widespread concern about the overfunding of Starr's investigation, as of independent counsel investigations generally. The machinery of federal criminal investigation and prosecution, with its grand juries, wiretaps, DNA tests, bulldog prosecutors, pretrial detention, broad definition of conspiracy, heavy sentences (the threat of which can be and is used to turn criminals into informants against their accomplices), and army of FBI agents, is very powerful; there is a fear that fed enough time and money, it can nail anybody. There is some truth to this, since there are literally thousands of federal criminal laws, many of them at once broad, vague, obscure, and underenforced, and since Americans tend not to be docile and obedient. If every American had an independent counsel on his tail, we would live in a police state. But whether or not the independent counsel law is wise or unwise (I shall argue in Chapter 7 that it is unwise), there is an argument for subjecting powerful public officials to a higher than average standard of law-abidingness. There are also grounds just explored for believing that even an ordinary prosecutor would have prosecuted a non-Presidential counterpart of Clinton.

Call Me Bubula

I expressed my unease at some of the contents of the Starr Report. I want now to express my unease at some of the contents of the 8,000 pages of evidence—evidence gathered by the Independent Counsel, mainly through interviews and grand jury testimony, and turned over to the House Judiciary Committee—that the Committee published as appendices and supplements to the Starr Report. My unease has nothing to do with the accuracy of the evidence, very little of which the President's lawyers and other defenders contested. Such challenges as they did mount, culminating in the portions of the 184-page submission to the House Judiciary Committee on December 8, 1998, that were devoted to the facts, were either picayune or unpersuasive. And remember that the White House preferred to go to trial in the Senate on the record compiled by Starr than to have live witnesses testify, who could be cross-examined—and when Monica Lewinsky, the star witness against Clinton, did finally testify, the President's lawyers declined to cross-examine her.

But the mountain of "evidence" assembled by the Independent Counsel's office is also an astonishing farrago of scandal, hearsay, innuendo, libel, trivia,[44] irrelevance, mindless repetition, catty comments about people's looks,[45] and embarrassing details of private life. Because grand jury transcripts, which constitute the bulk of the evidence, are ordinarily kept secret, even an experienced lawyer or judge is likely to be amazed (I was) by the rawness of these transcripts.

The redaction (lawyer-speak for deletion) of portions of the evidence by the staff of the House Judiciary Committee was clumsy. Some of the deleted materials had already been published in the Starr Report; the cat was out of the bag. Similarly, while an effort was made to excise

---

[44]For example, that the Watergate apartment in which Lewinsky lived with her mother became so infested with mice that the two women had to move out while the exterminators went to work. Or that President Clinton couldn't think of the name of Porky Pig's wife (it's Petunia) while doing a crossword puzzle, or that he collects frogs and "used to have this sort of really funny statue that was up on the bookshelf. It was this really weird thing. It was like a beast. It almost looked—they looked like cupie [Kewpie] dolls under a big mushroom, and it was raining." *Supplementary Materials,* note 37 above, vol. 2, p. 2637. Or that Linda Tripp, when she was still working at the White House, once went to the local McDonald's to get some food for some of the workers in her office and President Clinton said he wanted something too, namely a grilled chicken sandwich. McDonald's at the time didn't make grilled chicken sandwiches. Tripp begged the chef to make an exception and grill her a chicken filet. He refused, saying, "Lady, we don't do that here." "So I begged him again and here's a big line in back of me and the guy just looked at me and, goes, 'Lady, I don't care if this is for the President of the United States, we don't grill chicken sandwiches.' And I said 'I understand.' So I got a fried one." Id., vol. 3, pp. 4168–4169.

[45]For example:

Ms. Lewinsky: . . . I don't know when the last time you saw [name] was—

Ms. Tripp: Look, Monica. You cannot make a silk purse out of a sow's ear, so it really doesn't matter when I saw her.

Id., vol. 2, p. 2634. The woman's name appears in the passage that I have quoted. The entire passage should have been deleted; it is at once offensive to the person named and irrelevant to the investigation.

rumors about girlfriends of Clinton other than Monica Lewinsky and Gennifer Flowers, the redactors were not thorough and the key names are disclosed, along with such tidbits as that former Clinton girlfriends who do not turn against him are known as "graduates."[46] (Monica Lewinsky believed that Clinton and the White House staff did not treat her with the respect due a graduate.) The only consistent deletions are of telephone numbers, which is fine, and of expletives, which is absurd given the subject matter of the investigation and the fact that no child is going to read these fine-print volumes.

The more one reads in this multi-thousand page mélange (and here is evidence that the Republican majority of the House Judiciary Committee showed poor judgment in publishing so much, over the Democratic members' objections), the harder it is for even a legal professional to take the investigation of Clinton completely seriously. I will give just two examples.

Walter Kaye, the wealthy Democratic Party contributor who got Monica Lewinsky her internship in the White House (Kaye was a friend of Lewinsky's mother), had the following exchange with a grand juror and a prosecutor, Solomon Wisenberg:

The Foreperson: Can I ask you—
The Witness: Sure.
The Foreperson: —if you ever use the terminology "bubula"?
The Witness: I sure do.
The Foreperson: Thank you.
The Witness: I use it very often.
The Foreperson: Okay.
Mr. Wisenberg: How do you pronounce it?
The Witness: Do you know what the term means? Bubula, it's a Jewish term—in case you people don't know, I'm Jewish—and it's a term—I use it as an expression of endearment. I use it very often. I could have called her [Monica Lewinsky] bubula at some time . . .
The Foreperson: . . . Because maybe when you're hanging up on the phone with somebody, "Call me bubula." Do you ever—
The Witness: Say that again?

---

[46]In at least one instance, the name of a rumored girlfriend is clearly readable simply because the redactor didn't draw a sufficiently thick line through it. See id., vol. 3, p. 4024.

The Foreperson: "Call me bubula." Do you ever—

The Witness: Say to me? Nobody ever says it to me.

The Foreperson: No, no, no. But when you're winding up a telephone conversation.

The Witness: So I'll say, "Goodbye, bubula." I'll do that, absolutely right.

Mr. Wisenberg: "Give me a call some time, bubula."

The Witness: Bubula, absolutely right. I taught a lot of people Yiddish at the White House, a few words anyhow, and the Army. It's hard to believe, but—it's a term I use. How do I spell it? I don't know.

Mr. Wisenberg: Do you spell it with or without the "h"? I'm just kidding.

(Laughter.)[47]

A grand jury needs a few laughs from time to time to keep going; but the bubula[48] excursus, like the Jewish joke picked up on Lewinsky's computer and included in the volumes of evidence despite its manifest irrelevance, did not have to be published at taxpayer expense.[49]

My second example is a mite more serious. A Secret Service agent testified in a deposition that Bayani Nelvis, one of the President's stewards, told the agent (who was a pal) that "he was tired of cleaning up this crap, and this wasn't right, or something to that effect,"[50] and the agent got the impression that the reference was to lipstick on the President's towels in the bathroom off the Oval Office. This sets the interrogating prosecutor off on a minute inquiry into what the steward was holding in his hands. Was it just towels? More than one? How big? What color? Was it soda cans too? Maybe a plastic garbage bag? A replacement bag? How high? Maybe eighteen inches?

Q. And are they [the bags] clear or opaque?

A. They are semi-clear.

---

[47]Id., vol. 2, p. 2044.

[48]The correct spelling is "bubeleh" (the prosecutor was right about the h). It's a Yiddish diminutive for "grandmother." The grand juror's curiosity about the term may have stemmed from Monica Lewinsky's using the word "Baba" (probably a variant of "bubeleh" —and "baba" is the Russian word for grandmother) to denote Mrs. Clinton.

[49]The joke is: Question: Why do Jewish men like to watch pornographic movies backward? Answer: So that they can see the prostitute give back the money.

[50]*Supplementary Materials,* note 37 above, vol. 1, p. 323.

Q. Could you see what was inside the bag?

A. Really, I'm not sure anything was in the bag, you know. No, I couldn't. I couldn't see what was in the bag it was—he had it small in his hand.

Q. Did he have it crumpled up in his hand like from the top?

A. Yeah. It's possible the bag was actually the replacement bag. But he had the towels in his hands also.

Q. Why would he be coming out with a replacement bag?

A. Maybe to yell at me. I don't know. I don't know. I'm just—

Q. You know, when you take a garbage bag out, it may be folded or something.

A. Right.

Q. Was this thing opened up?

A. It was, it was, he was holding it in his hand more like this, elongated, if I remember correctly. And he had the towels in his hand.

Q. Could you tell whether there was anything in the plastic bag?

A. No, I could not. Not—I don't recall.[51]

One can imagine a murder or espionage case in which this kind of painstaking inquiry would be necessary. And it is easy to blame President Clinton for having compelled the Independent Counsel to inquire into the details of his relationship with Lewinsky in order to test the truthfulness of Clinton's denials of such a relationship and so to determine whether he had committed perjury in the Paula Jones case. But there is something a little crazy about turning the White House upside down in order to pin down the details of Clinton's extramarital sexual activities so that Paula Jones might have a shot at winning her long-shot suit for redress for an offensive but essentially harmless advance made (maybe) by Clinton before he became President.

One just *knows* that if the shoe were on the other foot—if everything were the same except that the President was a Republican—the Republicans would have denounced the investigation in the same terms that the Democrats used. And with perfect sincerity.

One begins to see why the whole Clinton-Lewinsky-Starr-impeachment business is so baffling. Even after unsubstantiated conjectures (such as Starr's being obsessed with sex, or Clinton's having tried to get Lewinsky a job so that she wouldn't tell the truth in the Paula Jones case) are put to one side, there are two diametrically opposed narratives

[51]Id., vol. 1, p. 324.

to choose between. In one, a reckless, lawless, immoral President commits a series of crimes in order to conceal a tawdry and shameful affair, crimes compounded by a campaign of public lying and slanders. A prosecutor could easily draw up a thirty-count indictment against the President. In the other narrative, the confluence of a stupid law (the independent counsel law), a marginal lawsuit begotten and nursed by political partisanship, a naive and imprudent judicial decision by the Supreme Court in that suit, and the irresistible human impulse to conceal one's sexual improprieties, allows a trivial sexual escapade (what Clinton and Lewinsky called "fooling around" or "messing around")[52] to balloon into a grotesque and gratuitous constitutional drama. The problem is that both narratives are correct.

Choosing to emphasize one or the other is legitimate. What is illegitimate is the confusion of popular and legal justice, a confusion perpetrated by the President's defenders, including academics and lawyers who should know better. By popular justice I mean the ideas of justice that are held by the average person untrained in law. By legal justice I mean the justice meted out by judges and other authorized officials. The two types of justice merge in systems such as that of ancient Athens or Maoist China in which the legal system is manned entirely by nonlawyers; they merged in Clinton's Senate trial. Popular justice has a tendency to degenerate into popularity contests, and it is in just such terms that the President's defenders cast the issue of his behavior. They called it "Starr v. Clinton" and asked the American people to pressure their representatives to acquit Clinton on the ground that Starr is less likeable. Implicitly, if Clinton were unpopular, say because the country was in a severe recession or because he was as dour as Nixon, and Starr had Clinton's charming television presence, it would be proper to impeach and convict Clinton, for he would be the loser in the court of public opinion.

Public opinion is relevant to impeachment given the composition of the tribunals, the House and the Senate. But we must bear in mind, not only for the sake of clarity of analysis but also to preserve the principle

---

[52]"We fooled around . . . Having sex is having intercourse." Id., vol. 2, p. 2664 (Monica Lewinsky to Linda Tripp). Clinton's defenders have fastened on this statement as evidence that Clinton was not lying when he denied in his Paula Jones deposition having sexual relations with Lewinsky. But "sexual relations" was a defined term and it unambiguously included the conduct in which Clinton engaged with Lewinsky.

that in a civilized society legal disputes are resolved without regard to the personal attractiveness of the disputants,[53] that whatever one thinks of Starr and his tactics, or however much one admires Clinton for his achievements as President, Clinton was guilty of serious crimes, and the behavior of the Independent Counsel's office, Linda Tripp, and Paula Jones's backers did not excuse or mitigate that guilt. Suppose X were prosecuted for raping Y. Would it be relevant that X was popular and successful, Y unpopular, yet the prosecutor unaccountably hostile to X? The answer is no, and importantly no, because legal justice must not be allowed to degenerate into popular justice. It is because the law, for this reason and also simply to keep the legal process manageable, tries to narrow the focus of disputes and exclude much that gives a legal dispute its color and urgency and emotional impact, that the sprawling mass of unsifted testimony published by the House Judiciary Committee is so disquieting to a legal professional.

Paradoxically, the pettifogging legalisms and diversionary arguments to which the President's defenders so often resorted during the impeachment proceedings (we shall see examples in subsequent chapters) were in the service of popular rather than legal justice. Many congressional Democrats were reluctant to support the retention of a criminal in the nation's highest office. The lawyers' arguments made it possible for them to argue that while the President's behavior may have been reprehensible, it was not (or at least not provably) criminal. The arguments provided the necessary figleaf.

The efforts to supplant legal by popular justice were not all on Clinton's side. The publication of the reams of grand jury testimony is a case in point, though it is hard to believe they could have been bottled up forever. The failure of the House of Representatives to adopt comprehensive procedural rules for Presidential impeachment *before* beginning its impeachment inquiry was also disrespectful of legal justice. It is bad enough from the standpoint of legal justice that the House is a partisan body. But that is inevitable. What is not inevitable is that the House, or its Judiciary Committee, should be making up the rules of procedure in the midst of the inquiry that the rules are to govern. Even if it would be too much to expect a legislature to make provision far in

---

[53]This is the core of the principle of "corrective justice," recognized since Aristotle as a cornerstone of the rule of law. See Richard A. Posner, *The Problems of Jurisprudence* 313–320 (1990).

advance for an event of such low probability (at least if history is a reliable guide) as a Presidential impeachment, the House had eight months between the outbreak of the Clinton-Lewinsky scandal and the submission of the Starr Report. In that time it could have promulgated rules of procedure so that when the impeachment inquiry proper began the rules would not be a political football. Clinton's defenders were right to object to the partisan manipulation of the rules during the impeachment inquiry and to make political hay out of the unfairness of such manipulation. The haymaking included efforts to stir a populist groundswell from outside the halls of Congress to drown the spectacle of populist justice within.

The Senate trial also suffered from an absence of detailed rules (see the next chapter), for example rules prescribing the burden of proof, rules of pretrial discovery, rules of evidence, rules on the proper behavior of Senators in an impeachment trial (like any judge or juror they should have been forbidden to comment publicly on the trial before it was over or to have secret contacts with the litigants—the White House and the House impeachment managers), and rules on the form of the verdict (can it include findings of fact, or just the bottom-line judgment of acquittal or conviction?). Because it lacked the necessary rules, the Senate had constantly to interrupt the trial to adopt rules for the next stage. These caesuras became occasions for partisan bickering, underscoring the failure of the impeachment proceeding to meet minimal standards of legal justice.

———————•———————

CHAPTER 3

The History, Scope, and Form
of Impeachment

History and Scope

The Constitution provides that the President and other federal officials shall be removed from office, and may be barred from holding a federal office in the future, upon impeachment by a majority vote of the House of Representatives and conviction by a two-thirds vote of the Senate of treason, bribery, or "other high Crimes and Misdemeanors."[1] The Senate may not impose any additional sanctions, although the impeached and convicted official remains liable to punishment in the ordinary course of criminal justice.[2]

The meaning of the quoted language is critical to whether President Clinton committed impeachable offenses. And since "high Crimes and Misdemeanors" is not defined in the Constitution and is not modern terminology (in modern legal parlance, a misdemeanor is a minor crime, generally a crime for which the maximum punishment is a year in prison), it is natural, though not necessarily fruitful, to look to history for guidance. Another possibly critical issue besides the meaning of the quoted phrase, one on which the constitutional text is also silent, is what procedures should be followed in an impeachment and in particular what standard of proof should govern the Senate's trial of an impeached official—whether guilt must be proved beyond a reasonable doubt, as in a criminal trial, or whether a lesser degree of certitude is sufficient.[3] It is natural to seek help with the answers to these questions, too, in history.

[1]U.S. Const., art. II, § 4; see also art. I, § 2, cl. 5; § 3, cl. 6.
[2]Art. I, § 3, cl. 7.
[3]The Senate has adopted "Rules of Procedure and Practice in the Senate When Sitting

Impeachment can be traced back to the fourteenth century in England. Parliament used it to get at high officials (and sometimes powerful private individuals) who bribed, intimidated, overawed, or were otherwise not amenable to punishment by, the regular courts; the monarch, however, was considered immune. The House of Commons, acting much like a grand jury, decided whether to impeach the official. If it did impeach him, the House of Lords tried him and if it convicted him could impose criminal-type punishments, including death, as well as removal from office. The fact that the trial was before a legislative body was not anomalous, not only because the English did not (and to a large extent still do not) have a robust notion of separation of powers but also because the House of Lords included, as it still nominally does, the principal royal judges.[4] The process of impeachment by the Commons and trial by the Lords was not a perfect substitute for a normal civil or criminal proceeding. The "grand jurors" (the Commons) and the "judge-jurors" (the Lords) were politicians to a greater degree than members of the regular judiciary were. It comes as no surprise that impeachment functioned in practice not only as a mode of legal punishment but also as a method for augmenting the power of Parliament relative to that of the monarch and his officials.

The colonial assemblies in Great Britain's American colonies used impeachment a great deal, especially in the seventeenth century, even though the British government did not recognize the right of colonial assemblies to impeach.[5] They did it anyway and the ensuing trial before the upper house (usually the governor's council), even the threat of trial, was often enough to induce the impeached official to resign. As in England, legal forms—in particular the right of the accused to notice of the charges and to a hearing in which he could confront his accusers

---

on Impeachment Trials," *Procedure and Guidelines for Impeachment Trials in the United States Senate,* S. Doc. No. 33, 99th Cong., 2d Sess. 2 (Aug. 15, 1986), but, as I noted at the end of the preceding chapter, they are brief and general and do not address the standard of proof. See Michael J. Gerhardt, *The Federal Impeachment Process: A Constitutional and Historical Analysis,* ch. 4 (1996).

[4]Nowadays the Appellate Committee of the House of Lords is England's supreme court. But the judges who compose it are not appointed from the ranks of the peers, who are the people entitled to sit in the House of Lords; they are professional judges, promoted to the Appellate Committee from the lower ranks of the judiciary.

[5]On impeachment during the colonial and revolutionary (that is, preconstitutional) periods, see Peter Charles Hoffer and N. E. H. Hull, *Impeachment in America, 1635–1805,* pts. 1–2 (1984).

and present witnesses in his defense—were adhered to. But, as in England, the process was often activated by political concerns. In a few colonial impeachments in the eighteenth century, before the Revolution, the subtext of the proceeding was a challenge to royal authority.

Impeachment was thus a familiar procedure to the framers of the Constitution. The argument for including it in the new charter of national government and making it applicable to the President, as well as to the Vice President, judges, and other civil officials of the federal government, was straightforward. The President was to have a fixed term of office; there ought to be some procedure for removing him before his term expired.[6] But if that procedure consisted, say, of a vote of no confidence by both houses of Congress, the President's position would be very weak; the legislature would be supreme, and thus the balance of powers that was the cornerstone of the edifice erected by the Constitution would be destroyed.

The solution was to create both procedural and substantive roadblocks to removing a President by impeachment. The principal procedural roadblock was the requirement of a two-thirds vote in the Senate to convict. It is a bit deceptive, since the harder it is to convict in the Senate, the easier it may be to impeach in the House; some of the moderate Republicans, whose votes to impeach President Clinton were essential, voted so in the hope and expectation that he would not be convicted by the Senate. The prohibition against the Senate's imposing any sanction on the impeached official other than removal from office and disqualification from holding a federal office of trust or honor in the future also slightly dilutes the effect of the two-thirds requirement, by lowering the stakes in an impeachment. At the same time, as with the prohibition against bills of attainder in Article I, section 9, of the Constitution,[7] the prohibition against the Senate's imposing criminal

[6]The Vice President was also to have a fixed term of office, and federal judges were to hold office "during good Behaviour," U.S. Const., art. III, § 1, that is, for life if they behaved themselves. Other civil officers of the federal government, though they did not have fixed terms, might exercise the kind of power that might make them difficult to control by the ordinary processes of law; yet the President might refuse to remove them. Apart from the two Presidential impeachments, however, federal judges are the only officials who have been impeached under the Constitution.

[7]Bills of attainder are criminal judgments rendered by legislatures and were used both in England and in the American colonies. The bill of attainder is an alternative device to impeachment by which a legislature can punish an official. On whether a legislative censure is a bill of attainder, see Chapter 5.

penalties on a President whom it convicts reduces the power of Congress to intimidate the President.

The substantive roadblock to impeaching and convicting a President was the limiting of the grounds of removal to high crimes and misdemeanors.[8] These terms were not defined, and had no settled usage. A "high" crime might mean a serious crime—or simply a crime committed by a high official.[9] "Misdemeanor" might mean "offence; ill behaviour; [or] something less than an atrocious crime."[10] If the word bore the last sense, which is also the modern sense, of a minor crime, the constitutional formula would be absurd: either "high Crimes and low Crimes" or "high Crimes and high low Crimes."

The constitutional convention rejected proposals to allow impeachment for "maladministration," "mal-practice," or "neglect of duty," lest such terms have the practical effect that the President, judges, and other federal officials would be serving at the pleasure of Congress.[11] But the convention did not intend to limit impeachment to crimes punishable in the regular courts.[12] Such a limitation would have been contrary to

[8]It has been argued that the grounds are not so limited, that the only significance of high crimes and misdemeanors is that they are a mandatory ground for removing the convicted President or other officer; removal is a discretionary sanction for Presidents or other officers impeached and convicted on lesser charges. Joseph Isenbergh, "Impeachment and Presidential Immunity from Judicial Process" (University of Chicago Law School, Jan. 1999, unpublished). Although this position is arguable from the text and background of the impeachment clauses of the Constitution, it is contrary to the modern understanding of these clauses and would greatly weaken the Presidency by eliminating any substantive barrier to Congress's removing a President it didn't like.

Professor Isenbergh had his Warholian fifteen minutes of fame when on January 26, 1999, in the midst of the President's trial, some Republican Senators were reported to be considering the possibility, on the authority of Isenbergh's paper (which had been posted on the University of Chicago Law School's Web site), of convicting the President but not removing him from office. Neil A. Lewis, "A Suggestion of Conviction Minus Ousting," *New York Times* (national ed.), Jan. 26, 1999, p. A17. The following day, the Senators dropped the idea. David E. Rosenbaum, "Lott Picks Six Scouts to Hunt Exit," *New York Times* (national ed.), Jan. 27, 1999, p. A17.

[9]Hoffer and Hull, note 5 above, at 102. Good discussions of the debates in the constitutional conventions over impeachment may be found in id., ch. 6, and in Gerhardt, note 3 above, ch. 1. Gerhardt also discusses the debates in the ratifying conventions. See id., ch. 2.

[10]"Misdemeanor," in Samuel Johnson, *A Dictionary of the English Language* (1755).

[11]Hoffer and Hull, note 5 above, at 97, 101. See, for example, *The Records of the Federal Convention of 1787*, vol. 2, p. 550 (Max Farrand ed., rev. ed. 1937).

[12]Hoffer and Hull, note 5 above, at 101–102, 118–119.

colonial and state practice.[13] And it would have left a gaping hole in the constitutional structure, owing to the fact that the Constitution provides no procedure other than impeachment for removing officials who do not serve at the will of the President, in particular the President himself, the Vice President, and federal judges. If the President moved to Saudi Arabia so that he could have four wives, intending to run the government of the United States by e-mail and telephone, he would have to be removed from office,[14] even though he would not be committing a crime by his absenteeism; and the only mode of removal would be impeachment. And likewise the totally incompetent judge who did not commit crimes: in other words, federal district judge John Pickering, alcoholic and lunatic but not criminal, who was the first official impeached and convicted under the new Constitution.

The only alternative to impeachment as a method of removing a tenured official—but it would come to the same thing—would be for Congress first to criminalize the official's activity and then impeach him for it.[15] But that would be formalism with a vengeance. Functionally, he would be impeached and convicted for noncriminal derelictions of duty. And the formalist trick would work only when the impeachable activity was of a continuing rather than a completed nature and one that the official could not discontinue without disabling himself from the effective performance of the duties of his office. If Congress attempted to criminalize an activity that the President had already discontinued, it would be violating the Constitution's prohibition against ex post facto laws.[16]

---

[13]This point is missed by Raoul Berger, *Impeachment: The Constitutional Problems* (1973), which argues from English precedent that impeachment was proper only for criminal conduct. It would be surprising if the framers of the U.S. Constitution had preferred English precedent to colonial and state precedent, with which they were intimately familiar; and Hoffer and Hull, note 5 above, ch. 6 and pp. 117–118, argue persuasively that they did not.

[14]The example is taken from Charles L. Black, Jr., *Impeachment: A Handbook* 33 (1974), and updated slightly (he didn't foresee e-mail).

[15]That is what Congress did to Andrew Johnson, the only President before Clinton to be impeached. It passed a law forbidding the President to appoint or remove certain officials and declaring violation of the law to be a "high misdemeanor." Johnson defied the law by removing Secretary of War Edwin Stanton and was promptly impeached, though the Senate acquitted him. See Michael Les Benedict, *The Impeachment and Trial of Andrew Johnson* (1973).

[16]U.S. Const., art. I, § 9, cl. 3.

In siding with Peter Hoffer and N. E H. Hull and Charles Black[17] against Raoul Berger and James St. Clair, who also argued the linguistic and historical case for confining "high Crimes and Misdemeanors" to crimes,[18] I am choosing a structural and pragmatic over a formalistic or originalist approach to constitutional meaning. Given the plain need to be able to remove the hypothetical self-exiled President or the totally incompetent judge (the pragmatic consideration),[19] and the absence from the Constitution of any provision for the removal of these officials during their terms of office (the structural consideration), the availability of impeachment to bring about the removal of a federal officer for serious abuse or complete neglect of office is inevitable and right, whatever history shows (though Hoffer and Hull's historiography is more persuasive than Berger's). This is regardless of which President people want to impeach. In 1974 the Republicans and Nixon's lawyer, St. Clair, were pushing for the narrow, formalist construal of "high Crimes and Misdemeanors" and the Democrats, including Clinton himself, and anti-Nixonians, such as Charles Black, were pushing for the broad construal. In 1998 the roles were reversed, with the Republicans taking the position of the Democrats in 1974 and the Democrats the position of the Republicans in 1974. Such role reversals are common because legislators and other politicians are not committed to consistency.

Impeachment by the House of Representatives has been rare in the history of the United States.[20] The only convictions by the Senate have

[17]And also Gerhardt, note 3 above, ch. 9.

[18]James D. St. Clair et al., *An Analysis of the Constitutional Standard for Presidential Impeachment* (1974). St. Clair was Nixon's lawyer in the impeachment inquiry that led to Nixon's resignation.

[19]The urgency of removing the totally incompetent judge is actually less, since his work usually can be split up among the remaining judges without much inconvenience.

[20]Nations whose constitutions are modeled on that of the United States invariably include an impeachment provision; nations that have a parliamentary system do not, since a prime minister can be removed by a vote of no confidence, although these nations do need, and have, procedures for removing judges. American students of impeachment are provincial; they do not study the foreign experience. They are also mesmerized by federal impeachment; state impeachments since the founding era are rarely discusssed. Yet all states but Oregon have impeachment provisions in their constitutions, often with additional grounds not found in the U.S. Constitution; and while state impeachment is rare, it is less rare than federal. See, for example, Wayne Greene, "History Notes State's Zeal for Impeachment," *Tulsa World,* Oct. 24, 1993, p. N1. See generally Robert F. Williams, *State Constitutional Law: Cases and Materials* 740–748 (2d ed. 1993).

been of judges, most of whom had committed serious crimes, such as taking bribes, though Pickering is an important exception. Andrew Johnson, Lincoln's Vice President and successor, was impeached in 1868, tried by the Senate, and acquitted by one vote. The proceeding against him is generally regarded as wholly political, in the sense of divorced from concerns about competence or probity. It revolved around the disagreement between him and the radical Republicans who controlled Congress over the pace and scope of Reconstruction. He did refuse to enforce or even comply with certain laws, but they were of dubious constitutionality.

President Nixon would have been impeached and convicted had he not resigned before the House of Representatives could vote on the recommendation of the House Judiciary Committee to impeach him.[21] He was charged with covering up, by methods constituting criminal obstruction of justice, the burglary by Republican operatives of the Watergate office of the Democratic National Committee, and with using the IRS, CIA, and FBI to harass and intimidate his critics and opponents. The cover-up was criminal but his enlisting of the agencies in his war against his political enemies, although a misuse of his office, was not criminal. Nixon's resignation is the closest thing we have had to the actual conviction of a President, and so the proceeding that led up to it exerts a gravitational force on lawyers who cannot think about a problem without a precedent to guide their thought. Yet it was illogical to argue, as many did during the debate over whether Clinton should be impeached, that because Clinton's misconduct did not involve any misuse of the powers of his office it was not impeachable. All that this showed was that his was a different form of misconduct from Nixon's.

Nor is it certain that Nixon himself should have been impeached, although, curiously, that he should have been was common ground among both Republicans who wanted Clinton impeached and Democrats who did not.[22] The Watergate burglary itself was a serious political crime, akin to election fraud; but Nixon was not complicit in the burglary, only in the cover-up. His participation in the cover-up was, of course, a misuse of the powers of his office, but it was to very little

[21]Actually, it is unclear whether resignation moots an impeachment proceeding, since if it did, the Senate would be disabled from barring the official from holding federal office in the future.

[22]See, for example, David Frum, "Yes, It *Is* Like Watergate," *Weekly Standard,* Sept. 28, 1998, p. 21.

effect; and some of the targets of the other activities for which he was impeached, such as Daniel Ellsberg, could be thought by reasonable people disloyal and a threat to national security. With respect to those activities (though not, I emphasize, Nixon's participation in the cover-up of the Watergate burglary), the gravity of Nixon's misconduct could be thought mitigated by considerations of the national interest, just as many people consider Clinton's misconduct to be mitigated by what they believe to be his excellent performance of his executive duties. And Nixon was not the first President to abuse the powers of the office. Those who think that the Cold War posed as much danger to the United States as World War II did might be inclined to compare Nixon's tactics toward opponents of his foreign policy to the deceptions by which Franklin Roosevelt aided Great Britain in violation of the Neutrality Act before the United States entered World War II. The same defense is possible of the Reagan Administration's illegal efforts (which President Reagan probably knew about, despite denials) to fund the Nicaraguan Contras, and achieve other foreign policy objectives (such as freeing the CIA's station chief in Beirut from his Hezbollah captors, who eventually killed him), by clandestine sales of weapons to Iran.

The analogy between Nixon and these other Presidents is just an analogy, and may not be a very good one. The Watergate burglary and its cover up cannot be defended on grounds of *raison d'état,* and such Nixonian adventures to which some of his other illegal and abusive acts might have been thought ancillary as the invasion of Cambodia may have weakened rather than strengthened U.S. national security and thus compounded rather than mitigated his domestic misconduct. I don't want to defend Nixon, but only to point out, much as Clinton's defenders did in Clinton's case, that while what Nixon did was wrong, it was not necessarily a grave enough wrong, given the circumstances, to warrant the extreme sanction of impeachment. Like Clinton, Nixon had won two elections—the second more decisively than Clinton's second—and it was a Congress controlled by the party that had lost those elections that was trying to push him out of office. Like Clinton, Nixon could point to arguably redemptive successes: in Nixon's case détente, the opening to China, and the consolidation and expansion of Lyndon Johnson's Great Society programs. If Nixon had had Clinton's charm and Clinton's booming economy he might have ridden out the storm—and that might not have been a constitutionally improper outcome.

A further difficulty in getting a handle on Presidential impeachment is the curious fact that the Constitution uses a unitary standard, high crimes and misdemeanors, for all federal officials. Yet it seems obvious that in most respects (an important qualification, to which I'll return) the threshold should be higher for the President than for, say, a judge. A judge who commits a felony violation of the income tax laws ought certainly to be impeached; but it is far from obvious that a President should be impeached for the same violation. It is even clearer that a judge who committed the criminal acts that Clinton committed in connection with the Paula Jones case and the ensuing investigation by the Independent Counsel, criminal acts more serious than tax evasion, should be impeached and convicted.[23] Yet this is not clear with regard to Clinton himself. This is not because we have many judges but only one President, and so can spare one of the judges more easily; or because they have longer terms, and so can do more mischief than a President, who must seek reelection after four years and even if reelected step down after four more. Because the President is one person rather than many and has vastly more power and responsibility than any judge, his abandonment of his office would be a far more serious "misdemeanor" than similar conduct by a judge even though the duration of the misdemeanor could not exceed four years. And while the most compelling argument against impeaching Clinton was that it would make future Presidents too subservient to Congress, impeaching judges could undermine judicial independence, which is as great a social value as Presidential power. As we shall see in the next chapter, there is respectable opinion that the President of the United States is too powerful an official; but few responsible people think that federal judges are too independent or, if they are, that impeachment is an appropriate method of dealing with the problem. Franklin Roosevelt was much criticized for his Court-packing plan; I am not aware that any serious people wanted to impeach the conservative Justices who were the target of the plan. The calm with which the stock market reacted to the impeachment and trial of President Clinton suggests that a slight raising or lowering of the threshold to Presidential impeachment is not perceived as potentially destabilizing.

[23]One judge, Walter Nixon, *was* impeached and convicted, in 1989, for perjury before a grand jury.

The impeachment threshold is lower for judges than for the President, at least in regard to crimes, for two other reasons. First, because judges are appointed rather than elected, the impeachment of a judge is less easily attributed to political motives, though there have been political impeachments of federal judges, as we shall see. The second and more important reason is the difference in the character of the judicial office from that of the President or most other executive officials (the Attorney General is an exception). The judge symbolizes law and so even his relatively minor crimes gravely undermine the system of legal justice. The President is recognized to be a politician. Politicians are expected to obey the law, but not to personify it.

That the meaning of "high Crimes and Misdemeanors" varies with the office makes it very difficult to pin that meaning down. The basic difficulty in interpreting the term in relation to a President is that the commission of a felony is neither a necessary condition of impeachment—the Saudi Arabia example[24]—nor a sufficient one, as it may be with a judge. A President's felony must reach some level of gravity or consequence, or maybe both, before it can justify impeachment; and the Constitution does not specify the level. So felonious conduct per se is not a sufficient condition for Presidential impeachment. And the Saudi Arabia example implies that a misuse of the powers of the office is not a necessary condition. The example is one of neglect rather than of abuse of power—King Lear or Richard II versus Macbeth or Julius Caesar—though for obvious reasons abuse of power was the principal concern of the framers of the Constitution,[25] as is suggested by their singling out treason and bribery from other high crimes and misdemeanors for special mention. The framers were particularly concerned about the possibility of the President's being bribed by a foreign power[26]—one of the accusations against President Clinton, arising from the funneling of Chinese government funds into the Clinton reelection campaign in 1996, that Kenneth Starr was *not* authorized to investigate.

In all the examples discussed thus far, the impeachable conduct, whatever its motivation or degree of culpability, is directly connected with the conduct of the office. They are all cases in which the President

[24]Which is also, however, true of judges and other officials, as we know from Pickering's case.

[25]Hoffer and Hull, note 5 above, at 101–102.

[26]See, for example, *The Records of the Federal Convention of 1787*, note 11 above, vol. 2, pp. 68–69 (remarks of Gouverneur Morris).

perverts, misuses, or relinquishes his official powers. None of them involves unofficial conduct. Nothing in the background of the Constitution's provisions on impeachment suggests that private conduct was a concern of the framers or ratifiers when they made "high Crimes and Misdemeanors" the criterion for impeachment. The concept of "good Behaviour," which is the criterion for judicial tenure, is at least consistent with such a concern; but the President's (shorter) tenure is not conditioned, not explicitly anyway, on his behaving himself.

Does it follow that if President Clinton, using none of the resources of his office and so being innocent of any misuse of Presidential power, had killed Monica Lewinsky with his bare hands in order to prevent her from cooperating with the Independent Counsel, he would not have committed an impeachable offense? This is difficult to accept; and if absence of a good historical pedigree for deeming such an offense a ground for impeachment is a fatal defect from the standpoint of a historicist or "originalist" understanding of "high Crimes and Misdemeanors," so much the worse for using history to guide constitutional interpretation. Constitutional history is useful in uncovering purpose and supplying clues and hints to meaning. But it is trumped by practical need. If Clinton committed murder, he could not remain as President and would have to be impeached and convicted if he refused to resign. His effectiveness as President would be destroyed. Americans will not be ruled by a Nero or a Caligula, however executively competent. And, to repeat, impeachment is the only method authorized by the Constitution for removing a President during his term of office. Even if he were convicted in an ordinary criminal trial and sent to prison, he would still be President until he either resigned or was impeached and convicted.

Prosecution and Pardon

If the President can be prosecuted in the regular courts on a criminal charge during his term of office, and if the hypothetical Presidential murderer can therefore be, and was, convicted and imprisoned, his impeachment could be based not on criminal activity or misuse of office but on simple incapacity to serve as President, as in the case of self-exile to Saudi Arabia. The question whether a crime unrelated to the office is a fit basis for impeachment would not arise, except during the awkward hiatus between arrest and conviction. No one knows, however, whether the President can be prosecuted in the ordinary way while he is in office. The Constitution is clear that he can be prosecuted after being impeached, convicted, and removed from office,[27] but it says nothing about before and a case has never arisen. The framers assumed that all federal officials would be subject to prosecution in the regular courts.[28] Countless officials who could be impeached have been convicted in the regular courts of ordinary crimes and removed afterward, without impeachment, because they serve at the President's pleasure and can thus be terminated at will. But since it would hamstring the President to subject him to criminal process while he is in office, a powerful practical case can be made that he should be immune.[29]

The case is reinforced by the structure of government created by the Constitution. Because (*pace* Eric Freedman)[30] an imprisoned President would have to be removed from office, subjecting him to the possibility of being prosecuted would in effect empower a prosecutor, plus a judge and jury, to impeach and remove the President, in derogation of the exclusive powers of impeachment and removal that the Constitution assigns to the House and Senate. Indeed, just the possibility of conviction might induce the President to give up his office as part of a plea bargain, as happened with Vice President Spiro Agnew. Kenneth Starr, had he persuaded one of his grand juries to indict the President, would in effect have preempted the impeachment process, since if in the criminal proceeding the President were convicted and sentenced to prison, he would have either to resign or to be impeached and removed from office. A local prosecutor could do the same thing.

The weakness of the structural argument is that it seems to imply, what almost no one believes, that judges also cannot be prosecuted in the ordinary way. Most of the judges who have been impeached and

---

[27]U.S. Const., art. I, § 3, cl. 7.

[28]Hoffer and Hull, note 5 above, at 101, 118.

[29]See, for example, Ken Gormley, "Impeachment and the Independent Counsel: A Dysfunctional Union," 51 *Stanford Law Review* 309, 315–324 (1999); Alexander M. Bickel, "The Constitutional Triangle," *New Republic,* Oct. 6, 1973, p. 14; also Alexander Hamilton, "Federalist No. 69," in *The Federalist* 462, 463 (Jacob E. Cooke ed. 1961). The contrary view is comprehensively argued in Eric M. Freedman, "The Law as King and the King as Law: Is a President Immune from Criminal Prosecution before Impeachment?" 20 *Hastings Constitutional Law Quarterly* 7 (1992).

[30]Who contends that "it may indeed be possible to conduct the Presidency from a jail cell." Id. at 53.

convicted were impeached after being convicted in the ordinary way. But the prosecution and imprisonment of a single judge has much less impact on the judicial branch than the prosecution and imprisonment of the President would have on the executive branch, and on the government and country generally.

If the President cannot be prosecuted while in office, this implies that he can be impeached and removed for a purely private crime, as in our murder hypothetical, where allowing the President to remain in office would be unthinkable. The President could, it is true, be prosecuted in the ordinary way after his term expired. There is little danger that the statute of limitations on a criminal prosecution might expire in the meantime; for when a potential defendant has a temporary immunity from suit, the statute of limitations does not begin to run until the immunity expires.[31] But if the President committed a heinous crime, especially at the beginning of his term, the public would not be content to allow him to complete his term and be punished in the regular course of the criminal law afterward—especially since the Constitution empowers the President to pardon any federal offender,[32] even in advance of prosecution,[33] as in the case of President Ford's pardon of Nixon and President Bush's pardon of Casper Weinberger. There is nothing in the pardon clause itself to suggest that the President cannot pardon himself. It reads, "he shall have Power to Grant Reprieves and Pardons for Offenses against the United States, except in Cases of Impeachment." He is forbidden to pardon himself in an impeachment case because that would enable him to nullify specific powers that the Constitution grants Congress—the power to impeach, and the power to convict, the President. But that is the only stated exception, and it does not reach the case in which the impeached but acquitted President grants himself a blanket pardon from ever being prosecuted for any federal crime that he has committed.

[31]See, for example, 11 U.S.C. § 362 (automatic stay in bankruptcy); 50 U.S.C. App. §§ 501–525 (suits by or against military personnel on active duty); Hilao v. Estate of Marcos, 103 F.3d 767, 772–773 (9th Cir. 1996); Cleghorn v. Bishop, 3 Haw. 483 (1873). These are all examples of temporary immunity from civil rather than criminal process. I can find no examples of the latter type, but I do not see why it should not be possible in an appropriate case.

[32]U.S. Const., art. II, § 2, cl. 1. The power is limited to federal offenses.

[33]Ex parte Garland, 71 U.S. (4 Wall.) 333, 380 (1866); Laurence H. Tribe, *American Constitutional Law*, § 4–11, p. 256 n. 10 (2d ed. 1988).

There is no case law on the question, of course, but it has generally been inferred from the breadth of the constitutional language that the President can indeed pardon himself,[34] and although this conclusion has been challenged,[35] it is unlikely that the present Supreme Court would be bold enough, in the teeth of the constitutional language, to read into the pardon clause an exception for self-pardoning. Unlikely, but not inconceivable. Despite the breadth of the language, the clause has been interpreted not to permit the President to pardon offenses not yet committed.[36] This is a judge-made exception; others are conceivable. It can be argued that the Constitution's express provision that an impeached President can be prosecuted after leaving office implies that he cannot pardon himself, because that would nullify the provision. There would be especially great pressure on the Supreme Court to reject the self-pardoning power if a President committed a heinous crime in a federal enclave—the District of Columbia, for example, which is indeed the most likely site of Presidential crimes, as in the Lewinsky matter itself—making it a federal crime and therefore placing it squarely within the literal scope of the pardon clause.

A practical argument in favor of the self-pardoning power is that the President can accomplish much the same thing indirectly by pardoning his accomplices. In many cases it is impossible to convict a criminal defendant without using the threat of prosecution to get his accomplices to testify against him. (Recall that the Independent Counsel's office used this technique on Monica Lewinsky.) This argument, combined with the absence of any clues in the text or history of the pardon power that self-pardoning is excluded, leads me to conclude that the President probably does have the power to pardon himself. If so, not only is the entire subject of criminally prosecuting Presidents rather academic; but impeachment is an essential remedy against a criminal President whether or not his crime involves the use of Presidential powers or indeed has any public dimension at all.

But could the commission by a President of a heinous crime have *no* public dimension at all? The example of a Presidential murder for purely private ends and using purely private means may not be conclu-

---

[34]Gormley, note 29 above, at 323.

[35]Brian C. Kalt, Note, "Pardon Me? The Constitutional Case against Presidential Self-Pardons," 106 *Yale Law Journal* 779 (1996).

[36]Tribe, note 33 above, § 4–11, p. 256 n. 10.

sive against the power of self-pardoning, but it does show that at some point the personal becomes the political. A President who having committed a murder refused to resign would have "abandoned" his office in the sense of having lost all authority to govern; he might as well have moved to Saudi Arabia. Many people believe that President Clinton's crimes, while not as serious as murder, were serious enough that he *should* have lost all authority to govern. But the public opinion polls suggested that he had not lost his authority to govern—that most Americans continued throughout the ordeal to accept his authority as President, something they would not have done had they thought him a murderer.

The Specter of Political Impeachment

It helps in thinking about what should constitute an impeachable Presidential offense to start from the end, with the remedy, which is removal from office. We should ask: What sort of conduct, criminal or noncriminal, warrants forcibly removing a President from office? From this perspective, and considering also the legalistic wording of the various sections of the Constitution dealing with impeachment, the emphasis that the framers placed on misconduct as the basis for impeachment, the rejection at the constitutional convention of the proposal to have Congress elect the President,[37] the colonial and state experience with impeachment, the practice of impeachment under the Constitution, and the structure of the Constitution, it seems reasonably clear that impeachment should not be used to express merely political disagreement between Congress and the President or other officials. This point has seemed to many students of impeachment to have been settled early in our constitutional history when the Republicans (that is, the party of Jefferson) resorted to "political" impeachment in an effort to remove the Federalist judges who had been appointed by Jefferson's predecessors.[38] The highwater mark of this effort was the impeachment of Su-

[37]A proposal extensively considered, and at first strongly supported. See, for example, *The Records of the Federal Convention of 1787*, note 11 above, vol. 2, pp. 119–121, 401–404.

[38]The Republicans should not be judged too harshly for this effort. They were trying to get back at the Federalist judiciary for enforcing the alien and sedition laws passed by a Federalist-controlled Congress to stifle Republican criticism of Federalist officials and laws. Turnaround is fair play in politics.

preme Court Justice Samuel Chase. His acquittal in 1805 put an end to the movement.[39] The specter of political impeachment recurred, however, in the impeachment of Andrew Johnson in 1868 and in unsuccessful efforts, culminating in an impeachment inquiry in 1970, to impeach the four-times-married hyper-liberal Supreme Court Justice William O. Douglas in 1970.[40] But it is only a specter. When in 1997 the Republican Congressman Tom DeLay (now the House Republican whip, and the leader of the effort to impeach Clinton) called for the impeachment of "liberal" judges appointed by President Clinton,[41] he was widely considered to have strayed well beyond the limits of a reasonable interpretation of the Constitution's provisions on impeachment.

The concern with political impeachment of judges is that it would make them timid and thus undermine judicial independence, a cornerstone of a liberal polity. The concern with political impeachment of Presidents is that it would make Presidents timid too. Since a President can be impeached by a simple majority of the House of Representatives, since a trial by the Senate would be a trauma for the President even if he were ultimately acquitted, and since it is not uncommon for the House to be controlled by a party different from the President's, adoption of the doctrine of political impeachment would nudge us in the direction of a parliamentary regime, in which the legislature is at least nominally supreme. And that, whatever its merits, is not the theory of the U.S. Constitution. True, the more political the impeachment process became, the less stigma would be attached to being impeached, and so the net increase in the intimidation of Presidents by Congresses might be slight. Our politics would be more turbulent, however, and the President weaker, than if the threshold to impeachment is kept very high.

The argument against political impeachment is stronger in the case of judges than in the case of the President. We want judges to be more independent from the other branches of government than Presidents. The President is supposed to get along with Congress; otherwise very little can be accomplished. Andrew Johnson was a disaster as President because of his contemptuous and confrontational attitude toward a

[39]Hoffer and Hull, note 5 above, ch. 12.

[40]Gerhardt, note 3 above, at 27, 29.

[41]See, for example, Ralph Z. Hallow, "Republicans Out to Impeach 'Activist' Jurists," *Washington Times,* March 12, 1997, p. A1; Editorial, "End Congress War on Courts," *Newsday,* Oct. 5, 1997, p. B3.

Congress controlled by the opposing party. In contrast, most Presidents faced with a Congress controlled by the opposition, including Clinton, have been able to govern effectively by judicious compromise. One might almost argue that Johnson had "abandoned" his office by failing to conduct it in the manner contemplated by the Constitution, which made the legislative and executive branches interdependent rather than independent. In this example we can see political impeachment blending insensibly into impeachment for noncriminal misuse or nonuse of Presidential power.

But Clinton cannot be compared to Johnson in this respect, and so we must ask whether Clinton's impeachment was an even purer, an even less defensible, political impeachment than Johnson's. The Democrats charged that it was, though they based this charge not on the articles of impeachment, which did not cite any policy disagreements or accuse the President of failing to cooperate with the Republican Congress (Democrats long criticized Clinton for being too cosy with the Republican majority in Congress), but on the alleged partisanship of the process that led up to impeachment. Their principal evidence, besides the role of impeachment-happy Congressman DeLay, is that only five Democrats joined the Republicans in voting to impeach Clinton, though a much larger number (thirty-one) had joined the Republicans in voting to initiate an impeachment inquiry. The evidence is not conclusive. The impeachment of Andrew Johnson was overtly political; he was charged with subverting Reconstruction legislation. Clinton's defenders emphasized the *non*political character of the conduct for which Clinton was impeached.

Of course the actual motives of many Republicans may have been darkly political. But this point has less force than Clinton's defenders tried to give it, and this for two reasons. The first requires us to consider more carefully how to understand "political impeachment." If it just means that party affiliation weighed heavily in the decision to impeach or not to impeach, so that, for example, if a Republican President had behaved exactly as Clinton had done he would not have been impeached by the Republican-controlled House, then the impeachment of Clinton was a political impeachment. But that is too loose a definition. No Presidential impeachment can fail to be suffused with politics. But there are degrees. Suppose that if Bush had done what Clinton did, the Republicans would have thought him worthy of being impeached but would have drawn back for political reasons from voting to impeach him. That would be a case of politics deflecting an impeachment rather than inspiring it. But if the Republicans didn't think that Clinton's conduct warranted impeachment but voted to impeach him anyway, that would be an example of a political impeachment, for the sole motive would be political. If this is the right test for calling an impeachment "political" (that politics was the sole motive for the impeachment), it is unclear whether the impeachment of Clinton should be deemed political; we don't know enough about the thinking of the Republican Congressmen.

The second reason for questioning whether the impeachment of President Clinton is properly described as a political impeachment is that Democrats may have been as strongly moved by political considerations in voting against impeachment as Republicans were in voting for it. They may have been more political than the Republicans in 1974, who joined Democrats in larger numbers in calling for Nixon's removal from office. In their heart of hearts the Democrats in Congress may have believed Clinton guilty of high crimes or misdemeanors but feared the effect that his impeachment and conviction might have on the Democratic Party or the boost it might give the Religious Right. The very charge of "partisanship" may have been a partisan ploy. The White House is reported to have been disappointed when on January 8, 1999, the Senate unanimously approved ground rules for the impeachment trial; "the White House had been trying to get Democrats [in the Senate] to forgo the display of bipartisanship."[42]

The fact that public opinion polls showed that most Americans were opposed to impeaching President Clinton is not good evidence that the Republicans were acting less from principle than the Democrats, who while criticizing Republicans for thumbing their noses at public opinion as manifested in public opinion polls argued inconsistently that Republicans were too responsive to the demands of their conservative constituents. One cannot have it both ways. Voters' preference either is or is not relevant to impeachment. If it is not, then polls fall out along with constituent pressures. If it is, the former cannot be considered a more authentic register of voters' preference than the latter. Responsiveness to constituents is an imperfect form of democracy (there is no perfect form of democracy), but one that might be preferred to the

[42]Alison Mitchell, "Senate, in Unanimity, Sets Rules for Trial," *New York Times,* Jan. 9, 1999 (national ed.), pp. A1, A10.

plebiscitary democracy of the public opinion polls; in the original constitutional scheme the House of Representatives was *the* populist branch of the federal government.

A deeper point (for critics of the impeachment were right to point out that a legislative body can be controlled by an electoral minority)[43] is that the political theory underlying the Constitution, today no less than in 1787, is that of representative rather than direct democracy. There are no federal referenda or initiatives. The people's political views are in all cases to be filtered through the refracting medium of their elected representatives. Opinion polls lack this filter, and are a poorer register of intensity of preference even than issue voting (as in a referendum or initiative), because it takes less effort to answer a telephone pollster's questions than to vote. The filtering function of representation is especially important when a legislative body is charged with a quasi-legal duty, such as deciding whether to impeach. It would be a curious argument that if a President's approval rating fell below 50 percent, he should be impeached.

Both Republicans and Democrats had frequent recourse to demagoguery in the public debate over impeachment. It is easier to find the holes in the Democrats' arguments, because the President's conduct placed Democrats on the defensive and how else does one defend the indefensible but with sophistries and obfuscations? Democrats both inside and outside of Congress (remember Carville and Mikva) contended that Clinton was being impeached for purely personal misconduct; that high crimes and misdemeanors are limited to abuses of government authority; that Clinton had not committed perjury or even lied (some Democrats suggested that it was believable that he had never fondled Lewinsky); that the issue was not perjury but merely what parts of Lewinsky's body the President had touched; that perjury cannot be proved without physical evidence—without it, the case is "he said/she

---

[43]Imagine a legislature composed of 100 members elected from districts of equal population. Fifty-one of the legislators belong to Party A, the other 49 to Party B. Party A has strong party discipline; as a result, a majority of the A's (26) controls the legislature. And each of those 26 was elected by a bare majority of the voters of his district. Then a shade over 13 percent of the electorate will control the legislature. This example is extreme, but helps to explain how the House of Representatives was able to vote impeachment despite what appears from the polls to have been the opposition of a majority of the electorate.

said" and such cases are not winnable;[44] that Clinton had apologized and "what more could he do?"; that the only wrong he had done was to his family; that he was not given an adequate opportunity to defend himself (as by cross-examining the witnesses who gave testimony damaging to him); that Starr was a greater scofflaw than Clinton and maybe sick in the head; that the impeachment of Clinton was in violation of the "plain meaning," or "letter," of the Constitution; that Democrats are free from partisanship while Republicans are consumed by it; and that Clinton is genuinely committed to liberal (in the sense of traditional Democratic) policies. All these contentions were false, as was the claim that the Republicans prevented the House from voting for censure in lieu of impeachment. After the presiding officer at the impeachment debate in the full House ruled that an amendment to the impeachment resolution to substitute censure was out of bounds, the ruling was appealed to the full House, which voted to uphold the ruling. Voting in favor of it were the moderate Republicans who the Democrats claimed were clamoring to vote for censure in lieu of impeachment. Party discipline was a factor; the moderates feared losing choice committee assignments if they defied the leadership. Yet it also appears that support for censure among Republicans in the House evaporated in the week preceding the impeachment debate and vote because of the President's continued refusal to admit that he had lied to the grand jury and in his deposition in the Jones case.

Democrats also claimed that the Republicans were trying to undo the results of the 1996 election. But that would have meant replacing Clinton with Robert Dole, not Albert Gore. Anyway, unless the President happens to be President pursuant to the Twenty-Fifth Amendment (like Gerald Ford, who had not been elected Vice President), impeaching and convicting him means removing an elected official from office before his term expires, so to complain that this is "undoing the election" is to complain about the Constitution, which no one has dared to do lately. If forcing Clinton from office would nonetheless have meant the undoing of the 1996 election, then forcing Nixon from office in 1974, which all Democrats approve, meant undoing the 1972 election *and* replacing an elected official by an unelected one (Ford) rather than by the people's choice for Presidential understudy (Gore).

---

[44]This seems to be a garbled version of the "two witness" rule that I touched on in Chapter 1.

Democrats complained that Starr's investigation had focused unduly on the Lewinsky matter but that the House Judiciary Committee had improperly tried to expand the focus of the impeachment inquiry beyond the matters in the Starr Report. They thus complained both that the inquiry was too truncated and that it was too protracted. In fact the inquiry added nothing to the Starr Report, and the Democrats were unable to identify significant mistakes in the report, though it is possible to argue (in fact convincingly) that some of the inferences Starr drew cannot be sustained if a higher standard of proof than the normal civil standard of a preponderance of the evidence is employed.[45] Democrats called for an end to the "politics of personal destruction," but did not retract their own attempts to destroy Starr (sex-obsessed sickie), Jones (trailer trash), and Lewinsky (stalker). Few of them criticized Larry Flynt, the publisher of the feminists' nightmare, the pornographic magazine *Hustler,* when he "outed" Speaker-designate Robert Livingston in an effort to derail the impeachment train, or when he tried to out Congressman Bob Barr, one of the House prosecutors in the impeachment trial. In the House, the Democrats criticized the Republicans for not calling any witnesses to the alleged misconduct, such as Lewinsky, Currie, and Jordan; in the Senate, the Democrats criticized the Republicans for wanting to call those very same witnesses. The Democrats criticized the House impeachment inquiry as too summary, and the Senate trial as not summary enough.

The impeachment of Clinton reflects something different from, though it is related to, increasing congressional partisanship: the rise of what Benjamin Ginsberg and Martin Shefter call postelectoral politics.[46] Writing in 1990, at a time when the Republicans had not controlled Congress for decades (except for the Senate between 1981 and 1987) and the Democrats had controlled the Presidency for only four of the previous twenty-one years, Ginsberg and Shefter claimed that the Republicans had obtained a lock on the Presidency and the Democrats on the Congress. They argued that this had reduced the importance of electoral competition between the parties and that as a substitute the parties had developed, with the complicity of the media and the federal

---

[45]That is not Starr's fault; he was not asked to advise on what standard of proof the House should use in deciding whether to impeach the President.

[46]Benjamin Ginsberg and Martin Shefter, *Politics by Other Means: The Declining Importance of Elections in America* (1990).

judiciary, "a major new technique of political combat—revelation, investigation, and prosecution" (p. 26). The authors were premature in pronouncing the demise of electoral competition; since 1993 the Democrats have controlled the Presidency and since 1995 the Republicans have controlled the Congress. But they were correct about the growth of revelation, investigation, and prosecution (what they call "RIP") as an alternative form of political combat aided by such institutional "reforms" as the independent counsel law. They demonstrated that both parties have used the technique equally (pp. 26–31), and they used the Nixon impeachment inquiry as an illustration of it (pp. 26–27). We can see it at work in the Clinton impeachment as well, and on both sides. Consider the "outing" of prominent Republicans as adulterers and the vicious attacks on Starr, as well as the machinations of the Clinton haters and the desire of some Republicans to "pay back" the Democrats for forcing Nixon from office, indicting officials of the Reagan Administration over the Iran-Contra affair, blocking Robert Bork's appointment to the Supreme Court, and giving Clarence Thomas a hard time when he was nominated to the Court. RIP creates a climate favorable to political impeachment. It is notable that the Republicans took a much softer line on obstruction of justice in the Iran-Contra affair and on sexual harassment in the Thomas confirmation fight, while Democrats who had thundered rule-of-law rhetoric in the Iran-Contra controversy became very quiet about the rule of law in the debate over Clinton.

Granted the inappropriateness of political impeachment of Presidents, as I have defined the term, it does not follow that politics is an illegitimate factor in impeachments. We must consider first the original structure of the Constitution and then its current structure. In the original Constitution the only officials directly elected by the people were the members of the House of Representatives. The President and Vice President were elected by the Electoral College, the members of which were appointed by the states; the Constitution did not (and does not) indicate the method to be used by states in making these appointments. The Senators were elected by the legislatures of their states. The members of the Cabinet and all the other officials of the executive branch, along with the judges, were appointed by the President, subject to the Senate's concurring. The members of the House of Representatives, the only directly elected branch of the federal government, were like the Roman tribunes—the people's watchdogs. The power to impeach complemented the investigative powers of the House. It was thus a democratic power, especially when directed against life-tenured judges.[47] Political considerations were certain to figure in the decision of a popular assembly to impeach an official—all the more so since the House was responsible not only for filing the bill of impeachment but also for prosecuting the case against the impeached official in the Senate.[48] As we saw in the last chapter, prosecutors are understood to have discretion as to whom to prosecute and for what, and it is a discretion the exercise of which might in appropriate circumstances be influenced by political considerations.

The Senate, in contrast, like the Roman Senate or the English House of Lords, was conceived to be a council of notables, a deliberative rather than merely a representative body. This is shown by the fact that the Constitution entrusted it with sole responsibility for ratifying treaties and confirming the President's judicial and executive appointments.[49] It was natural therefore to repose judicial responsibilities in it, especially since the Justices of the Supreme Court, who might have been thought the more logical judges of an impeachment, were appointed by the President. Concern was also expressed in the constitutional deliberations that, because there would be fewer Justices than Senators, they might be more easily corrupted or intimidated.[50] The Senate could not be expected to decide cases of impeachment without regard to politics any more than the House of Lords could be expected to. But the political tincture might be relatively slight, especially since the President himself, not being directly elected, would find it difficult to accuse any Senators who voted to convict him of trying to reverse the people's choice.

Much has changed in the constitutional structure, both formally and informally, since the eighteenth century. The sheer increase in the size of the Senate, from 26 Senators to 100, has made the Senate a less efficient judicial tribunal,[51] while the increased workload of the Senate

[47]Hoffer and Hull, note 5 above, at 259–260.

[48]This is not stated in the Constitution, but is implied by the fact that the impeachment clause casts the House in the role of accuser and the Senate in that of judge and makes no independent provision for a prosecutor in the Senate trial. In English and American impeachment practice before the Constitution was adopted, the impeaching body (the lower house) conducted the prosecution in the judging body (the upper house).

[49]Hoffer and Hull, note 5 above, at 106.

[50]See *The Records of the Federal Convention of 1787*, note 11 above, vol. 2, p. 551.

[51]Concern that trials of impeachment would degenerate into "carnival" trials had been expressed as early as the 1790s and the first decade of the 1800s, when the Senate had only thirty-two members. Hoffer and Hull, note 5 above, at 261.

owing to the enormous growth in the size of the federal government has made the trial of a President (in which the Senators are reluctant to delegate most of the process to committees or staff, as they do when judges are impeached)[52] a more onerous and distracting senatorial task. In addition, Senators are now directly elected by the people, as is the President in effect. They are therefore more political and the President better able to oppose impeachment and conviction by reference to his popular mandate. In addition, the elimination of property qualifications for voting has made democratic politics more populist, while the rise of scientific polling and the instantaneous mass dissemination of comprehensive information concerning political issues have pushed us in the direction of direct as distinct from representative democracy. People expect to have a strong voice in the resolution of specific issues of national concern formally entrusted to legislatures (such as impeachment), and not merely in the selection of officials to resolve those issues on the basis of the officials' own judgment. The populist cast of modern American democracy has given rise to concerns that our politics have become insufficiently deliberative.

As a practical matter, then, politics is bound to play a larger role in Presidential impeachments today than when the Constitution was written and ratified—and for the further reason that whatever the framers may have intended by the term high crimes and misdemeanors, two hundred years of fortunately quite limited experience with impeachment have not yielded precise guidelines on when the process can properly be deployed against a President. The vaguer a law is, the more likely it is to be applied in light of the values, including the political preferences, of the persons charged with applying it, who in this instance are elected officials, rather than in conformity with objective legal rules.

It is nevertheless arguable from the legalistic language in which the impeachment provisions of the Constitution are cast that the Constitution requires the Senators, however much it goes against their grain or imperils their chances for reelection or their legislative effectiveness, to conceive their duty in impeachment trials as being strictly judicial and nonpolitical.[53] But this position is difficult to maintain once it is

---

[52]See Gerhardt, note 3 above, at 116–117.

[53]A nice piece of symbology is the meeting on January 8, 1999, of the Senate in the Old Senate Chamber to discuss the procedures for the trial of President Clinton. The

admitted, as I think it must be, that impeachable offenses are not limited to crimes and that not all crimes are impeachable offenses. In deciding whether a crime is serious enough to warrant removing the President from office, or whether some bizarre conduct (such as moving to Saudi Arabia) that is not criminal nevertheless warrants removal, Senators cannot avoid taking political factors into account, because those factors bear on Presidential effectiveness. If a President were revealed to be a producer of child pornography, the determination of whether this activity, or more precisely the public revelation of it, would so reduce his effectiveness as President as to warrant his compelled removal from office would be at once a political judgment and a proper, indeed decisive, consideration for an impeachment trial.

The closest analogy to the trial of a President before the Senate may be the trial of the Nazi leaders before the Nuremberg Tribunal. Though composed primarily of professional judges, the Tribunal was far from being a regular court; and the legal standards under which the defendants were tried were ad hoc. Most of the procedural formalities of law, however, were observed, so that guilt and innocence were reliably and publicly determined. While the U.S. Senate is not a court, and while high crimes and misdemeanors cannot be specified in advance,[54] so long as the normal procedural formalities of a trial are scrupulously observed everyone will know whether an impeached President is actually guilty of what the House and Senate consider impeachable offenses. We shall see, though, that the procedures actually employed, especially in the Senate trial of Clinton, were not well designed to assure an accurate determination of guilt or innocence.

The chief difference between the Nuremberg trial and an impeachment trial lies in the enormity of the conduct that was on trial at Nuremberg. So appalling had the behavior of the Nazi leaders been that the only practical choice in dealing with them was between administrative punishment with no pretense of legality and a legal process that could not be brought into complete conformity with fundamental norms of legality. The latter course was preferable for a variety of practical reasons, including the need to create a credible public record and

---

Old Senate Chamber was the courtroom of the Supreme Court until the construction of the present Supreme Court building in 1935.

[54]Imagine a newly elected President asking White House Counsel for a list of "high Crimes and Misdemeanors" so that he could avoid risking being impeached.

the traditional German respect for legalism.[55] Impeachment by the House of Representatives and the trial of the impeached official in the Senate are specified in the Constitution; the process thus has the requisite pedigree; the problem is the lack of definition of impeachable conduct and the political makeup of the tribunals. The problem of inadequate procedures that plagued the Senate trial of President Clinton is not inherent; the Senate could have run a better trial. But the departures from due process that are inherent in impeachment proceedings argue, along with the disruption of government and the disturbance of the balance of powers between branches of government that the impeachment and trial of a President might engender, for resolving doubts against impeachment.

Procedural Issues Raised by the Impeachment and the Trial

The most important issue relating to the form of a Presidental impeachment proceeding is the standard of proof in both the House and the Senate: the amount of evidence and degree of confidence required to impeach and to convict, respectively. Despite its importance, the issue is ignored both in the Constitution and in the rules of the House and of the Senate, and no effort to resolve it was made in the Clinton impeachment proceeding. It was left to the judgment of the individual members.

If there were a rule, what should it be? The standard for an indictment or other criminal charge is probable cause to believe the defendant guilty, and usually the only evidence laid before a grand jury is the evidence of guilt that the prosecutor has gathered. And in an impeachment, the role of the House corresponds to that of a grand jury. But because the trial of a President before the Senate is such a costly and disruptive process, it seems clear that the House ought to believe that the President is guilty, not merely that he may be, before it votes to impeach and by doing so asks the Senate to undertake the burdens of conducting a trial.[56]

[55]See the excellent discussion in Judith N. Shklar, *Legalism: Law, Morals, and Political Trials* (1986 ed.), esp. pp. 155–170.

[56]This appears to have been the view of most of the members of Congress who voted to impeach President Clinton, but not all—especially not those who, having voted for impeachment, urged the Senate not to convict the President.

I say "asks" rather than "compels" because nothing in the Constitution, in the history of impeachment, or in the counterpart processes of the criminal justice system requires the Senate to suspend its independent judgment of whether the charges against the President (or other impeached official) actually warrant a trial. Just as a regular criminal court can dismiss an indictment as insufficient without putting the defendant to the bother of a trial, so the Senate can properly dismiss articles of impeachment lodged with it by the House if it concludes that even if all the facts alleged in them are true they do not warrant removing the impeached official from office. But it is reluctant to do this because it would be a slap in the face of the House of Representatives. (This assumes that the House and the Senate are controlled by the same party.) That is another reason why the House should be convinced of the President's guilt in order to impeach: otherwise it externalizes the political costs of the impeachment process by passing the buck to the Senate. The effort to do this was unmistakable in the case of the moderate Republicans who having voted for impeachment then publicly announced that they thought the Senate should not convict the President.

The general belief that the burden of proof required for impeachment should indeed be higher than the burden of proof required for an ordinary indictment made the House of Representatives reluctant to rubber-stamp the Starr Report, as a grand jury would surely have rubber-stamped it had Starr submitted the report to a grand jury and asked it to indict Clinton. But the House was unable to formulate procedures for conducting a responsible factual inquiry. The House is no more a prosecutorial agency than the Senate is a court. It lacks staff, structure, procedures, and traditions consistent with the competent and expeditious performance of the prosecutorial function. This was not a critical deficiency in the Clinton impeachment, because the evidence marshaled by the Independent Counsel was comprehensive and largely uncontested. The House was free to focus its inquiry on the issue, one not of fact but of legal and political judgment, whether the conduct revealed in the Starr Report was a proper basis for impeachment.

The Democratic minority on the House Judiciary Committee originally proposed that the Committee take up the issue of defining "high Crimes and Misdemeanors" first, before getting into the facts, and that the Committee confine its attention to allegations of wrongdoing in the

Starr Report and so give a bye to allegations involving Kathleen Willey, other women, and Whitewater-related matters. The Republican majority would have been wise to accept the Democratic proposals regarding sequence and scope. The charge of excessive partisanship leveled against the Republicans would have been largely defused, and the boomerang effects of hastily releasing the evidence that Starr had given the Committee,[57] including the videotape of the President's grand jury testimony, avoided. Moreover, the Republicans' effort to broaden the impeachment inquiry beyond the matters dealt with in the Starr Report fizzled.

It is less clear whether the Committee should have agreed to the Democrats' proposal for a cut-off date in December, though as things turned out the Committee beat the date with time to spare. The fear was that a rigid deadline would give the White House and the Committee's Democrats an increased incentive to use stalling tactics. The fear became plausible when, with impeachment approaching, the Committee Democrats demanded that "fact" witnesses (witnesses to the alleged crimes, as distinct from witnesses on issues of law and policy) be called.

Eschewing any sort of factual inquiry—resting entirely on the Starr Report for its source of the facts—would not have required the House to accept the inferences from the evidence narrated in the report. For the House had to decide not only whether Clinton had committed particular acts, as found by Starr's investigation, and not only whether those acts constituted impeachable offenses, but also whether the evidence of those acts was sufficiently compelling to be likely to convince the Senate. That would depend on the standard of proof in the Senate trial. Obviously the burden of proof should be on the House in the sense that the President should be acquitted if the Senate concluded that it was no more likely that he was guilty than that he was innocent. The difficult question is whether the burden of proof should be the criminal burden, requiring proof beyond a reasonable doubt; the normal civil burden, which requires proof by a mere preponderance of the evidence (proof merely that the defendant is more likely guilty than not guilty); or the intermediate civil burden, used mainly in fraud cases, which requires proof of guilt by clear and convincing evidence.

The choice affects the balance between two types of legal error: the error of acquitting a defendant who is in fact guilty and the error of

---

[57]Too hastily for proper editing, as we saw in the last chapter.

convicting a defendant who is in fact innocent. The lighter the burden of proof on the prosecutor (or plaintiff, if it is a civil case), the likelier is the second type of error (convicting an innocent defendant) and the less likely the first (acquitting a guilty defendant). The heavier the burden of proof, the likelier the first type of error (acquitting the guilty) and the less likely the second (convicting the innocent). The weighting of the two types of error ought to determine, or at least strongly influence, the choice of the burden of proof to impose on the prosecution. Unfortunately, they are difficult to weight in the context of a Presidential impeachment. Forcing a President from office before his term expires is a fearful move, done only once (to Nixon) in the more than two centuries of United States history. But failing to remove a President who had in fact committed high crimes or misdemeanors would be a fearful abdication of constitutional duty and might endanger the nation by leaving in the Presidency someone manifestly incapable of discharging the duties of his office. The fact that the House must, as I argued, satisfy itself that the President is guilty, and not merely that he may be guilty, and the fact that a two-thirds vote in the Senate is required to convict, provide considerable protection against conviction of an innocent President. Maybe requiring proof beyond a reasonable doubt, or, as Charles Black proposed, proof by "an overwhelming preponderance of the evidence,"[58] would give a guilty President too much protection.

The proper standard of proof may depend on the precise offense with which a President is charged. If it is abuse of the powers of the office, a lighter burden of proof may well be proper on the theory that the risk to the nation of erroneously retaining in office a President who abuses his powers is symmetrical with the risk to the nation of erroneously removing him. But where, as in Clinton's case, the offenses charged are criminal offenses unrelated (or only subtly or tenuously related) to the exercise of Presidential powers, it would be anomalous, or at least peculiar, to convict on less evidence than would be required in an ordinary criminal case. It is true that conviction by the Senate does not result in imprisonment or a fine. But removal from the Presidency, especially when conjoined with possible disqualification from ever again holding a federal office, is a heavy punishment. This is particularly clear when

---

[58]Black, note 14 above, at 17. This sounds much like proof by clear and convincing evidence, a preferable formulation because it is more familiar.

the full social costs of impeachment are considered and not just the costs borne by the President.

The choice of the standard of proof matters only in close cases, but in some though not all respects the case against Clinton was close. Some of the charges against Clinton, such as that he helped Monica Lewinsky get a job in New York in order to prevent her from testifying truthfully in the Paula Jones case, could not be proved beyond a reasonable doubt on the basis of the evidence that was before the House and Senate, that is, the evidence that the Independent Counsel had gathered (as modestly supplemented, in the Senate, by the testimony of the three witnesses that the House prosecutors were permitted to depose). Most of the charges that I discussed in the first chapter, however, could be proved beyond a reasonable doubt on that evidentiary record. So if proof beyond a reasonable doubt that the President committed a crime required that he be impeached and convicted, the House was right to impeach President Clinton and the Senate should have convicted him.

But we have seen that the simple approach of making Presidential impeachment and conviction mandatory if the President commits a crime would be unsound. A fuller inquiry into the President's conduct and the surrounding circumstances than that undertaken in the first chapter is therefore necessary. The conduct of the Independent Counsel and of other prosecutors, or persecutors, of Clinton (including "Clinton haters"), which was the subject of the second chapter, may be relevant, and likewise the broader moral and ethical issues raised by the President's conduct, which are the subject of the next chapter. These issues bear not only on the gravity of his criminal conduct but also on the effect of that conduct on his effectiveness as President, and so on whether Clinton can be compared to the President who moves to Saudi Arabia so that he can have four wives. There is also the question whether high crimes and misdemeanors can be excused on the basis of excellence in the President's discharge of the executive duties of his office, another question examined in the next chapter.

Clinton's defenders wanted to head off a trial in the Senate by converting the prosecution of the articles of impeachment into a motion for censure. When this effort failed, they sought to limit the trial to the evidence that had been obtained in the Independent Counsel's investigation. There is nothing wrong in principle with such a mode of trial, though the reasons that Clinton's lawyers and other defenders gave for wanting to do it in this case were nonsensical—that the Senate would be defiled or the public scandalized by hearing Monica Lewinsky describing her trysts with the President, and that a trial with witnesses would last months. The defenders' real concern was that live witnesses would create a more vivid impression of the President's wrongdoing even if their testimony was identical to what it had been before the grand jury[59]—and of course it might be different. The concern proved to be unfounded; the testimony of the three witnesses who eventually testified in the Senate trial did not harm Clinton.

If there were bad reasons for a paper trial (a trial without live witnesses), there were also bad reasons against it, such as that the credibility of a witness cannot be assessed without seeing the witness testify so that his or her demeanor (mainly, body language and the tone and pace of the testimony) can be assessed. What a witness's demeanor reveals is not whether the witness is lying, but whether he's a good actor.[60] That is one reason it was a blunder for the House Judiciary Committee to release the tape of Clinton's grand jury testimony. The best argument against a paper trial was the unwieldiness of the record—thousands of pages,[61] mostly of grand jury testimony gathered, as we saw in Chapter 2, under the loosest constraint of relevance, that were highly repetitious. Much evidence relevant when the Independent Counsel was trying to prove that the President had lied in denying a sexual relationship with Lewinsky became irrelevant when the President admitted the relationship. Although the prosecuting and defending lawyers in the Senate trial were able to point the Senators to relevant passages in the evidentiary record, thus sparing them from having to try to read the

[59]This would be an example of the salience or availability heuristic. See Chapter 2.

[60]There is evidence that lies are more likely to be detected if the trier of fact just reads a transcript of the witness's testimony rather than hearing oral testimony. Michael J. Saks, "Enhancing and Restraining Accuracy in Adjudication," 51 *Law and Contemporary Problems*, Autumn 1988, pp. 243, 263–264.

[61]The reported number is 60,000, but this is misleading. The House Judiciary Committee published five volumes of testimony and other evidence (including some materials that are not really evidentiary, such as the Independent Counsel's legal analysis of obstruction of justice law), amounting to some 8,000 pages. Because the published volumes use a condensed format for much of the grand jury testimony, a format in which each published page contains four to six pages of the original transcript, 8,000 is an underestimate of the total number of pages; but I would be surprised if the total normal page equivalents in the published volumes exceeded 30,000 pages. The other 30,000 pages, I surmise, are phone company records, visitor logs, and other documents that the Senators need not have felt obliged to read.

whole record, it would have been more efficient, certainly for focusing attention on the few key areas of factual disagreement, to let the witnesses tell their stories. Most of the facts bearing on the charges against the President were uncontested; no testimony was required to establish those facts. So far as the contested facts were concerned, it is difficult to see who besides Lewinsky, Betty Currie, Vernon Jordan, Linda Tripp, Frank Carter (Lewinsky's first lawyer, the one recommended by Jordan), Bill Richardson, Ronald Perelman, and of course Clinton himself had relevant testimony to give. Only Lewinsky, Currie, Jordan, and Clinton had a lot of relevant testimony to give,[62] and Clinton refused to testify. The witness phase of the trial need not have lasted more than a few days, even if more than three witnesses had been permitted.

In their effort to head off the calling of witnesses, the President's lawyers offered, in the guise of a generous concession, to stipulate to the admissibility of the entire evidentiary record that Starr had compiled. It was not much of a concession. All it meant was that they would not challenge the admissibility, under the rules of evidence (primarily the hearsay rule), of particular parts of the record. Since the Senate has not adopted rules of evidence to guide impeachment trials,[63] just as it has not adopted a standard of proof, it is difficult to see on what basis such challenges could be made; and they would only anger the Senators and the public by reinforcing the impression that the President's case rested entirely on legal technicalities. The President's lawyers were un-

---

[62]Sidney Blumenthal, the only witness to testify in the Senate trial besides Lewinsky and Jordan, did not have relevant evidence to give, if I am correct that the President could not be found guilty beyond a reasonable doubt of obstruction of justice in having lied to his aides knowing that they would be called before the grand jury. Probably the House prosecutors selected Blumenthal as a witness in order to make the President look as bad as possible; for it was in speaking to Blumenthal that Clinton had embellished his denial of a sexual relationship with Lewinsky by claiming that she had sought an affair with him in the hope that it would dispel her reputation as a stalker. The House impeachment manager who questioned Blumenthal was able to extract from him an acknowledgment that the President had indeed lied to him. Limited to three witnesses by the Senate, the House managers had to choose between Currie and Blumenthal and chose the latter. This was probably a mistake. If one may judge from Currie's grand jury testimony, her denial of having initiated (surely at the President's direction) the return of the President's gifts to Lewinsky would have been disbelieved, solidifying the proof of witness tampering.

[63]The Senate should adopt the Federal Rules of Evidence. They are both sensible and flexible, and would provide a familiar framework for keeping an impeachment trial from running off the rails.

willing to stipulate to the *facts* alleged in the Starr Report—that would have been a real concession. Indeed, it would have been more than could reasonably be asked, since some of the fact findings in the report cannot be considered proven to a high degree of certitude.

The Republicans and Democrats compromised on the issue of witnesses. They decided in effect to have a two-week trial on the documentary record and then decide whether to call witnesses. This seemed at the time a sensible compromise and it won the unanimous support of the Senators, thus bolstering (according to public opinion polls taken immediately after the compromise was announced) the credibility of the process in the eyes of the public. In the event, the "trial on the documentary record" turned into a rehash of issues that had been thoroughly canvassed before the House Judiciary Committee. It was like an enormously distended appellate argument, with the Starr Report taking the place of the trial court's decision, the usual springboard for an appeal. Once again the prosecution made a tactical mistake, this time by giving speaking roles to all thirteen House managers. This facilitated the efforts of the President's lawyers to make the case for removing the President from office seem niggling by splintering the case into dozens of petty charges none of which viewed in isolation seemed to warrant so fell a sanction. The Senate gave much too much time to each side (twenty-four hours!—at least three times what was necessary) and refused to allow the House managers to reserve some of their time for rebuttal, a departure from normal trial procedure that made it more difficult for the Senate and the television audience to form a crisp idea of the issues in controversy. At last, on February 6, a month into the trial, there was a genuine evidentiary hearing, at which the opposing sides dueled with the aid of excerpts from the videotaped depositions of the three witnesses.[64]

The trial, considered as a whole, was a travesty of legal justice.[65] Although most of the Senators pretended not to have made up their minds, their public comments during the course of the trial indicated otherwise. And as the trial moved toward its conclusion, more and more Senators began announcing publicly how they intended to vote. The Senators are neither judges nor lay innocents; and with a few exceptions

---

[64]145 Cong. Rec. S1290 (Feb. 6, 1999).

[65]But not because excerpts from videotaped depositions were used in lieu of live testimony. That is the wave of the future for trials in general.

they are neither able nor willing either to concentrate on a trial involving complex legal and factual questions or to subordinate political concerns to legal and constitutional concerns—in a word, to rise above partisanship. Democratic Senators had *ex parte* contacts with the White House (the defense), Republican Senators with the House managers (the prosecution). Had the trial conformed to the elementary principles of due process, all the Senators would have been disqualified from participating from the start, or expelled after their public statements and *ex parte* contacts demonstrated their unfitness by reason of partiality or inattention, or both, to play a responsible judicial role. The framers of the Constitution, who entrusted the Senate with judicial responsibilities in impeachment cases, had in mind a differently constituted body—smaller, more leisured, less political. Because the Senators were so terribly fidgety having to sit still hours on end listening to arguments that would not affect their vote, the excessively generous allotment of time to the lawyers to argue the case was pure torture.

The most serious procedural failure was the failure to impose a gag rule. As a result, the normal order of a trial—hearing, then verdict—was reversed, just as in Alice's trial in *Alice in Wonderland*. Having made up their minds before hearing the evidence and arguments, the Senators were inattentive as well as biased adjudicators.

A novel procedural issue was injected into the impeachment proceedings when Professor Bruce Ackerman of the Yale Law School, in testimony before the House Judiciary Committee on December 8, 1998, argued, by analogy to the process for enacting legislation, that a bill of impeachment lapses when the Congress that issued it expires.[66] The analogy is weak. Legislation to be valid requires the concurrence of both houses of Congress; that is bicameralism. The impeachment process is not legislative, but adjudicative, and does not require concurrence. The houses are assigned different tasks: the House of Representatives to determine whether the President (or other official) should be tried; the Senate to conduct the trial. The Senate doesn't have to agree with the House to put the President on trial, and the House doesn't have to agree with the Senate for him to be convicted, whereas both houses must agree on the text of a bill for it to be enacted into law. Ackerman's position would create the anomaly that between the first Tuesday in

[66]He has published an expanded version of his testimony as a short book. Bruce Ackerman, *The Case against Lameduck Impeachment* (1999).

November and the first week in January (when the new House convenes) a President could not be impeached no matter what enormities he had committed, if it were infeasible for the Senate to complete a trial of the President before the session ended. It would be like requiring a grand jury to indict and a petit jury to convict within the same term of court, or aborting a trial because the grand jury that had indicted the defendant had since expired.

Ackerman's argument is even more unreasonable than the example I just gave suggests. Despite the title of his book, *The Case against Lame-duck Impeachment,* he does not argue that a lame-duck House lacks the power to impeach. Although section 1 of the Twentieth Amendment, which reduced the term of lame-duck Congresses (and Presidents) by making the terms of Senators and Representatives end on January 3 following congressional elections, was motivated in part by hostility to lame-duck sessions of Congress, the amendment did not abolish such sessions. Ackerman uses that hostility, rather, to argue that the concurrence requirement for legislation (the House and the Senate must pass a bill in the same session) should not be relaxed for impeachments.[67] But the requirement of concurrence is not limited to a lame-duck Congress, that is, a Congress that is in session even though the election for the new Congress has taken place. On Ackerman's view, if the House of Representatives impeached the President in June, before the election, but the trial in the Senate was still going on when Congress's session ended in December, the impeachment would be void even though the impeaching House had not been a lame duck.

Even worse, Ackerman's proposal, though motivated by hostility to lame-duck impeachments, does not eliminate the possibility of them. If the President was impeached after the November election and the Senate hurried up and completed the trial in December, finding him guilty, he would have been impeached and convicted by a lame-duck Congress but the conviction would be valid.

Ackerman argued that Chief Justice William Rehnquist, as the presiding officer at the Senate trial,[68] would have to rule on whether the lame-duck House of Representatives could impeach Clinton, although Ackerman acknowledged that the ruling could be overridden (as the

---

[67]Id. at 11, 13.

[68]The Chief Justice of the United States presides at impeachment trials of the President. U.S. Const., art. I, § 3, cl. 6.

Senate's impeachment rules provide) by a majority vote of the Senate. The argument is unsound. The function of the Chief Justice is to preside as the chairman of a meeting governed by Robert's Rules of Order presides; that is, to keep order. He is to rule on objections to evidence and other matters relating to the conduct of the trial, subject (as under Robert's Rules) to appeal to the Senate; he is not to rule on issues going to the validity of the proceeding, such as whether the impeachment was lawful. The Constitution assigns the Chief Justice to preside over trials of Presidents not because he's a judge but because the Vice President, who presides over all other impeachment trials even though he is not required to be a lawyer, let alone a judge, would have a conflict of interest in presiding over the trial of the President.[69]

If the limitation of the Chief Justice's authority in impeachment trials isn't clear as a matter of law (I think it is clear),[70] it is clear as a matter of political theory. It would undermine the judiciary to put a single judge, even one as exalted as the Chief Justice of the United States, in the position of having to determine whether the President shall be tried by the Senate and possibly convicted and removed from office, or let off without a trial. That is one reason impeachments are not tried before the Supreme Court or convictions in impeachment trials reviewed by the courts.[71] It was apparent from Rehnquist's behavior at the trial of President Clinton that he interpreted his powers narrowly. He made few rulings, none either substantive or remotely likely to affect the outcome.

---

[69]Michael J. Gerhardt, "The Constitutional Limits to Impeachment and Its Alternatives," 68 *Texas Law Review* 1, 88, 98 (1989).

[70]Ackerman's argument that the Chief Justice can rule on the validity of the impeachment of Clinton rests on a footnote in Bruce Ackerman, *We the People*, vol. 2: *Transformations* 467–468 n. 63 (1998), paraphrased in Ackerman, note 66 above, at 74–77. The footnote, which is about Chief Justice Salmon Chase's conduct of the impeachment trial of Andrew Johnson, disclaims any suggestion that the "limited position of procedural leadership" that Chase did claim is a precedent for future impeachment trials. Ackerman, above, at 468 n. 63. Chase is in any event remote from being a model of how a Chief Justice should preside at a Presidential impeachment. He had Presidential ambitions himself and communicated to wavering Senators his belief that Johnson should be acquitted. Benedict, note 15 above, at 136–137.

[71]Hamilton warned against "the additional pretext for clamour, against the Judiciary, which so considerable an augmentation of its authority [as giving it responsibility to try impeachments] would have afforded." "Federalist No. 65," in *The Federalist*, note 29 above, at 439, 443.

The issue of lame-duck impeachment was rendered largely moot by a vote in the House of Representatives on January 6, 1999, after the new Congress convened. The vote was on reappointing the impeachment managers who had been appointed by the lame-duck House to present the case for impeachment at the Senate trial. The Democrats argued that the new House should refuse to reappoint the impeachment managers. Had the argument prevailed, it would have undone the lame-duck impeachment. It failed; the managers were reappointed by a vote of 223 to 198. This cannot be judged a ringing endorsement of lame-duck impeachment, since it would have been a terrible slap in the face of the managers and the rest of the reelected Congressmen who had voted for impeachment in the previous Congress. In any event, the Senate ignored Ackerman's argument completely.

A novel procedural issue arose in the Senate trial when the President's lawyers argued that the articles of impeachment were unconstitutionally vague. This may seem a surprising argument; recall from Chapter 1 that the two articles between them allege seven specific respects in which the President committed perjury before the grand jury (Article I) or otherwise obstructed justice (Article III). However, three of the four "specific" charges in Article I are not very specific: that the President lied to the grand jury about the nature of his relationship with Lewinsky, about the truthfulness of his deposition in the Paula Jones case, and about "his corrupt efforts to influence the testimony of witnesses and to impede the discovery of evidence in" that case.

Ordinarily, a lack of specificity in an indictment is easily cured by requesting the prosecutor to file a bill of particulars. But if an indictment is really vague—so vague that it provides little guidance to the scope of the charges against the defendant—it may not be curable by a bill of particulars. The bill would be drafted by the prosecutors, not the grand jury that had issued the indictment; and if the indictment were truly vague, it would be impossible to determine whether the prosecutors were prosecuting the charges authorized by the grand jury or the charges that they considered best to charge whether or not the grand jury would have agreed. The parallel concern in the case of vague articles of impeachment is that the impeachment managers might be prosecuting charges different from those approved by the House of Representatives and thus bypassing the House, in derogation of the constitutional role of the House in the impeachment process. The concern is greater than in the case of a vague indictment. Grand juries usually rubber-stamp the indictments proposed by the prosecutors; so a prosecutor has little reason to exploit the vagueness of an indictment by adding charges not presented to the grand jury. But the House was not a rubber stamp of its Judiciary Committee. It voted down two of the four articles of impeachment proposed by the Committee—from whose ranks the impeachment managers were drawn. And if the House ought to be convinced that the President is guilty, and not merely that he may be guilty, before impeaching him, there is an argument for making it deliberate with specificity rather than permitting it to write a blank check either to its Judiciary Committee or to the impeachment managers.

These are good arguments, but they don't have much application to Clinton's impeachment. It is true that Article I was broad; it encompassed all the lies that the President may have told the grand jury. But there were so many lies that an attempt to specify them (or embody each in a separate article) would have bogged the proceedings down—and remember that the Democrats wanted the proceedings to be expedited. It is unrealistic to think that Article I would not have passed had the lies been spelled out. Article III was not vague at all.

The President's lawyers argued that the managers strayed beyond Article I's broad bounds by repeatedly asserting that the President had lied in his deposition in the Jones case, even though the House had voted down the proposed article of impeachment that charged lying in the deposition. This argument misconceives both the grounds for voting down that article and the relation between the President's deposition and his grand jury testimony. The article was voted down not because the Republican majority thought the President had *not* lied at his deposition, but because of doubts about the materiality and gravity of his lying in testimony that was tangential to a mere civil case. These lies remained material to Article I, which charged lying before the grand jury, because the President had repeated much of his deposition testimony to the grand jury and had affirmed the truthfulness of that testimony. These were lies only if the deposition testimony contained lies.

CHAPTER 4

Morality, Private and Public

Intelligent evaluation of the moral dimensions of the Clinton-Lewinsky mess requires distinguishing between *private morality* and *public morality*. The former term refers to the duties that the moral code of a society imposes on people regardless of their office or job, the latter to the duties that the code imposes on people who occupy particular offices (not necessarily public). A lawyer has special moral duties—the domain of "legal ethics"—by virtue of his or her profession, as well as the moral duties that are common to all persons in his society. And so with every other profession and vocation, including that of a political leader.

The distinction between private and public morality was stressed, and precisely in the context of political leadership, by the nineteenth-century economist and philosopher Henry Sidgwick,[1] and more recently by (among others) F. G. Bailey.[2] But their emphasis is on the tensions, conflicts, or trade-offs between the two types of morality, as when a leader's

[1] See Henry Sidgwick, *Practical Ethics,* ch. 3 (1898). A related contrast, that between an ethic of ultimate ends (as in the Sermon on the Mount) and an ethic of responsibility (the proper ethic for a political leader), is explored in Weber's essay "Politics as a Vocation," reprinted in *From Max Weber: Essays in Sociology* 77, 117–128 (H. H. Gerth and C. Wright Mills trans. 1946).

[2] F. G. Bailey, *Humbuggery and Manipulation: The Art of Leadership* (1988). See also the essays by Stuart Hampshire, Thomas Nagel, and Bernard Williams in *Public and Private Morality* (Stuart Hampshire ed. 1978). The tension between private and public morality is, as emphasized in C. A. J. Coady, "Dirty Hands," in *A Companion to Contemporary Political Philosophy* 422 (Robert E. Goodin and Philip Pettit eds. 1993), part of a larger issue, that of moral dilemmas (or "dirty hands"), discusssed extensively by Sartre and other philosophers.

role-related lying, cruelty, or other normally reprobated behavior is defended by reference to *raison d'état*. Bailey argues that "leaders everywhere are like deans, inescapably polluted by what they do, and, since leadership is by its very nature defiling, it follows that moral judgments are as appropriate in this regard as they are about foul weather."[3] "Leadership . . . is part villainy."[4] "No one succeeds in politics without getting his hands dirty."[5] This is a point often made about lawyering as well, and many plausible examples could be adduced from the conduct of the lawyers involved in the investigation and impeachment of President Clinton. But Bailey is being too colorful; once it is accepted that we must have leaders, the "villainy" *inseparable* from the exercise of leadership cannot be real villainy.[6]

This qualification turns out to be relevant to the Clinton-Lewinsky imbroglio, as we shall see. But I want to emphasize other relations, which have received too little emphasis, between public and private morality. These are the additive relation, that is, the additional moral duties (not the possible license for immorality or amorality that is Sidgwick's and Bailey's focus) that occupying a public office imposes on a person; the spillover from private to public morality (when does a breach of the former contaminate the latter?); and the compensatory relation—not when does public morality *require* a breach of private morality (the issue emphasized by Sidgwick and Bailey), but when can an unrelated breach of private morality be redeemed by outstanding performance of the duties imposed by public morality. The last question gestures to the difference between an Aristotelian and a Kantian sense of "character," the former emphasizing achievement and the latter moral goodness. It also points to the distinction, basic to Machiavelli's political theory, between Roman and Christian virtue.[7]

To help fix the distinction between public and private morality, consider once again Charles Black's example of the President who moves to Saudi Arabia so that he can have four wives. There are two violations of the moral code, though Black does not distinguish them. The first is polygamy, the second absenteeism. The first is a violation, in the first

[3]Bailey, note 2 above, at ix.

[4]Id. at 174.

[5]Michael Walzer, "Political Action: The Problem of Dirty Hands," in *War and Moral Responsibility* 62, 66 (Marshall Cohen, Thomas Nagel, and Thomas Scanlon eds. 1974).

[6]Coady, note 2 above, at 423–425.

[7]See Harvey C. Mansfield, *Machiavelli's Virtue* (1996).

instance at least, of private morality; the vast majority of Americans consider polygamy immoral for anyone, or at least any American, regardless of his vocation. The second is a violation of public morality; the President is expected to perform the duties of his office, with the exception of occasional official trips abroad, in the United States.

But the qualification "in the first instance" is important. Compliance with the American moral code might be a duty attached to the office of the President as well as being obligatory on private individuals and on public officials in their private life. A President who took multiple wives might be thought to be violating the duties of his office, one of which, it could be argued, is to be a moral exemplar—not a saint, who would be unfitted by his saintliness for the rough and tumble of political leadership, but a good example to the population at large, a "role model." If this is right, it implies that a President's immoral personal behavior (personal in the sense of not involving the exercise of governmental powers) might violate the moral duties attached to the office of the Presidency as well as his private moral duties, though this may depend on whether such behavior is likely ever to become public knowledge. We may have here a true instance of the adage that what you don't know can't hurt you. If no one ever found out about a President's moral failings, those failings could not impair his status as a role model.

Private Morality

In the contrition phase that followed President Clinton's grand jury testimony, Clinton and his defenders were vague about what exactly had been "wrong" in his conduct.[8] The vagueness was deliberate. He was afraid to confess to perjury and the other obstructions of justice that he had committed. Not only would a confession have strengthened the legal case for impeachment (though it now appears that it would have weakened the political case), but it could be used as evidence against him should he ever be tried in a regular court, though presumably he could avert that danger by pardoning himself before he leaves

---

[8]Here is how his lawyers put it in the 184-page brief that they submitted to the House Judiciary Committee on December 8, 1998: "What the President did was wrong. As the President himself has said, publicly and painfully, 'there is no fancy way to say that I have sinned.' The President has insisted that no legalities be allowed to obscure the simple moral truth that his behavior in this matter was wrong; that he misled his wife, his friends and our Nation about the nature of his relationship with Ms. Lewinsky."

office; we saw in the last chapter that it is probable, although not certain, that a President does have the power of self-pardoning. All that he confessed to was, first, having unspecified sexual contact with Monica Lewinsky, and, second, misleading his family, friends, Cabinet officers and other subordinates, and the American people, by publicly and privately denying, between January 21 and August 17, 1998, that he had had any kind of sexual relationship with Lewinsky.

Oddly, these "wrongs" to which he confessed may not have been violations, at least serious violations, of either private or public morality. Although some Americans, particularly religious ones, consider oral sex, masturbation (especially mutual masturbation) whether in the form of phone sex or otherwise, and the use of an object as a phallic substitute to be immoral, most do not. Oral sex, both fellatio and cunnilingus, "has become a nearly universal technique for the vast majority of people."[9] Clinton and Lewinsky both seem to regard oral sex as closer to petting than to intercourse, and I don't know on what basis they could be thought "wrong" to think this. As I intimated in Chapter 1, it is not beyond the realm of the possible that some day welfare and public health authorities, concerned with the risks of unintended pregnancy and of sexual transmission of disease, may want to encourage the substitution of oral for vaginal sex by couples that do not want to produce a child.

The vast majority of Americans disapprove of adultery[10] and most of them consider oral sex between a married man and a woman not his wife to be a form of adultery. But if pressed, most of these people would probably admit that their view assumed that the wife disapproved, or would disapprove if she knew about it; and not all wives disapprove of their husbands' adultery. But passing this perhaps esoteric point, disapproval of adultery is tempered by recognition of its commonness. In a pluralistic society, a practice that is common enough tends to become normative. So high a fraction of men are adulterers,[11] including highly respected Presidents, such as Franklin Roosevelt and John Kennedy, who were in office at a time when adultery was more reprobated than it is today, that it is difficult to consider Clinton's relation with

---

[9]Edward O. Laumann et al., *The Social Organization of Sexuality: Sexual Practices in the United States* 107 (1994).

[10]Id. at 22.

[11]Roughly 20 to 25 percent of married men. Id. at 213–216.

Lewinsky—involving as it did, moreover, a form of sex less threatening to marriage than vaginal intercourse[12]—a serious immorality just by virtue of his being a married man. A complicating factor, but one that I shall not attempt to weigh, is that Clinton has had other adulterous affairs apart from the one with Lewinsky, some of which involved full intercourse; he admitted in his deposition in the Paula Jones case to having had intercourse with Gennifer Flowers.

Many radical feminists believe that sex between a male superior and a female subordinate is sexual harassment per se because of the imbalance of power between them. Most Americans would reject this view if they read Monica Lewinsky's testimony. I have been over this ground in Chapter 1 and will not repeat myself beyond reminding the reader that Clinton cannot fairly be accused of deception, seduction, overreaching, exploitation, taking advantage of an innocent or naive girl, retaliation, threats, or promises, in relation to Lewinsky. It is true that the relationship turned out to be a disaster for her. But Clinton cannot be charged with having *deliberately* not warned her of this possibility. Careless, even reckless, he may be; but if he had had an inkling of what might ensue from their affair, he would never have gotten involved with her. Maybe he should have foreseen the collision between the affair and the Paula Jones suit, filed well before the affair began. But this is to accuse him of carelessness or obtuseness rather than of sexual harassment.[13] Clinton is an intelligent and well-educated person and an experienced and successful politician, but even intelligent and experienced people do dumb things. People will be scratching their heads for many

---

[12]One of Lewinsky's friends, to whom she had confided the details of her relationship with the President, speculated that because Clinton "has a bond with Hillary . . . he wanted to be, you know, truer to his wife than he had been and [vaginal] intercourse would make it that much more difficult." *Supplementary Materials to the Referral to the U.S. House of Representatives,* H. Doc. No. 316, 105th Cong., 2d Sess., vol. 1, p. 1075 (Sept. 28, 1998).

[13]Clinton's self-described "friend" Alan Dershowitz contends that Clinton's decision to have sex with Monica Lewinsky was "foolhardy." Dershowitz finds it "difficult to imagine any action more reckless than Oval Office sex with a young blabbermouth." But "when people have succeeded so often in the past in achieving both immediate gratification and long-term avoidance of consequences, they miscalculate the odds and act as if they can have their cake and eat it too." Alan M. Dershowitz, *Sexual McCarthyism: Clinton, Starr, and the Emerging Constitutional Crisis* 7–8 (1998). "He [Clinton] wanted sex with deniability. What he got was unsatisfying sex with unconvincing deniability." Id. at 7.

years over how Clinton could have allowed himself to become involved with Monica Lewinsky—almost as fatal an infatuation as Antony's with Cleopatra, and with less excuse.

If Clinton made a *practice* of having sex with his subordinates, this would certainly be objectionable, as is now pretty universally recognized in American law and morality, even if there was no element of coercion. It would distract and upset his female subordinates with whom he did not have sex; they might fear that their more complaisant counterparts were gaining a vocational advantage. So might some of his male subordinates. It would give the workplace an atmosphere of favoritism and intrigue, undermining a sense of professionalism. (Notice that this example straddles the line between private and public morality. It is a violation of the moral duties of a superior officer to have sex with subordinates, but it is a violation independent of the nature of the office.) There is some evidence that President Clinton does have such a practice. Certainly that is what Monica Lewinsky believed (and she named names imperfectly deleted in the volumes of published testimony), as did some of the Secret Service officers who testified. It is the basis of that peculiar definition of "graduates" that Lewinsky and Tripp bandied about in their taped telephone conversations. But it has not been proved, so I shall disregard it.

In refusing to take a stand on whether adultery is wrong or oral sex wrong or sex with a subordinate (unless habitual) wrong, I am avoiding what might seem one of the most interesting and important issues presented by Clinton's actions: the "real," the "objective," moral valence of those actions. I am doing this because, as I have argued elsewhere,[14] the tools do not exist for resolving normative issues *about* the moral code—such issues as whether Americans ought to abandon their hostility to polygamy or female genital mutilation or infanticide, or reject abortion, fornication, and physician-assisted suicide. Even if my skepticism is excessive, it would hardly be appropriate to punish Clinton not for violating the prevailing moral code of modern American society but for failing to comply with what a minority of Americans consider a better moral code, for example the code implied by Catholic natural law doctrine, which condemns oral sex even within marriage.[15]

---

[14]See Richard A. Posner, *The Problematics of Moral and Legal Theory*, ch. 1 (1999).

[15]Applying that doctrine to Clinton's dalliance with Monica Lewinsky, William Bennett says it matters that "the president acted [with Lewinsky] sexually more like an alley cat

Even less "wrongful" than adultery or oral sex, once we put sectarian doctrine to one side, was Clinton's "misleading" his family, friends, and associates, and the public at large. For it is unlikely that many of them *were* misled or that those who were (with the possible exception of his daughter) incurred any lasting harm as a result. Most people disbelieved his denials from the outset, and the closer people were to Clinton and therefore the more they knew about his history and proclivities the less likely they were to believe the denials. The leaks from the Linda Tripp tapes were convincing; the acts alleged of Clinton were in character for him; and his initial denials, before the impressive television denial of January 26, 1998 ("I did not have sexual relations with that woman, Miss Lewinsky"),[16] were evasive and unconvincing. His wife must know him well enough by now to have seen through his denials. (If so, that makes her an accomplice in her husband's scheme of deception.)[17] What many people doubtless believed, perhaps including Clinton's lawyers, Cabinet members, and other Clinton agents and supporters, was that Clinton's denials would never be *proved* false; for these people didn't know about the semen-stained dress; nor, in all likelihood, did he (or he thought she must have cleaned it). Maybe the Secretary of State and other high officials, while no doubt secretly disbelieving Clinton (these are sophisticated people), thought it important to the nation's prestige or security that he get away with his lie. They have not said so, however, and it would not be very convincing. This is not to say that they should have felt obliged to resign. A President could be forced from office if enough members of the executive branch resigned in protest, but this would be an unconstitutional method of removal. It would be like a parliamentary vote of no confidence. The only constitutional method of forcing a President from office is impeachment. But President Clin-

---

than an adult." William J. Bennett, *The Death of Outrage: Bill Clinton and the Assault on American Ideals* 25 (1998). Do cats engage in oral sex? That's news to me, but I take it that Bennett means only that animals do not have a sense of sexual propriety. Bennett, incidentally, is the brother of Clinton's lawyer in the Paula Jones case (Robert Bennett)—putting one in mind of brothers fighting on opposite sides in the Civil War.

[16]*Appendices to the Referral to the U.S. House of Representatives,* H. Doc. No. 311, 105th Cong., 2d Sess., vol. 2, p. 1961 (Sept. 18, 1998).

[17]Notably in the television interview on January 27, 1998, in which she denied that her husband had "had an adulterous liaison in the White House and lied to cover it up" and attributed the charge to "a vast right-wing conspiracy." She also said, however, that if the charge were proved to be true, it "would be a very serious offense." Id., vol. 2, pp. 1973–1974. Did she mean it? If so, has she changed her mind? She isn't saying.

ton's Cabinet members could have said nothing, as a number of them did, without thereby disserving the national interest. Those who repeated Clinton's denial of an improper relationship with Monica Lewinsky can only be regarded as willing victims of the President's deceits.

His daughter may have believed his denials. Children like to think well of their parents. But if Clinton thought he could convince her of the truth of his denials and didn't think he would ever be forced to retract them, then he was not hurting her by not telling her the truth. If he knew that the truth would come out, then he was hurting her, by undermining her trust in him and branding himself a liar as well as a rake in her eyes. But as I say, he probably thought he could keep the truth bottled up. After all, there are still people who believe that Alger Hiss was not a Soviet agent.

Clinton may, as we shall see, have committed a serious wrong in lying even if the people to whom he lied knew that he was lying. But he has not confessed to lying, only to misleading. He was clever to confess to the moral wrongfulness of precisely those aspects of his conduct that were least wrongful, and perhaps not wrongful at all.

But it may have been a superficial cleverness. It placed Clinton on the defensive in a two-front war. One front was the moral, the other the legal. By admitting moral wrongdoing, Clinton enabled the Republicans to focus on his legal wrongdoing, his obstructions of justice. That Clinton had done wrong became the consensus, the benchmark. The Republicans then hammered at the legal wrongdoing, where Clinton's defenses were weak: they amounted, after the stripping away of his lawyers' obfuscations, to the contention, defensible certainly but unedifying, that his crimes were not serious enough to compel his removal from office.

An incontestable breach of private morality for which President Clinton did *not* apologize was involving other people in his questionable activities, subjecting them to possible legal expense and criminal jeopardy. His clearest "victim" was Betty Currie, whom he may have enlisted (he has certainly created the appearance of having done so) in a conspiracy to obstruct justice in the Paula Jones case and conceivably in the ensuing grand jury investigation of him. Vernon Jordan may be a similar victim; and one of the President's stewards, and perhaps others of his staff, again including Currie, may get into trouble for denying to the grand jury that they knew anything about the President's hanky-panky with Lewinsky. But maybe anyone who gets close to a President, or at least this President, is playing with fire and should know it, for

> The cease of majesty
> Dies not alone, but, like a gulf doth draw
> What's near it with it; it is a massy wheel,
> Fix'd on the summit of the highest mount,
> To whose huge spokes ten thousand lesser things
> Are mortis'd and adjoined; which, when it falls,
> Each small annexment, petty consequence,
> Attends the boisterous ruin. Never alone
> Did the king sigh, but with a general groan.[18]

It is unrealistic, however, to expect low-level staffers to foresee the legal risks involved in working for the President.

Involving others in criminal or criminal-seeming activity was not the President's only breach of private morality. He slandered Monica Lewinsky, calling her a liar and a stalker. He condoned, perhaps actively encouraged, slanders of Paula Jones and Kenneth Starr, though since it is not certain (although it is likely) that these slanders are false,[19] we should perhaps reserve judgment. His slanders of Lewinsky, however, were false.

Through his defenders, Clinton encouraged perjury by permitting them to say in public that "no one" is prosecuted for the kind of conduct

---

[18]*Hamlet,* act III, sc. 3, ll. 16–23.

[19]Now that the Paula Jones case has been settled, we may never know whether her charge that Clinton solicited her for oral sex is true. But the circumstances of the settlement suggest (no stronger word is possible) that it is true. The case was settled for a hefty sum ($850,000), suggestive of guilt, in mid-November 1998, after the danger that Clinton would be forced from office seemed to have passed. Clinton must have thought there was a good chance that the court of appeals would reverse the district court and remand the case for trial, and that he would lose at trial; otherwise, for the sake of vindication—of removing one of the blots from his escutcheon—he would probably have fought on.

In saying that Jones's claim that Clinton solicited her for oral sex is probably true, I do not mean to suggest that her entire story is probably true. Judge Wright found that Jones had exaggerated the harm that she had suffered from the incident in an apparent effort to ward off the dismissal of her suit on the ground, which the judge found persuasive, that the incident had been too inconsequential to sustain the suit. See Jones v. Clinton, 990 F. Supp. 657, 675, 677 n. 21, 678 (E.D. Ark. 1998). Judge Wright, incidentally, is a Republican who was appointed to the bench by President Bush.

in which he engaged. Since this is false, some people may find themselves in prison as a result of public statements made on Clinton's behalf. Clinton is not responsible for every irresponsible such statement, but he is responsible for the irresponsible statements by his lawyers and aides. He could have turned them off with a word. Or he could have stated publicly, without necessarily admitting that *he* had engaged in perjury or other obstructions of justice, that these are serious crimes which should be and are punished. As late as December 1998, a defender of Clinton who should have known better was publicly describing the charges against Clinton as "highly technical charges for which no ordinary citizen would ever be punished."[20]

The volume and brazenness of Clinton's lies are impressive. To keep on lying after no one believes you does not mislead, but it shows contempt for truth and truthfulness. That is why liars are reprobated even when everyone knows they are liars and therefore no one is deceived. It is why the technique of the Big Lie is offensive even when almost everyone sees through it. Truth is an important social value, so we want people to respect rather than flout it. That may have been one reason the moderate Republicans on whom Clinton placed such faith in the run up to impeachment fell away from him when he refused to admit that he had lied. It is understandable why he refused. But it made it seem as if, like Pontius Pilate, he views truth as a purely instrumental value. It made him disquietingly postmodernist even to those who have never heard of postmodernism.[21] It reminded one of how tyrants exhibit their power by forcing their subjects to express agreement with lies that no one believes, such as that the tyrant is benign and the nation a democracy. And it brought to mind a long history of equivocation by

---

[20]Jeffrey Rosen, "Stop, in the Name of the Law," *New York Times* (national ed.), Dec. 6, 1998, § 4, p. 19. The immediate referent of "highly technical charges" is the charges brought against Michael Espy, a former Clinton Cabinet member, by another independent counsel. But the clear implication of the article, in which Rosen pleaded for Clinton not to be impeached, is that the charges against Clinton were of the same character.

[21]Republican Congressman Bob Inglis, during the December 10, 1999, hearing before the House Judiciary Committee, actually attacked Clinton as a "relativist," which is pretty close to a postmodernist. But Inglis ruined it all, in my eyes at least, by tracing Clinton's relativism back to—Oliver Wendell Holmes, who, in the Congressman's words, "basically said let's abandon the search for truth and let's do relative justice between people, because there is no truth out there to find." I find the idea of Clinton as Holmes's avatar passing odd.

Clinton—over the draft, over smoking marijuana, over pre-Presidential adulteries.

Clinton made a travesty of the religious rite of atonement by asking for forgiveness and absolution without offering to incur any cost,[22] thus putting one in mind of another phony repenter, Shakespeare's Claudius.[23] Claudius is frank in acknowledging his crimes (the murder of the king and marriage with the king's widow, with whom he had been carrying on an adulterous, and arguably an incestuous, affair) to himself. "O, my offense is rank! It smells to heaven." He tries to pray for forgiveness, but realizes that this is impossible because

> . . . What form of prayer
> Can serve my turn? "Forgive me my foul murder"?
> That cannot be, since I am still possessed
> Of those effects for which I did the murder:
> My crown, mine own ambition, and my queen.
> May one be pardoned and retain th'offense?

The answer, of course, is "no." Clinton, too, wants to be pardoned and retain the offense. When it began to seem clear, on the basis of the results of the November 1998 mid-term elections (one of the many false dawns that punctuated the ordeal), that Clinton would not be forced from office, he dropped the contrition act and became his old smiling

[22]See *Judgment Day at the White House: A Critical Declaration Exploring Moral Issues and the Political Use and Abuse of Religion* 11 (Gabriel Fackre ed. 1999); Steve Kloehn, "To Err Is Clinton, But Is Public Divine?" *Chicago Tribune* (Chicagoland final ed.), Aug. 23, 1998, p. C1. Jean Bethke Elshtain, "Politics and Forgiveness: The Clinton Case," in *Judgment Day at the White House,* above, at 11, describes Clinton as an exemplar of "contrition chic . . ., meaning a bargain-basement way to gain publicity, sympathy, and even absolution by trafficking in one's status as victim or victimizer." Don Browning notes that some people seem to think that "if Clinton confesses to what he is not being charged with, he should be exonerated for all actual charges against him." Don S. Browning, "Missing the Point on Clinton," in *Judgment Day at the White House,* above, at 39–40. And Akhil Amar remarks of the President, "he mouthed words of contrition without really exhaling." Akhil Reed Amar, "Take Five: Why Clinton Should Consider a Sabbatical," *New Republic,* Feb. 8, 1999, pp. 13, 14. The Clintons' pastor, in his book-length plea for forgiving the President, depreciates the gravity of the President's acts, J. Philip Wogamon, *From the Eye of the Storm: A Pastor to the President Speaks Out* 57, 132 (1998), while providing no evidence whatever for the sincerity of the President's repentance. His book is a kind of clergyman's brief for a member of his flock, complementing a lawyer's brief for his client.

[23]*Hamlet,* act III, sc. 3, ll. 36–72.

self. Just as he was forced to admit to his relationship with Monica Lewinsky by flunking a DNA test rather than by experiencing pangs of conscience, so he was forced to put on sackcloth and ashes by the public relations fiasco of his uncontrite confession of August 17 rather than by a sudden realization that he was indeed a liar and a lecher. When the immediate crisis passed, so did the affectation of contrition.

President Clinton made fools of the naive clergymen whom he persuaded to participate in his atonement rite. In repeatedly lying under oath, he repeatedly swore falsely to God—and has steadfastly refused to acknowledge having done so. He acknowledged being guilty of engaging in conduct that was barely culpable, shamelessly denied being guilty of the culpable conduct that the evidence proved he had engaged in, refused to admit having ever told *any* lies to anybody about his relationship with Monica Lewinsky, and, after repenting, immediately redoubled his efforts to avoid having to suffer any adverse consequences from his misconduct. It has been reported that, during his Senate trial, he was—in very un-Christian fashion—plotting revenge against the House prosecutors.[24] He flaunts his religiosity, but gives religion a bad name.

Clinton's obstructions of justice, too, were violations of private morality. This is not to say that *every* criminal act is immoral. To deduce the moral code from the criminal law would put the cart before the horse. The law criminalizes a number of serious breaches of the moral code, though not all. But it also criminalizes a number of morally neutral acts, some of which I noted in Chapter 1; a number of acts that used to be considered immoral but are no longer, at least by most of the population, such as fornication, which is still a crime in a number of states;[25] and many acts, such as manufacturing adulterated food or drug products, that would be immoral if done intentionally but that are punished criminally even if done unintentionally. Deliberately obstructing justice, however, is not morally neutral.

Particular laws, or their application in particular cases, can often be criticized on moral grounds. Many people believe that it was immoral to punish for contempt of Congress the people who, when they were

---

[24]Richard L. Berke and James Bennet, "Clinton Vows Strong Drive to Win a House Majority, Advisers Say," *New York Times* (national ed.), Feb. 11, 1999, p. A1.

[25]See Richard A. Posner and Katharine Silbaugh, *A Guide to America's Sex Laws,* ch. 7 (1996).

subpoenaed in the 1950s to testify before the House Un-American Activities Committee, refused to inform on their friends who were members of the Communist Party. But President Clinton did not argue that he was morally justified in lying in order to protect Monica Lewinsky's reputation, and he could not argue persuasively that the dubious merits and political antecedents of Paula Jones's suit justified him in lying, though it might conceivably have justified his refusing to cooperate with her lawyers. He did argue that even a President should have a modicum of privacy and not be asked about his sex life, but again this would not justify lying; it would justify only refusing to answer the questions.[26] The people who refused to name names to the House Un-American Activities Committee were not lying; they were refusing to cooperate with what they believed to be an illegitimate, although lawful, inquiry.

With all these "moral defenses" to criminal conduct inapplicable to Clinton's case, we are left with the fact that obstructing justice, whether by perjury, suborning perjury, or witness tampering, is a serious crime.[27] And as a lawyer, and a bright one, Clinton cannot plead ignorance (a plea that might be good in morality, though rarely in law) that his conduct constituted obstruction of justice.

Many people believe, however, that his obstructions of justice should have been, if not justified or condoned, at least excused or forgiven because of the circumstances. Particular weight is laid on their origins in a sexual escapade and on the assumed malicious and political motivations, and procedural irregularities, of Clinton's persecutors. Members of the legal profession, professionally disposed to believe that the laws which punish obstruction of justice in its myriad forms undergird our system of legal justice, are apt to think that the circumstances at

---

[26]"Perjury is not a permissible way of objecting to the Government's questions. 'Our legal system provides methods for challenging the Government's right to ask questions and lying is not one of them.' " United States v. Wong, 431 US. 174, 180 (1977). See also Sissela Bok, *Lying: Moral Choice in Public and Private Life* 176 (1978). Earlier I acknowledged an exception for the case in which a refusal to answer is tantamount to an admission. But if Clinton had told Paula Jones's lawyers, "None of your business," when they asked him about his relations with women, most people would probably have taken his statement at face value.

[27]See, for example, United States v. Mandujano, 425 U.S. 564, 576 (1976) ("perjured testimony is an obvious and flagrant affront to the basic concepts of judicial proceedings").

most mitigated the gravity of Clinton's behavior, but did not excuse that behavior. Many members of the general public, however, seem, whether rightly or wrongly, to evaluate obstruction of justice in more nuanced terms. (Others, however, are apathetic, confused, uninformed, or lawless—let us not mistake any of these dispositions for nuance.) They focus on the precise conduct constituting the obstruction and on the "justice" (in a lay, not legal, sense) of the legal proceeding that is obstructed. An obstruction of justice that involves violence, the threat of violence, or bribery will be condemned regardless of the nature of the legal proceeding that is obstructed. But if, as in Clinton's case, that proceeding should never have been instituted in the first place, then the lay public, lacking the legal professional's tendency to think of obedience to law as a good of transcendent value, is apt to be forgiving. The proceeding that Clinton obstructed was the Paula Jones case. We cannot be certain how much truth there was in Jones's charges; but whether much or little, the legal basis of her suit was shaky, as we have seen. And to this shaky suit, as we have also seen, Clinton's affair with Lewinsky was tangential—while the grand jury investigation of Clinton was a pendent to his deposition in the Jones case.

It is easy to sympathize with someone who is *gratuitously* placed in a position where he would be humiliated if he told the truth and punished if he did not; and that is a possible though not inevitable light in which to view Clinton's situation. Arguably the President of the United States should be held to a higher standard than the ordinary citizen, but the argument crosses the line from private to public morality.

Consider, as further bearing on the gravity of the President's conduct, the public reaction, including the reaction of conservative Republicans, to the grant of comprehensive immunity to Monica Lewinsky. The proof that Lewinsky committed and suborned perjury is even more conclusive than the proof that Clinton committed such crimes. Yet as a result of the grant of immunity, Lewinsky will not be punished for them. Of course everyone understands that to nail a really big criminal, the little criminals must sometimes be given a pass. But when this happens, the little criminals do not become objects of sympathy; they are still hated criminals. Many people dislike Monica Lewinsky—but not because she, like Clinton, is a criminal. They dislike her for her role in precipitating a year's worth of political upheaval. Maybe they *should* dislike her for her criminal acts as well. But remember that I'm using as my standard the nation's current moral code, not the higher code to which a moral rigorist—and many judges—would like to hold people.

Even judges have a certain ambivalence about perjury in civil litigation. It is not unusual for one judge to say to another that he or she has just presided at a trial at which several of the witnesses were obviously lying, or that the witnesses seem to have coordinated their stories or to have been "well coached" by the lawyers. I have heard expert witnesses referred to as "paid liars." These comments are generally not made in a tone of indignation, and they very rarely lead to a referral to the Department of Justice to inquire into the possibility of an obstruction of justice. Part of this reaction is due to the difficulty of proving perjury in most cases, and part to the fact that judges like other professionals grow moral calluses. But part is due to a sense that the court system has been designed, or at least has evolved, to be robust in the face of the known inefficacy of the oath and of the threat of prosecution for perjury and other obstructions of justice and as a result the frequency of these crimes. It would be nice if they were less frequent, but fortunately they are less costly to society, less feared, and less dangerous than many other felonies.

But this analysis is incomplete too, and not only because the President perjured himself in a criminal investigation as well as in a civil investigation. The analysis treats lying under oath in a legal proceeding as an either-or phenomenon, whereas actually there is a spectrum of such lying. It reaches from the barefaced lie at one end to the phony "I don't remember" (phony if the witness does remember) at the other. The more barefaced the lie, the greater the liar's risk of being prosecuted for perjury. The effect of perjury law, here operating in tandem with the laws against witness tampering and subornation of perjury, is thus to nudge witnesses away from the barefaced and toward the shamefaced end of the perjury spectrum. The latter type of lie is generally easier to catch out. When a witness testifies that he does not remember what obviously he does remember, the lie is transparent and thus harmless; put differently, a lie uttered in a form that renders it unbelievable is the equivalent of truth. So perjury law does play an important role in reducing the cost and uncertainty of litigation, though not so much by deterring perjury as by altering its form from the more to the less difficult to see through.

Most of President Clinton's lies were of the unbelievable "I don't remember" variety, but not all. His denial that he touched Monica Lewinsky erotically was not buffered by a "I don't remember," which would have immediately revealed its falsity.[28] It was not the sort of perjury that is inconsequential because transparent.

I have been emphasizing the perjury; but the President's conduct must be evaluated as a whole, with due attention to the other obstructions of justice, to the other lies both public and private, to the slanders, to the stonewalling, to the enlisting of others in the scheme to obstruct justice, to the phony contrition. Perhaps the most compendious moral assessment is that the President demonstrated a radical deficiency in moral courage, what Clausewitz, describing the moral dimensions of leadership, called "*courage d'esprit*" and defined as "the courage to accept responsibility, courage in the face of a moral danger."[29] The critical question is whether the President's breaches of private morality have a public dimension warranting impeachment and removal from office.

Public Morality

EXECUTIVE MORAL DUTIES

In considering the moral duties that are attached to a particular office, here that of President of the United States, we must distinguish between the *executive* moral duties of an office and its *exemplary* moral duties. The former are the moral duties relating directly to the performance of the various executive and administrative tasks that the Constitution, laws, and custom assign to the President. These tasks include commanding the armed forces, managing foreign affairs, appointing federal officials, formulating executive and legislative policies, working with Congress, and overseeing the operations of the executive branch, including law enforcement. The moral duties (broadly defined) attached to these tasks include diligence, prudence, judgment, moral courage, integrity, fairmindedness, and conformity to fundamental American principles such as legality and equality. So far as Clinton's affair with Lewinsky and its sequelae are concerned, I cannot find any significant intersection with the President's executive actions until the attack on Iraq in December 1998.

[28]At one point in his grand jury testimony, when he was asked whether Lewinsky was lying in testifying that he had touched her erotically, he did say that this was not his recollection; but at other points in his testimony he dropped the qualification. Unless he is as promiscuous as Don Juan, it is unbelievable that he would forget this detail.

[29]Carl von Clausewitz, *On War* 102 (Michael Howard and Peter Paret eds. 1976).

Contrary to myth, the Presidency is not and should not be an office whose occupant works around the clock, immersed in details. There is no indication that President Clinton's affair with Monica Lewinsky, or even the first seven months or so of its legal and political aftermath, reduced the time that he devoted to his official duties or dangerously distracted him from them.[30] Only when impeachment loomed and then was voted did the crisis become almost totally consuming of his time and energy (though his defenders denied this). It would be bootstrapping to argue that a President should be convicted and removed from office because impeachment and trial are so time-consuming. It is likewise untrue that the Chief Justice's judicial and administrative duties are so consuming that the operations of the Supreme Court or the federal judicial system generally would be disrupted if he had to preside at a Senate trial that lasted more than a few weeks. Months, yes, but there was no reason for the trial of President Clinton to last months. It lasted six weeks, and if well managed would have been even shorter yet covered more ground.

There would have been no aftermath, time-consuming or otherwise, to the President's sexual affair with Lewinsky had it not been for the Paula Jones case and the Independent Counsel's investigation of obstruction of justice in that case—both proceedings that the nation could have lived without. It was important to the nation's welfare neither that Paula Jones be able to press her marginal sexual harassment case (marginal because she sustained no lasting harm from being propositioned by the President,[31] even assuming that she was propositioned in exactly the manner she has alleged) nor that Clinton's affair with Monica Lewinsky be made public. To avoid unduly narrowing the field from which public officials are selected and inflicting gratuitous emotional suffering on them and their families, officials should be allowed as much privacy as private persons except where an infringement of privacy is nec-

---

[30]Compare Senator Charles W. Jones, who beginning in 1885 "missed 2 years of Senate meetings. He had been smitten with love for a wealthy woman and spent all his time in Michigan wooing her." J. Patrick Dobel, "Judging the Private Lives of Public Officials," 30 *Administration and Society* 115, 130 (1998).

[31]She may have sustained lasting harm from suing the President. That would be consistent with Ambrose Bierce's definition of litigation as "a machine which you go into as a pig and come out of as a sausage." *The Devil's Dictionary,* in *The Collected Writings of Ambrose Bierce* 187, 293 (1946).

essary to enable the public to evaluate the official's ability to perform his official duties.[32]

Granted, that is a potentially large exception when we consider that private sexual peccadilloes can make a public official vulnerable to blackmail. Clinton placed himself in a position in which Lewinsky could blackmail him—and she did blackmail him, threatening to expose their relationship if she didn't get a good job. It is fortunate that Lewinsky was not a foreign agent[33] or a fisher for government contracts or for an important government job for which she was unqualified.

A greater concern is the President's lies. It may be that "everyone lies about sex," but a President caught in a barefaced public lie delivered with all the apparent sincerity of President Clinton's emphatic January 26, 1998, televised finger-wagging denial of having had any sexual relationship with Monica Lewinsky, and repeated until exposed by irrefutable physical evidence, whereupon it spawned subordinate lies (such as the denial of having lied) repeated long after the public had ceased to believe them, may no longer be able to speak credibly on public matters. *Any* denial by Clinton is now apt to be greeted with skepticism—notably his denial that the timing of the bombing campaign against Iraq in December 1998 was a tactic to stave off impeachment.[34]

Now it is true that Americans no longer believe that politicians have any commitment to telling the truth. Even the conservative moralist

---

[32]As argued in Dennis F. Thompson, *Political Ethics and Public Office*, ch. 5 (1987). The Supreme Court gave qualified support to this view in Nixon v. Administrator of General Services, 433 U.S. 425, 455–465 (1977), holding that ex-President Nixon had a substantial interest in keeping from the public view the purely personal contents of his Presidential papers and tapes. For more on the *Nixon* case, see the discussion of censure in the last section ("Proportionality and Alternative Punishments") of the next chapter.

[33]When the scandal first broke, several newspapers in the Arab world accused Lewinsky, who is Jewish, of being an agent of the Israeli secret service, assigned to weaken President Clinton's authority so that he could not force Israel to make concessions to the Palestinians.

[34]The attack began the day before the impeachment debate in the House was scheduled to begin and ended a few hours after the House voted to impeach the President. So lacking in credibility had the President become over the course of the impeachment proceedings that when, shortly after his acquittal by the Senate, he was publicly accused by Juanita Broaddrick of having raped her many years earlier, he did not offer a public denial—which would merely have reminded people of his public denials of affairs with Gennifer Flowers and Monica Lewinsky—but instead referred reporters to his lawyer's denial. In this instance the slang term for a lawyer—"mouthpiece"—really fit.

William Bennett will say only that "most presidents do not . . . lie under oath."[35] He does not say that most Presidents do not lie. This is not necessarily to be regretted. It can be argued that candor in a statesman, while occasionally a smart tactic, ought not to be part of his job description. This is an area in which the correct standard of public morality probably is "lower" than the correct standard of private morality—an area in which, indeed, a private virtue of truth telling[36] may be a public vice.[37] It is the number, publicness, transparency, solemnity, and gratuitousness of President Clinton's lies, both under oath (whether or not technically perjurious—some were, some weren't) and not under oath, that sets him apart from other Presidents. If anything, the essential triviality of his objective in lying—saving his own skin—aggravates the offense. It is one thing for a Lincoln or a Roosevelt to lie, or even to violate the law, under conditions of civil and world war respectively, and another for a lesser figure in calmer and easier times to lie for purely private gain. No one supposes that Lincoln or Roosevelt should have resigned to atone for their violations of law or morality; many people think that Clinton should have. Even Nixon, and, more plausibly, Reagan in the Iran-Contra affair, could argue reasons of state in extenuation of illegal acts committed in time of (cold) war;[38] Clinton couldn't.

Thus while it is true, as Clinton's defenders argue, that a President's illegal use of his official powers is more dangerous to the country than his private immoralities, it is not the whole truth. For it is also true, as defenders of Lincoln, Roosevelt, and other lawbreaking Presidents have argued, that the illegal use of official powers can confer benefits on the nation that exceed the costs. This is something that private immoralities cannot do, which is why it is fallacious to argue that because no one supposes that Lincoln or Roosevelt should have been impeached for committing illegal acts, Clinton should not be impeached for his illegal acts. His were all social cost and no social benefit; theirs were some social cost but more social benefit.

---

[35]Bennett, note 15 above, at 68.

[36]Itself overrated, as argued in David Nyberg, *The Varnished Truth: Truth Telling and Deceiving in Ordinary Life* (1993).

[37]However, Sidgwick, note 1 above, denied this.

[38]See, for example, Michael J. Malbin, "Legalism versus Political Checks and Balances: Legislative-Executive Relations in the Wake of Iran-Contra," in *The Fettered Presidency: Legal Constraints on the Executive Branch* 273, 274–283 (L. Gordon Crovitz and Jeremy A. Rabkin eds. 1989).

It is beside the point to argue that Clinton should have been allowed to conceal his affair with Lewinsky. I agree that he should have been; and if he had been, he wouldn't have had to (more precisely, he wouldn't have been tempted to) lie about the affair and then lie about having lied. The point is that by December 1998, after eleven months of lying about the affair, his credibility had fallen to a point at which his ability to conduct the nation's affairs was impaired. It had fallen not because of his original lies but because of his obdurate refusal to come clean about them.

By then he had also, as I pointed out earlier, shown a lack of moral courage. Clausewitz thought moral courage an essential trait in a military leader, and the President is the commander in chief of the armed forces of the United States. But it is a deep question whether a person's moral character is likely to be uniform, and hence whether his conduct is likely to be morally consistent.[39] The same person might display moral courage in one area of his life and moral cowardice in another. Clinton's personal conduct may not be of a piece with his official conduct, in which event it would be precipitate to infer from his moral cowardice in regard to the Lewinsky business that he is a moral coward in the performance of his official duties.

Among the possible intersections between the public and the private Clinton is his use of his office to extract concessions that other litigants do not enjoy, such as being allowed to have his lawyers present when he testified before the grand jury. And it is most unlikely that Monica Lewinsky would have received a job offer from Ambassador Richardson but for her ex-lover being the President. Or from Revlon; Vernon Jordan testified that he worked hard to get Lewinsky that offer because he was trying to help the President of the United States.

A more interesting point is that in consequence though not in motive, the President's illegalities constituted a kind of guerrilla warfare against the third branch of the federal government, the federal court system, which had rejected his argument that he should be entitled to immunity from civil suits until the end of his term. The Supreme Court said that Paula Jones could proceed with her suit against the President. The President did his damnedest to shipwreck the suit and thus nullify the Court's action.

---

[39]See Posner, note 14 above, at 53.

EXEMPLARY MORAL DUTIES

The least ambiguous intersections between the Clinton-Lewinsky mess and the conduct of official business were those three telephone conversations between Clinton, while being fellated by Lewinsky, and Congressmen, concerning public business. If Aristotle was right that it is impossible to think about anything while absorbed in the pleasures of sex,[40] then Clinton was allowing his affair with Lewinsky to interfere with public business. But of course the real significance of these incidents (and likewise of what might be thought the President's violation of his constitutional duty to "take Care that the Laws be faithfully executed")[41] lies elsewhere, in what I am calling the exemplary moral duties attached to the Presidency. These are of three types, though all are closely related. The first concerns the President as role model; the second the dignity of the office; the third the importance of avoiding scandal.

The President is not merely the principal executive officer of the federal government, like the prime minister in a parliamentary system of government; he is the head of state; and it is natural to think of the head of state as constituting a powerful example for the population. At a time when divorce in America was stigmatized, a divorced man could not become President. This was not because anyone thought that being divorced would prevent a person from performing the executive functions of the Presidency. It was because a divorced President would have been considered a bad example. People might have said, "If the President can be divorced, I can be divorced." And today they might say, "If the President can be a serial adulterer, and lie repeatedly under oath, I should be able to do likewise."

Whether Presidents *are* role models in the sense (the only sense, it seems to me, that matters) of actually influencing the behavior of other people I do not know. It is possible to think of them as existing outside the usual moral boundaries, in much the same way that the gods in Homeric mythology were conceived of as existing outside the moral boundaries of human society. The gods' code of conduct was not deemed normative for human beings, and perhaps a President's code of conduct is not deemed normative for other American citizens. The Ho-

[40]Aristotle, *Nicomachean Ethics*, bk. VII, § 11, in *The Complete Works of Aristotle*, vol. 2, p. 1821 (Jonathan Barnes ed. 1984).

[41]U.S. Const., art. II, § 3.

meric gods were more powerful than human beings, but more primitive morally; perhaps we should begin to see our politicians in that light. The more that citizens disdain politicians, the less likely they are to imitate their behavior. It can be argued that today exemplary moral duties are more firmly attached to judicial office than to the Presidency. I alluded to this possibility in Chapter 3, in discussing the impeachment of judges who commit crimes.

Some Presidents have been role models, George Washington[42] and Abraham Lincoln being the outstanding examples. (The contrast in this respect between our first and our current President is particularly striking. A further irony is that President Clinton was acquitted by the Senate on Lincoln's birthday.) Governing in a comfortable era in which to be President, Clinton is unlikely ever to be a revered role model; his achievements are too limited in relation to his character flaws. But although there have been many undistinguished Presidents, it is difficult to think of any who were "bad" role models in the sense of setting a bad example that actually influenced the attitudes or behavior of a significant number of other people—that made us worse than we would otherwise be. Grant and Harding were bad Presidents, but does anyone suppose that their "badness" damaged the nation's moral fabric? We seem never to have had a charismatic bad President, a Napoleon or a Hitler type. Some people think Nixon was evil; did his evil rub off on the rest of us, and lower the moral tone of American society? I haven't heard that. To the extent that Nixon was admired for his foreign policy successes, it was in spite of rather than because of his bad qualities.

Only Clinton haters think Clinton evil, and they have not made their case. More important, no one seems to admire or even envy Clinton for his illegalities and immoralities, because they have yielded no triumphs, even the transient sort associated with the military victories of a Napoleon or a Hitler. Clinton's misconduct has repeatedly gotten him into trouble. Luck (notably in his political enemies), skill, and some further misconduct have enabled him to dig himself out every time, making him the Huck Finn or Br'er Rabbit of Presidents. But it's not as if his delicts, his pratfalls, his character flaws weird enough to have incited a search for psychiatric explanations, are somehow organic to

---

[42]See, for a superb brief account of Washington's career and character, and their meaning for us, Joseph Epstein, "George Washington, an Amateur's View," 51 *Hudson Review* 21 (1998).

his successes, as Lincoln's illegal suspension of habeas corpus during the Civil War was part and parcel of a successful, desperate, and morally and politically justifiable effort to save the Union.[43] Clinton is not admired for his illegalities.

William Bennett's example of how "Clinton's behavior has started seeping into the culture" is bathetic:

> In Columbus, Ohio, ads for a car dealer named Bobby's use a Monica Lewinsky look-alike (complete with "Secret Service" agents) saying, "Hi, I'm the new intern . . . If you want to get serviced late at night during the week, Bobby's open all the way until midnight."[44]

The advertisement is mildly vulgar, but Clinton did not invent vulgarity, and vulgarity is not a threat to American values. The advertisement is not, as Bennett believes, a symptom of moral decline, but merely of a lack of culture, refinement, and sophistication—the areas where Europe has America beat. But Bennett, as it happens, is no fan of European sophistication. What is best about Americans, he says, is that "morality is central to our politics and attitudes in a way that is not the case in Europe." It is our moral streak that "liberated Europe from the Nazi threat and the Iron Curtain" (p. 17). This is incorrect. American participation in World War II and the Cold War was motivated (primarily anyway) by national interest rather than by considerations of morality. Nor is morality central to our politics and attitudes. Freedom and wealth are.

This is not to deny that the rule-of-law values that Clinton has flouted are important ingredients in America's success; they are essential to the freedom and wealth that distinguish the United States from most other nations. Because American society is so heterogeneous, it relies very heavily on law to hold everything together. Bennett is right that "it would be a travesty, and frightening, to legitimize Mr. Clinton's ethics and the arguments made on their behalf" (p. 131). But no one outside of a few Hollywood wiseacres has proposed doing that. Clinton's conduct is almost universally condemned, even those aspects of it that don't seem all that horrible. The issue is how severely to punish it. To allow him to serve out his term does not, as Bennett implies, mean that we

[43]The Constitution permits habeas corpus to be suspended in times of rebellion, U.S. Const., art. I, § 9, cl. 2—but by Congress, not by the President.

[44]Bennett, note 15 above, at 43.

"approve . . . his actions" and by doing so "become complicit in his lies" (p. 130).

Moralistic conservatives like William Bennett and Robert Bork believe that the United States is deteriorating morally. They point to the divorce rate, the crime rate, the high percentage of births out of wedlock, and the other familiar social problems, which are indeed more serious than they were forty years ago. Yet during this period, American Presidents have been on the whole persons of good moral character. Bennett instances Eisenhower, Carter, and Reagan, and could easily have added Ford and Bush, and, if *apparent* moral character counts, even Kennedy and Johnson, leaving only Nixon in the reprobates' camp with Clinton. The men of good or at least seemingly good character presided over the alleged moral decline, while Clinton has presided over a period not only of extraordinary prosperity but also of marked improvement in most social indicators.[45] It is very difficult for pious people like Bennett to believe that people can behave themselves without having a strong sense of moral seriousness, but apparently they can.

Of course, if you compare Bill Clinton to George Washington, or the One Hundred and Fifth or One Hundred and Sixth Congresses to the First Congress, you will never again be able to say "We've come a long way, baby," without a smirk. If the founders of the nation aspired with some success to emulate the ideals of Republican Rome, our current political class invites comparison with a later stage of the Roman polity. But Bennett and Bork are wrong to think the American *nation* either decadent or even in serious danger of infection by the moral and intellectual rot that may be eating away at the vital organs of the political class.

A point related to, though I think distinct from, concern with a bad role model is the limitation of Americans' tolerance for personal misconduct on the part even of a President whose official performance is admired. If the President committed a *very* serious crime—very serious

[45]For an illuminating graphic summary, see Karl Zinsmeister, Stephen Moore, and Karlyn Bowman, "Is America Turning a Corner?" *American Enterprise,* Jan./Feb. 1999, p. 36; also Gregg Easterbrook, "America the O.K.," *New Republic,* Jan. 4 and 11, 1999, p. 19. The 1990s have seen dramatic declines in black teenage births and black births out of wedlock, the abortion rate, teen sex, divorce, the percentage of people on welfare, black poverty, crimes (both homicide and other violent crimes, and property crimes), teen suicides, school dropouts, federal spending as a percentage of the Gross Domestic Product, and of course the federal deficit.

as ordinary people judge crimes, not as judges and lawyers do—even one wholly personal, the people would not tolerate it. He would have to be either punished in the ordinary course of criminal justice, and then impeached and removed from office because incapable of filling it at all, or impeached and removed in advance of ordinary punishment. Intolerable behavior would render the President wholly ineffective. President Clinton's behavior did not reach that level in the eyes of most Americans.

Talking on the phone to members of Congress while being fellated was not even a minor crime; but it displayed a deep disrespect for the Presidency. It has been said that President Reagan always put on a necktie before entering the Oval Office, as a sign of respect for the *sanctum sanctorum* of the Presidency, the chapel of our civic religion.[46] The Presidents have been called "the high priests of the American civil religion."[47] President Clinton may be said without hyperbole to have defiled the Oval Office by his antics in the adjoining spaces in his office complex, antics that included not only sex with Lewinsky but also those phone calls to the Congressmen, the enlisting of Betty Currie as a kind of procuress, and the dodging, at times farcical, of minders and Secret Service agents. Clinton's disrespect for the decorum of the Presidency, especially when combined with the disrespect for law that he showed in repeatedly flouting it and with his barefaced public lies, constitutes a powerful affront to fundamental and deeply cherished symbols and usages of American government, an affront perhaps unprecedented in the history of the Presidency. Imagine a President who urinated on the front porch of the White House or burned the American flag; these acts could be thought metaphors for what Clinton did. He compounded the outrage when, in response to questions put to him by the House Judiciary Committee in November 1998 in an effort to pin down his version of the facts, he repeated his lies once again. By this time, no thinking person doubted that he had lied; in repeating his lies, he was thumbing his nose at Congress and the American people.

It is on the ground of disrespect for his office and for decency in the conduct of government that the most powerful case for impeachment

[46]This is another of the ironies that abound in the Clinton affair, in light of Monica Lewinsky's choice of the necktie as the appropriate gift for her lovers because of the expertise she had acquired from working in a tie shop during college.

[47]Robert Shogun, *The Double-Edged Sword: How Character Makes and Ruins Presidents, from Washington to Clinton* 2 (1999), quoting Walter Dean Burnham.

and conviction could have been pitched.[48] But neither Starr nor the Republican majority of the House Judiciary Committee attempted to do this. This may be a symptom of a change in expectations concerning political leadership that Max Weber's concepts of charisma and rationality can help us see. When people are ignorant and fearful, they want to believe that their leaders are people of superhuman capability to whom they can thus safely entrust the management of the multitudinous problems that overwhelm them.[49] They seek a charismatic leader, an authority figure, a Great Father, "a symbolic leader, the one figure who draws together the people's hope and fears for the political future."[50] (Sometimes a madman may best fit the bill!)[51] When people are prosperous, secure, sophisticated, and self-assured, as an unprecedented number of Americans are today, they seek, not inspired leadership—not the actualization of the *Führerprinzip*—but just sound policies and rational management.[52] They know (they are sophisticated) that most Presidents have been rather ordinary people; that even the greatest of them were not quite so extraordinary as they have been traditionally represented to be; that charismatic leaders often are dangerous; and that the American nation is highly resilient to variance in the quality of government leaders. They see in Clinton a generally competent, articulate, intelligent, well-educated, empathetic, and (if only intermittently) skillful professional politician and a man who, if perhaps personally

---

[48]By the time his credibility had been dangerously eroded by his reiterated lies, it was too late to base impeachment on what, if evident earlier, would also have been a strong ground. Remember that the only articles of impeachment approved by the House charged perjury before the grand jury and other obstructions of justice. The two articles the House did not approve dealt with perjury in the Paula Jones deposition and lying to the House Judiciary Committee in answering the eighty-one questions that the Committee had propounded to the President.

[49]"In times of distress, we turn to authority." Ronald A. Heifetz, *Leadership without Easy Answers* 69 (1994); see also id. at 65. This attitude of submissive passivity to leadership is parodied in two of Kafka's parables, "The Refusal" and "The Problem of Our Laws." See Franz Kafka, *The Complete Stories* 263, 437 (Nahum N. Glatzer ed. 1971).

[50]James David Barber, *The Presidential Character: Predicting Performance in the White House* 4 (1972).

[51]Robert S. Robins, "Introduction to the Topic of Psychopathology and Political Leadership," 16 *Psychopathology and Political Leadership* 1, 18–20 (1977).

[52]John R. Zaller, "Monica Lewinsky's Contribution to Political Science," *PS: Political Science and Politics,* June 1998, pp. 182, 184, argues in like vein that Clinton's undiminished popularity in the wake of the Lewinsky scandal is due to the fact that today's "public stays focused on a bottom line consisting of peace, prosperity, and moderation," a mindset that Zaller distinguishes from wisdom or virtue.

contemptible, is not dangerous or extreme. Nixon, rightly or wrongly, was thought dangerous, and his fall was followed by a raft of legislation aimed at limiting Presidential powers,[53] though this was partly a response to Lyndon Johnson's high-handed and secretive conduct of the Vietnam War as well. Clinton's disgrace is apt to be followed by measures, notably allowing the independent counsel law to expire, designed to increase the President's power. Many people who have no use for Clinton feared the possibly destabilizing effects of impeachment and conviction of a President. They did not think that removing this lame duck, kept on a short tether by a Congress controlled by the opposition, worth the bother. They thought the costs would exceed the benefits.

The last exemplary moral duty of a President is the simplest; it is to avoid scandals that reduce a President's effectiveness. Even if most people do not and should not care whether the President is a role model and do not and should not care about preserving the dignity of his office, even if Presidents should be entitled to a considerable measure of privacy, and even if President Clinton has such a disciplined mind that he could avoid being distracted and consumed by the mess he found himself in as a consequence of his affair with Monica Lewinsky, a President has a duty to avoid becoming enmeshed in a scandal that is likely to weaken his effectiveness. Whether rightly or wrongly, Clinton was conducting the affair against a background of social, legal, and political institutions, events, and attitudes that created a substantial risk of an explosive scandal that would impede the functioning of the Presidency. In running that risk, for wholly personal rewards (the furtive pleasures of the affair itself), the President exhibited a high degree of personal irresponsibility. That was a personal failing. What I want to emphasize is that the avoidance of scandal is also a public duty—a precondition to the effective discharge of the President's other public duties. Political capital that President Clinton might have expended on worthwhile Presidential projects and policies had to be diverted to saving his political hide.

Redemption by Achievement?

The President committed breaches of public morality. Their gravity is open to debate. But even if they are very grave, we must consider whether they might be excused by reference to the President's other

[53]James L. Sundquist, *The Decline and Resurgence of Congress*, pt. 2 (1981).

qualities or achievements. The case for such a redemptive possibility can be formulated in several different ways: as a need for balancing moral weaknesses against moral strengths; as a recognition of inherent human weakness ("original sin"); as a frankly pragmatic balancing of moral weaknesses against strengths in other areas of human activity; or as the adoption of a Greek (both pre-Socratic Greek and Aristotelian), as distinct from a Christian or Kantian, conception of character, blurring the line between moral and other qualities.[54] The third and fourth formulations overlap, because a President's moral duties include qualities such as prudence and judgment that are talents as much as or more than they are moral qualities.

The general view of Clinton is that after a rocky start[55] he became, and remained (at least until impeachment week when he bombed Iraq), a good President in the sense of effectively discharging the executive duties of the office. And those duties, as we saw earlier, have a moral dimension. Even with regard to the exemplary moral virtues, Clinton is not a total failure. Many Americans consider him an effective and probably a sincere exemplar of such qualities as sympathy and tolerance, and an eloquent though perhaps hypocritical spokesman for many traditional American values. In addition to these positive moral qualities, which are not negligible though most people think them outweighed by his now well-documented moral failings, Clinton has displayed intelligence, energy, flexibility, imagination, enormous resilience, and an ability to establish rapport with foreign leaders. Probably most of America's success during the period of Clinton's Presidency owes little to Clinton. How likely is it that the country would be less secure and prosperous today if George Bush had been reelected in 1992 or Bob Dole elected in 1996? One would have to be mad with partisanship to answer, "Very." But any conspicuous failures would have been blamed on Clinton regardless of his causal responsibility for them. When it comes to judging Presidents, generals, and other leaders of complex and uncertain ventures, we have more than a trace of the ancient Greek attitude that good luck is praiseworthy and bad luck blameworthy.

[54]See, for example, J. Patrick Dobel, "Political Prudence and the Ethics of Leadership," 58 *Public Administration Review* 74 (1998), listing and discussing the suite of ethical and prudential "virtues" that can reasonably be demanded of a political leader.

[55]Well documented in *The Clinton Presidency: First Appraisals* (Colin Campbell and Bert A. Rockman eds. 1996).

Yet at the same time and further complicating an already dauntingly complex task of assessing this President, we must consider the atrocious judgment that he exhibited in relation to the Lewinsky affair and the ensuing investigation—so atrocious as to shake one's confidence in his executive competence. He was dumb in placing his trust in the discretion of Monica Lewinsky, about whom he knew nothing when he began their affair; in failing to take greater precautions to prevent discovery; in failing to realize that the affair might be dragged into the Paula Jones case; in failing to settle that case before he was deposed by Jones's lawyers; in failing, at the slight monetary and slighter political costs of risking the entry of a default judgment against him, to refuse to answer the Paula Jones lawyers' questions about Lewinsky; in agreeing to appear before the grand jury and then lying to it instead of refusing to answer questions about sex;[56] in failing to make a properly abject apology to all and sundry after his grand jury testimony; in making a televised address to the nation the evening of that testimony without taking time to cool off and think through his situation; and in repeating, after the House Judiciary Committee recommended impeachment, his incredible denials, which were as if designed to drive away the moderate Republicans, who demanded that he confess to lying.

Some of his other tactics, such as trying to brazen it out after the scandal first broke and diabolizing Kenneth Starr, may have been sensible (though repulsive). The results of the poll that Dick Morris commissioned the night the news of the scandal broke indicated that a majority of Americans wanted Clinton to leave office if the news was true. Later, as the shock value of the news diminished with time, they changed their mind; but Clinton cannot be criticized for having failed to foresee this. The blunders that I have listed cannot be reinterpreted as clever tactics, however, and they undermine one's confidence in Clinton's ability to cope with a domestic or international crisis. It is arguable that the behavior of the President in regard to Lewinsky and the ensuing investigation and impeachment proceeding has been so strange and shocking that we can no longer trust his ability to perform his public duties competently. So strange and shocking that it might make us readier to believe some of the charges of misuse of office that have been made against him, such as that the bombing of Iraq in December 1998 was intended to deflect people's attention from the impeachment pro-

[56]This was probably his single biggest mistake in the whole mess.

ceedings or that the White House traded away militarily sensitive technology to China in exchange for illegal contributions to the President's 1996 reelection campaign.

But I have questioned this "uniformity" thesis—that all of a person's actions are of a piece, so that one's behavior in public life can be reliably predicted from one's behavior in private life. If, moreover, *all* the qualities that we value in a person and particularly in a President, and not only the narrowly moral, are fairly to be considered aspects of "character" and are to be added to each other and then the bad qualities netted out to provide a summary assessment, who is to say how "bad" a person President Clinton is? There are some crimes and immoralities so outrageous that they not only clearly outweigh the person's good qualities but dissuade us from doing the necessary moral arithmetic. It would be in bad taste to say of Hitler, "Yes, he was evil, but he should get at least *some* credit for the autobahns, for his rhetorical skills, and for his love of animals and his mother." Clinton's misdeeds do not rise to the level at which Americans refuse to weigh a person's good qualities against his bad. Or perhaps I should say, do not *yet* rise to that level. A number of the ethical shadows that surround Clinton, shadows unrelated or only distantly related to his affair with Lewinsky and its criminal aftermath, have yet to be dispelled. When all is known, Clinton may be revealed as a more serious violator of public morality than the public record compiled to date establishes.

What makes it difficult, in trying to make an overall assessment of President Clinton's character, to view him simply as a person in whom the elements are fearfully mixed, is his shamelessness, his evident lack of conscience, his self-absorption, and his apparent belief that the end justifies the means even when the end is the petty one of burnishing his historical reputation.[57] These are deeper failings of character than sexual incontinence and a proclivity for lying. An Augustinean believes

[57]William Bennett has offered the following summary assessment of Clinton's character: "He systematically uses, and then destroys, women. He has contempt for the truth and for the meaning of words. He has radically lowered the standards of what we consider permissible behavior. He is willing to manipulate and disfigure even Christian forgiveness to advance his own ends. He is a man of breathtaking self-indulgence and self-absorption, forever aggrieved, always the victim, more sinned against than sinning, never responsible for the trouble in which he finds himself. He routinely makes others pay a very high price for his misconduct. A man of enormous political talent and considerable charm, he is a malignant presence in American politics and culture." William J. Bennett, "What We've Learned," *Wall Street Journal*, Feb. 10, 1999, p. A22.

that because we are all burdened by original sin, none of us can achieve moral perfection. But what should be within our capacity is recognition of our imperfection, sincere repentance for our bad acts to which that imperfection conduces, and meaningful efforts to improve our conduct in the future. This capacity for moral growth appears to be missing from President Clinton's makeup. The absence was conspicuous in his speech to the nation on August 17, 1998, after his grand jury testimony. It was apparent that he was admitting his relationship with Monica Lewinsky only because it had (he was guessing correctly) been proved by irrefutable physical evidence; that his reaction to being caught was anger, not shame; that he would blame everyone but himself for the stew he was in; and that he would continue to lie to the extent that physical evidence would not contradict him. In the months that followed, the lies became ever more brazen as the evidence that they *were* lies mounted; the White House machinery of slander, propaganda, and disinformation more active and unscrupulous; the President's legal defense more crabbed, cynical, picayune, and hypertechnical; his apologies more perfunctory; and his entourage more unsavory.

The calculus of character may depend on how one weights the various elements that compose a political leader's character. If you agree with Aristotle (and William Bennett) that an important, perhaps the most important, function of politics is to promote virtue (even more emphatic versions of this view are found in Plato, Calvin, Rousseau, and many other distinguished political thinkers),[58] or with Adam Smith that effective political leadership depends on authority rooted in admiration, you will be inclined to judge Clinton more harshly than if you take the view of Machiavelli and thus think that the aim of politics should be to place at the head of the nation the person who through intelligence, guile, and ruthlessness can advance his nation's interests most effectively in competition with other nations—though even Plato believed that political leaders were entitled to lie.

And yet one doubts that Machiavelli would actually have approved of President Clinton, all cultural differences to one side. Machiavelli's view is not, as it is sometimes taken to be, that of an amoralist. It is rather the view of someone who has a particular conception of public morality, one founded on a harshly realistic assessment of politics. It is

[58]See, for a helpful discussion, Mary P. Nichols, *Citizens and Statesmen: A Study of Aristotle's* Politics, ch. 5 (1992).

a view that can help us to see that a character flaw that is *organic* to a strength is much easier to justify in moral terms than one unrelated to a strength. Ruthlessness is a condition of achievement in a political leader when tough measures are required in the national interest. To be ruthless would therefore be a duty that public morality thrust on him, and it would be hypocritical to "blame" him for possessing it. Lechery and lying about it don't lend themselves to being justified in this way. They seem rather the splinters of a fractured personality. (Some observers consider Clinton to have the most *abnormal* personality of any President since Nixon.) Clinton was not lying for the state. Even less was he telling Plato's "noble lie."

The "separability thesis" that I have just been expounding may explain a part of our unease with crediting Hitler with his sincere love of animals, and so on. Building limited-access highways, protecting endangered species, and being charmed by children do not require waging aggressive war and committing genocide. Similarly, balancing the budget, reforming welfare, and supporting capital punishment do not require perjury and philandering. We have a clue here to the unease that pragmatism engenders in moralists, a theme I pursue further in the next chapter. There is something unsettling about forgiving or even lightening the guilt of a monster because of his accomplishments, unless the elements that made him a monster (perhaps an utter indifference to public opinion, or utter absence of pity) were essential to those accomplishments so that we can say that he had the weaknesses of his strengths.

A third position concerning a political leader's character, to be contrasted with the Aristotelian and the Machiavellian, is that of Locke. In advocating a strictly limited role for government, he implicitly "gave up" the quest for rulers of superior virtue, whether Christian or Roman. Locke's position is both most in tune with the thinking of the Constitution's framers and most likely to commend itself to a majority of modern Americans, although the second point is firmer than the first. There is a current in American thinking of the founding period—it is best illustrated in the person of George Washington, in Hamilton's conception of the Presidency, and in frequent appeals to the ideals, heroic and even militaristic, of classical republicanism[59]—of a fusion of Aris-

[59]See, for example, Cass R. Sunstein, "Beyond the Republican Revival," 97 *Yale Law Journal* 1539, 1564–1565 (1988).

totelian and Machiavellian conceptions.[60] At the moment, that fusion is pretty dead. Americans today neither feel sufficiently embattled to want a Machiavellian President nor look to government to save the nation from moral depravity or even expect government to be staffed by people more virtuous than themselves.[61] "Romantic pomposity about the state"[62] leaves them cold. Many of them would agree with William Godwin that "it is to be hoped that mankind will never have to learn so important a lesson [what is virtue and what is offense], through so incompetent a channel [as government]."[63]

They demand of Presidential "character" nothing more exalted than executive competence and flair in a person sufficiently well socialized not to unravel the legal and moral fabric of the society by his personal or political behavior. "For most people, politics is not terribly interesting. They don't really care what their President is doing as long as he's not screwing them."[64] It is a credit to the nation's founders that, imbued as they were with classical conceptions of political virtue,[65] they designed a governmental system that could be operated successfully by politicians not well endowed with it.

I must be cautious here and elsewhere in speaking of what "the American people" seek, demand, etcetera. Public opinion is not uniform on most of the matters discussed in this book or even readily divisible into two or three schools of thought. The "people" cannot be divided neatly into those who hate Clinton and want him removed from office, those who love him (or hate his enemies), and those who recognize his character flaws but do not think them sufficiently relevant to his public duties to warrant his removal from office. The people include as well

[60]Cf. J. G. A. Pocock, *The Machiavellian Moment: Florentine Political Thought and the Atlantic Republican Tradition* 545–548 (1975).

[61]The two points are connected. "It is in times of war that republican virtue . . . is most powerfully displayed; it is war that tends to unite the citizenry in dedication to the public good; and it is war that might serve as the model, even in times of peace, for the subordination of private interests to the general good." Sunstein, note 59 above, at 1564.

[62]Coady, note 2 above, at 426.

[63]William Godwin, *Enquiry concerning Political Justice and Its Influence on Morals and Happiness,* vol. 2, p. 303 (3d ed., F. E. L. Priestley ed. 1946).

[64]"The Year of the Goat," *American Enterprise,* Jan./Feb. 1999, pp. 23, 25 (remarks of Andrew Ferguson).

[65]See Carl J. Richard, *The Founders and the Classics: Greece, Rome, and the American Enlightenment* (1994). On Washington, see, for example, id. at 69–72.

the ignorant, the alienated, the confused, the "tuned out," the lawless,[66] and a large number of people who say they would not have voted for Clinton had they known what he was really like and would not vote for him again if he could run for a third term, but prefer putting up with two more years of him to changing horses in midstream.

All this said, character in the conventional sense is still an asset in a President; it is still the case that "people may follow leaders because they trust their integrity, judgment, and competence."[67] Long before the Lewinsky mess, Clinton's character flaws (his "personal baggage," as it was sometimes called) were recognized as a drag on his Presidency.[68] The leader's character is a more valuable asset in the American governmental system, in which one person doubles as head of state and head of government, than in a parliamentary system, in which the monarch or president is the head of state and a different official, the prime minister, is the head of the government.[69] The function of the head of state is to "symbolize the nation"; he "stands for the things that the members of society have in common"; he "personifies the ideal of the polity."[70] The head of government, in contrast, is primarily a manager. The Constitution does not give the President as much managerial power, at least in domestic affairs, as prime ministers typically have. So, to be effective, the President has to be able to draw on the moral capital that he accrues as head of state. He thus *needs* a better character than a prime minister does (which may help explain why most Europeans who followed the Clinton-Lewinsky scandal could not understand what all the fuss was about). President Clinton squandered his moral capital, but he has other assets that may make him on balance, even in his damaged state, a more effective President than, say, Carter, a man of sterling character in the conventional sense.[71]

This discussion lends perspective to William Bennett's claim that "it

---

[66]Even today, the outlaw is a romantic figure to many Americans.

[67]Erwin C. Hargrove, *The President as Leader: Appealing to the Better Angels of Our Nature* 35 (1998).

[68]Bert A. Rockman, "Leadership Style and the Clinton Presidency," in *The Clinton Presidency,* note 55 above, at 325, 332–336.

[69]See the illuminating discussion in David F. Prindle, "Head of State and Head of Government in Comparative Perspective," 21 *Presidential Studies Quarterly* 55 (1991).

[70]Id. at 56.

[71]This comparison may be unfair to Carter, and exaggerate the relation between the

matters if we treat a president as if he were a king, above the law."[72] At one level, this is simply a misreading of Clinton's escape from being thrown out of office. Clinton has not been treated like a king; he's been treated like dirt; he has been made ridiculous and pathetic; he remains vulnerable to criminal prosecution and may eventually find himself in the humiliating position of having to pardon himself in order to escape a prison term. He may have succeeded all unwittingly in destroying the mystique of the Presidency once and for all, though Starr, the House Judiciary Committee, and the media were the President's accomplices in the work of destruction through their relentless publicizing of the details of Clinton's extramarital sexual activities. Past Presidents invested heavily in enhancing Presidential mystique, in order to augment their political power,[73] in other words to become more—kinglike. Clinton disinvested. Yet this may not matter to the strength, prosperity, or moral health of American society; it may even conduce toward the attainment of these goods by making government more transparent to the governed.

Bennett's reference to treating the President like a king is unintentionally ironic. Like Machiavelli, Bennett wants the nation's chief executive to behave and present himself in such a way as will make him an exemplary figure, one worthy of veneration,[74] "our surrogate king, the symbol of our past and greatness."[75] Bennett desires this not because a better performance in the head of state role might enhance a President's effectiveness as the head of the government, but because a President who personifies the nation's moral aspirations can inspire the peo-

---

success of a President and his actual abilities, as forcefully argued in Stephen Skowronek, *The Politics Presidents Make: Leadership from John Adams to George Bush* (1993). (With specific reference to Carter, see id. at 361–406.) Skowronek's book is a milestone in scholarly demythologizing of the American Presidency. Its tone is in sharp contrast to the traditional literature of Presidential studies and political science, illustrated by Barber's and Hargrove's books, see notes 50 and 66 above, which exalts the inspirational or charismatic nature of Presidential leadership over executive competence and underrates the importance to a President's success or failure of sheer luck.

[72]Bennett, note 15 above, at 50.

[73]See, for an excellent discussion, Forrest McDonald, *The American Presidency: An Intellectual History*, ch. 15 (1994).

[74]See Niccolò Machiavelli, *The Prince*, chs. 18, 21 (Harvey C. Mansfield trans., 2d ed. 1998).

[75]Harold M. Barger, *The Impossible Presidency* 13 (1984).

ple to be better. Bennett, the stern moralist, has at root a *theatrical* conception of the Presidency.[76]

Speaking of theater, anyone who doubts that we are in a new era, so far as the representation of officials to the public is concerned, has only to ponder the cultural significance of the four yellow stripes on each sleeve of Chief Justice Rehnquist's robe. American judges, including the Justices of the U.S. Supreme Court, have for as long as anyone can remember worn plain black robes. A few years ago the Chief Justice became bored with his plain black robe and added the yellow stripes, inspired by the costume worn by the Lord Chancellor in a production that Rehnquist had seen of Gilbert and Sullivan's operetta *Iolanthe*. It was in this regalia that Rehnquist presided over the trial of President Clinton by the United States Senate. The yellow stripes are a striking visual feature and drew a good deal of comment, all duly noting their comic-opera origins. The most solemn form of American trial was thus presided over by the highest judge in the land *dressed in a funny costume.* Maybe (though I greatly doubt it) the Chief Justice was signaling what he thought of the proceeding.[77] Whatever his intentions, the appearance he presented makes it difficult to believe that the American people any longer expect their officials to be more dignified, aloof, and impressive than themselves. Our current symbol of *gravitas* is Joe DiMaggio.

The Chief Justice's costume has a particular significance in light of the assiduous efforts of bench and bar to preserve the mystique of adjudication and adjudicators. Many judges believe that the nonjudicial branches of government—legislatures, executive officials, administrative agencies, even the military—should be transparent to public scrutiny. Very few believe that this transparency should extend to the judicial branch. Judges who almost certainly do not believe that an executive branch official (the President, for example) should be able to assert the attorney-client privilege with respect to their communications

---

[76]His conception was curiously echoed by a column in the *Wall Street Journal,* in which the columnist lamented the "sorry little drama [Clinton's trial], populated with too many wimps and sycophants and not enough John Waynes. It was a tale of anti-heroes." George Melloan, "Ruminations about a Recent Event in Washington," *Wall Street Journal,* Feb. 16, 1999, p. A23. John Wayne was not a hero; he was an actor.

[77]Gilbert and Sullivan fans will recall that the Lord Chancellor in *Iolanthe* is in love with a ward in Chancery—which might be thought a parallel to a sexual relationship between a President and an intern.

with government lawyers, because government lawyers represent the government, not individual officials, believe that a similar privilege, casting the judges' law clerks in the role of attorney and the judge in the role of client, should cloak the operations of the judiciary in secrecy.[78] The Chief Justice of the United States evidently does not consider the judiciary's authority quite so brittle; and against the costs, if there really are costs, of diminished judicial mystique must be traded off the possible benefits of public scrutiny in improving the selection and performance of public officials. A more businesslike, less sacerdotal, conception of judges and Presidents alike might get us better government, not worse as Mr. Bennett fears.

Consider two further paradoxes. The first is the paradox of the lubricious details in the Starr Report and in the voluminous evidentiary materials published by the House Judiciary Committee. On the one hand, President Clinton was excoriated for lowering the dignity of his office. On the other hand, his prosecutors lowered it further by publicizing the details of his undignified conduct.

The second paradox is that most of Clinton's defenders believe that not merely his personal reputation, but also his place in history, has been fatally diminished by the Lewinsky episode and its aftermath. The implication is that one can be a good President, yet, by virtue of character failings somehow not inconsistent with being a good President, fail to cast a historical shadow. It is, perhaps, the ultimate in pragmatism: we shall defer punishing the malfeasant until we have wrung the last bit of benefit from him; we shall wait until he leaves office and then punish him by despising him.

[78]See, for example, Alex Kozinski, "Conduct Unbecoming," 108 *Yale Law Journal* 835, 842–845 (1999).

CHAPTER 5

Should President Clinton Have Been Impeached, and If Impeached Convicted?

Having examined both the meaning of the key constitutional phrase "high Crimes and Misdemeanors" and the morality as well as legality of President Clinton's conduct in the Lewinsky matter, I am ready to consider whether he should have been impeached for and convicted of those offenses, criminal or otherwise, that could have been proved with sufficient certitude on the basis of the public record. Later in the chapter, I consider alternative sanctions, such as censure.

No Shortcuts to the Answer

The questions that give this chapter its title may be unanswerable, and this for two reasons. The first is the uncertainty of the constitutional standard. As with many vague legal standards, it has a definite core. A President who tried to betray the country to a foreign power or to establish a dictatorship, or who abandoned his office, or committed particularly heinous criminal offenses even if not ones related to (or committed with the aid of) his office, would be impeachable without the need for an elaborate inquiry into his motives or the motives or conduct of his opponents. Equally clearly, a President who merely took actions that Congress opposed on partisan political grounds should not be impeached. We may never have enough information to decide which of these poles President Clinton's obstructions of justice and related misdeeds are nearer to. The fact that obstructing justice is felonious is relevant but not determinative. It is neither so grave a crime as to make it imperative that the perpetrator be removed from office nor so trivial a one as to make removal a clearly excessive sanction. Judgment becomes even more uncertain when Clinton's other misconduct besides obstruction of justice is factored in, notably the disrespect that he has displayed for the institution of the Presidency, for the truth, and for the Congress, and when to the stew is added his successes as President.

There are no shortcuts that would enable a free-wheeling, wide-ranging, and unavoidably indeterminate analysis of imponderables to be avoided. Some have been suggested. In testimony before the House Judiciary Committee on November 9, 1998, Cass Sunstein argued "that a false statement under oath is an appropriate basis for impeachment if and only if the false statement involved conduct that *by itself* raises serious questions about abuse of office" (emphasis added).[1] In other words, perjury can only be an aggravating factor. A President could not properly be impeached for perjury in connection with a traffic accident in which he was involved or for perjuring himself to help a friend in a negligence suit, because the Presidential conduct giving rise to perjury in these cases would not involve an abuse of the powers of his office.

The suggested line slices between Clinton and Nixon. Two of the three articles of impeachment of Nixon that the House Judiciary Committee recommended to the full House primarily charged obstruction of justice in various forms, much as in Clinton's case, but in Nixon's case the act sought to be covered up was political rather than personal. It is not a difference that can easily be elevated to a general principle. Sunstein himself makes an exception for the case in which the President murders someone even though for private purposes and with private means. He does not suggest—it would be absurd to suggest—that the exception for private wrongs that warrant impeachment could be limited to murder, that no other crime could qualify. And so what is offered as a bright-line standard for impeachment dissolves on inspection.

Consider as a further indication of its sponginess how the standard would apply if Clinton had been impeached for committing criminal fraud in the Whitewater matter, years before he became President. He is accused of having abused the powers of his office, but the office was the governorship of Arkansas. Does that count? (I should think not—

---

[1]He later expanded his testimony into an article. See Cass R. Sunstein, "Impeaching the President," 147 *University of Pennsylvania Law Review* 279 (1998).

and a pre-Presidential fraud with or without abuse of office would be a good example of a crime unlikely to be serious enough to count as a high crime or misdemeanor.) For that matter, Paula Jones accused Clinton of such an abuse—of using a state trooper (named as a codefendant with Clinton in the Jones suit) as his procurer. Clinton could even be accused of having abused his office as President by using his secretary, Betty Currie, a government employee, to help him conceal his relationship with Monica Lewinsky from his staff and the Secret Service.

Sunstein's approach can also be criticized as unduly depreciating the gravity of obstructing justice. Suppose the President's best friend were a child molester, and the President gave perjured testimony at the friend's trial for sexual molestation and as a result of this testimony the friend was acquitted and went on to commit further crimes of that character. Or suppose that the President, driving with customary carelessness on the back roads of his ranch, kills a child. He has not committed a crime, but he is sued for negligence and perjures himself by denying that he was driving and bribes a witness to back up the denial. Or suppose the President fathers an illegitimate child, is sued for child support, and defends against the suit with the aid of DNA test results that he has forged. In all these cases there would be sustained, intense, and legitimate outrage at a President who was setting himself above the law to the injury of others with no shadow of justification or excuse. To apply to these cases Sunstein's test, which puts all obstructions of justice arising from private misconduct beyond the reach of the impeachment power, would circumscribe that power too narrowly. Only if they were committed toward the end of the President's term (and maybe not even then, given the possibility of a Presidential advance self-pardon) would the public conceivably be content to allow him to finish his term and then be punished in the ordinary way.

There is also a textual point, made by Richard D. Parker in his testimony before the House Judiciary Committee, also on November 9, 1998. The Constitution lists "bribery" along with treason as high crimes and misdemeanors, yet it is easy to imagine a President bribing someone for purely personal reasons; I gave an example in the preceding paragraph. To argue that bribery by a President is not an impeachable offense unless the bribe is connected to official actions would do considerable violence to the constitutional language, though the reference in Article II, section 4, to "bribery" was based on a concern with the President's accepting bribes rather than giving them.[2] Implicitly, Sunstein is reading "high Crimes and Misdemeanors" to mean treason, bribery to do an official act, criminal or other grave abuses of Presidential power, and murder and other especially heinous crimes even if accomplished with purely private means and for purely private objectives, but never obstruction of justice unless it is incidental to one of the aforementioned offenses.

One might try to defend the idea of confining impeachable offenses to public acts but making an exception for heinous private acts as follows: a President who would commit murder would do anything. In other words, a private act might be generalizable to the public sphere because of what it would tell us about the decency, self-control, or other relevant dimensions of the President's character. I suggested in the last chapter that this view assumes greater moral consistency in the behavior of an individual than it is realistic to expect; one could be a private monster but a public saint. But if I am wrong about this, then the inference from private to public conduct cannot reasonably be confined to cases in which the private conduct is a particularly heinous crime. For as I also argued in that chapter, Clinton's private conduct in the Lewinsky matter has been sufficiently shocking to raise questions about his capacity to conduct public business responsibly—unless we are willing (and I am more willing than Sunstein is) to accept a Jekyll and Hyde view of President Clinton.

The search for a simple, definite rule of impeachability must be abandoned. Unfortunately, once that is done, it becomes bafflingly difficult to situate Clinton's case in the welter of arguably relevant considerations. On the one hand, he committed repeated and varied felonious obstructions of justice over a period of almost a year, which he garnished with gaudy public and private lies, vicious slanders, tactical blunders, gross errors of judgment, hypocritical displays of contrition, affronts to conventional morality and parental authority, and desecrations of revered national symbols. And all this occurred against a background of persistent and troubling questions concerning the ethical tone of the Clinton Administration and Clinton's personal and political ethics.

---

[2]The Iran-Contra affair was arguably a case of bribery *by* the President—in that case, of Iran to get it to release hostages being held by Iran-supported terrorists in Lebanon.

On the other hand, Clinton acted under considerable provocation—perhaps provocation so considerable that few people in comparable circumstances would not succumb—in stepping over the line that separates the concealment of embarrassing private conduct from obstruction of legal justice. And, astonishingly, his illegal and immoral actions seem not to have had untoward consequences for the nation as a whole. Maybe it's too soon to tell and what we should fear is a gradual erosion of public respect for the norms of legality and morality. Alas, no methodology exists for determining the effect of unpunished bad behavior by prominent people on conduct generally. A clearly guilty O. J. Simpson was acquitted of murder in 1995, yet this seems not to have interrupted the steady decline in the nation's murder rate. This may be because, although acquitted, he did not get off scot-free. He was disgraced, ostracized by most respectable people (though he has a gaggle of admiring cronies), compelled to pay a huge civil damages judgment, and deprived of the lucrative earnings opportunities that he had enjoyed before his arrest; and at this writing, his custody of his children has been revoked. He is a pariah. That may be the destiny of President Clinton, although he has better opportunities for eventual redemption than Simpson does.

An Analysis of Consequences

The lack of a definite standard of Presidential impeachability makes it natural to focus on the consequences of impeaching and convicting. Let us try to compare the likely bad consequences with the likely bad consequences of alternative courses of action, including intermediate sanctions, such as censure.

Concern was expressed that a trial in the Senate would paralyze the federal government for the duration, and that the duration might be months unless the Senate let the President cop a plea because the public had wearied of the whole business. These fears would have seemed chimerical to anyone familiar with trials. A well-managed trial (including discovery and other pretrial proceedings) of the charges in the two articles of impeachment approved by the House could not have taken months, because very few facts were contested. There is no need or occasion for evidentiary hearings on matters not in dispute. With 8,000 pages of largely uncontested evidence already in the public record, a full trial should not have taken more than a month. The actual trial, with its truncated evidentiary hearing, was completed in less than six weeks. Not truncated, merely well managed, it would have taken even less time.

An analogy can be drawn between impeachment and the Continental European system of criminal procedure. In that system the trial, in the sense of an evidentiary hearing with live testimony, is preceded by a comprehensive investigation by an examining magistrate, who lays his findings, in the form of a dossier or report, before the judge or panel of judges that is to conduct the actual trial. Armed with the dossier, the trial panel calls witnesses only as needed to fill gaps or resolve conflicts. Starr's eight-month investigation of the Clinton-Lewinsky matter yielded a comprehensive and meticulous dossier consisting of the Starr Report itself and the thousands of pages of testimony and other evidence to back it up. The House of Representatives, after initial indecision, sensibly forbore to augment the evidence that the Independent Counsel had collected. When the case moved to the Senate, the Senate was in the position of the trial court in a Continental litigation. The only good reason for the Senate to hold any evidentiary hearings was to fill the gaps (if any), and resolve the conflicts (which were few), in the dossier that it had received from the Independent Counsel via the House of Representatives. The uncontested facts could have been presented to the Senators in the form of a stipulation.

The fear of governmental paralysis during a Senate trial even of brief duration was also overstated. Most of the work of government is done below the political level, and much that goes on in the legislative branch nowadays consists of mulcting and placating various interest groups and raising campaign funds for the next election. Some Senators may have been concerned about the length of the trial because they were afraid that it would go on for a long time *and they would not be missed.* And one should really speak of *incremental* paralysis; when government is divided between a Congress controlled by one political party and a lame-duck President of the other party with only two years left in his term, paralysis is likely to have set in already.

Another bad argument against a trial was that it would defile the Senate to have Monica Lewinsky and Linda Tripp testifying in the "well" of the Senate about sex. In the wake of the undignified squabbling in the House over impeachment, Senators plumed themselves on being statesmen "above" being blown about by the partisan passions that had convulsed the lower chamber. The pretense soon wore thin.

And one has only to think back to the Bork and Thomas Supreme Court confirmation hearings to realize that the modern Senate is a populist body rather than the conclave of notables envisaged by the framers of the Constitution more than a century before the Seventeenth Amendment ordained the popular election of Senators. Much that goes on in the Senate, as in any political body, is not much more edifying than an illicit sexual affair. One recalls Bismarck's comparison of the making of legislation to the making of sausage—the result may be tasty, but the process is unsavory.

The biggest concern expressed by Clinton's defenders was that whatever the length or outcome of the Senate trial, the Presidency—already weakened by the independent counsel law and the Supreme Court's decision in the Paula Jones case—would inevitably be weakened further if Clinton was impeached. A long trial ending in conviction and therefore removal from office would have weakened the Presidency the most; it would have established a precedent bound to influence the behavior of future Presidents. But even a very short trial ending in acquittal would not wipe away the obloquy of impeachment.

In other words, the less secure an official's tenure in office, the weaker the official is, and the greater the threat of impeachment, the less secure his tenure is. Security of tenure is one reason, along with his "head of state" status noted in Chapter 4, that the President of the United States, despite the two-term limitation and his limited legislative power, is on average more powerful than the prime minister in a parliamentary democracy; the latter can be removed at any time by a simple majority of the legislature, which usually, moreover, is effectively unicameral.[3]

But there is an assumption buried here that should make us cautious about applying the analysis to the impeachment of President Clinton. It is that before Clinton was impeached there was a fixed threshold for impeachment, and impeaching him lowered it. Because only three Presidents (counting Nixon, as one should) have ever been impeached, and

[3]See Anthony King, "Foundations of Power," in *Researching the Presidency: Vital Questions, New Approaches* 415, 423–425 (George C. Edwards III, John H. Kessel, and Bert A. Rockman eds. 1993); and, on the relation of security of tenure to power, Anthony King, "Executives," in *Governmental Institutions and Processes* 173, 195 (Fred I. Greenstein and Nelson W. Polsby eds. 1975). The qualification in the text—"on average"—is important. " 'No Canadian,' commented one civil servant and minister, 'would want their prime minister to be as weak as the American president.' " Patrick Weller, *First among Equals: Prime Ministers in Westminster Systems* 200 (1985).

two the Senate acquitted, and because the meaning of "high Crimes and Misdemeanors" is unclear, the impact of an impeachment on the threshold is itself unclear. When Andrew Johnson was acquitted, a precedent was created that is generally thought to have *raised* the threshold of impeachment. A book on Johnson's impeachment, published, ironically, just a year before the fall of Nixon, stated that Johnson's acquittal by the Senate had made it "almost inconceivable that a future president will be impeached and removed."[4] If Johnson hadn't been impeached in the first place, this precedent favorable to Presidential power would not have been created. President Clinton's acquittal by the Senate may similarly make it "almost inconceivable that a future president will be impeached and removed." Even though the opposition party controlled both houses of Congress, it could not muster even a simple majority for conviction. Clinton's acquittal has certainly reduced the likelihood of a future President's being impeached for purely personal misconduct. And it has reduced any temptation a future House of Representatives may have to impeach a President, even when the prospects for conviction by the Senate are dim, on the theory that "anything can happen" in a trial. That may be true of a real trial, but it seems not to be true of a Senate trial, where, in effect, the verdict *precedes* the trial.

Even if it were true that every Presidential impeachment must weaken the Presidency, it would remain a question whether such a weakening is a bad thing. Many students of American politics, representing all points of the political compass, believe that everything good in American government comes from the President because there is only one President (unity of command) and he is elected by the whole nation (democratic legitimacy and accountability), while Congress is pummeled and riven and blown hither and yon by interest groups, regional parochialism, pork-barrel politics, and the sheer transaction costs of coordinating a multimember bicameral assembly.[5] There is probably

---

[4]Michael Les Benedict, *The Impeachment and Trial of Andrew Johnson* 180 (1973). To similar effect, see Sidney M. Milkis and Michael Nelson, *The American Presidency: Origins and Development, 1776–1793* 178 (2d ed. 1994).

[5]See, for example, Grant McConnell, *Private Power and American Democracy* 351–352 (1966); Gary L. Rose, *The American Presidency under Siege* (1997). See generally Michael A. Fitts, "The Paradox of Power in the Modern State: Why a Unitary, Centralized Presidency May Not Exhibit Effective or Legitimate Leadership," 144 *University of Pennsylvania Law Review* 827, 829–830, 841–855 (1996). In periods of divided power (that is, the Presidency controlled by one party and the Congress by another),

something to this, maybe a lot, even though parliamentary governments can be as strong, decisive, and effective as presidential government. England since the eighteenth century and Germany since the creation of the Bonn government after World War II have had a number of powerful prime ministers.[6] There was even a short-lived movement in the United States in the late 1970s and early 1980s to amend the Constitution to move the United States in the direction of parliamentary government in order to make government stronger by reducing deadlocks between Congress and the President.[7] The movement was probably misconceived. Arthur Schlesinger has argued convincingly that the success of parliamentary government depends on institutions that do not exist in the United States, such as strong political parties.[8]

But the issue that impeaching a President raises is not whether to amend the Constitution to substitute a parliamentary for a presidential system; it is whether to allow a slight shift in the institutional balance of power within the framework of the existing Constitution. In the 1970s, after the fall of Nixon, Congress chipped away at the President's powers, particularly in foreign affairs, yet this did not prevent Reagan from becoming a strong President, with an active and effective (if occasionally illegal!) foreign policy, in the following decade. Writing during the Reagan Presidency, the distinguished political scientist Theodore Lowi thought the Presidency was still too strong.[9] Clinton's successes

the members of the party that controls the Presidency tend to favor a strong Presidency, while the members of the party that controls the Congress argue that a strong Presidency is a danger. Compare Arthur M. Schlesinger, Jr., *The Imperial Presidency* (1973, with 1989 epilogue) (a Democrat writing during two Republican Presidencies), with Terry Eastland, *Energy in the Executive: The Case for the Strong Presidency* (1992) (a Republican writing during a Republican Presidency). On the politically partisan character of Presidential studies, see Richard Rose, "Evaluating Presidents," in *Researching the Presidency,* note 3 above, at 453, 473–475.

[6]See, for example, Michael Foley, *The Rise of the British Presidency* (1993).

[7]See, for example, Lloyd N. Cutler, "To Form a Government," 59 *Foreign Affairs* 126, 139–143 (1980); Schlesinger, note 5 above, at 461–462. On the stability and effectiveness of parliamentary versus presidential regimes, see Arend Lijphart, *Democracies: Patterns of Majoritarian and Consensus Government in Twenty-One Countries* 68–85 (1984).

[8]Schlesinger, note 5 above, at 463–470. Similarly, the success of "presidentialism" in the United States may depend on institutions that do not exist in most other countries. See Juan J. Linz, "The Perils of Presidentialism," 1 *Journal of Democracy* 51 (1990).

[9]Theodore J. Lowi, *The Personal President: Power Invested, Promise Unfulfilled* (1985).

as President may well be due, paradoxically, to the strength of Congress, which prevented him from governing from the Left, as was his initial impulse. It is sheer speculation that Clinton's impeachment and its sequelae will bring about a dangerous weakening of the Presidency. The shift in the balance of power as a result of Nixon's de facto impeachment was slight, and may have had nothing to do with the impeachment inquiry as distinct from the revulsion at the high-handed way in which Nixon and before him Lyndon Johnson had conducted the Indochinese war.[10]

What is more, Clinton's struggle may have undone the Democratic efforts, which began in the Nixon Administration, to clip the President's wings. Democrats now *oppose* the independent counsel law, a Democratic initiative that weakened the Presidency, and now *support* unilateral Presidential military action, which they had sought by the War Powers Resolution and other now ignored methods to curb. Clinton's impeachment rallied Democrats to the cause of Presidential power!

The case of Nixon, who was (in effect) convicted, is a better example of the effect of impeachment on Presidential power than the case of Andrew Johnson, who was acquitted. Whether Johnson's impeachment and trial had any effect on the Presidency is deeply uncertain.[11] It is true that he had no strong successors until Theodore Roosevelt a quarter of a century later; but the nineteenth-century Presidency was a weak office. And while Albert Castel has argued that "the presidency [under Andrew Johnson] in an institutional sense plummeted to the lowest point of power and prestige in its history" and did not rebound immediately, he attributes this dip to Johnson's "blunders and obstinacy" rather than to the impeachment and trial. And he attributes the weakness of Johnson's successors to "historical circumstance" rather than to anything specific to Johnson.[12]

It has been conjectured that the near conviction of Johnson made his successor, Grant, even more subservient to Congress than was his nat-

---

[10]For remember that it spilled over into Laos and Cambodia—the legally most questionable features of the war.

[11]What is less doubtful is that Johnson's acquittal gave a shot in the arm to the white South and helped do in Reconstruction. See, for example, Hans L. Trefousse, *Andrew Johnson: A Biography* 332–334 (1989). With nice irony, the Johnson impeachment was North versus South; the Clinton impeachment was (to a degree) South versus North. It will be interesting to see what if any political effects Clinton's acquittal will have.

[12]Albert Castel, *The Presidency of Andrew Johnson* 230 (1979).

ural bent.[13] But James Sundquist's careful analysis of the balance of power between President and Congress in the nineteenth century attributes neither the Johnsonian nadir nor the weakness of the nineteenth-century Presidency to the impeachment, but rather to a variety of other factors. He notes as well the weakness of a number of Johnson's predecessors, which obviously cannot be blamed on Johnson's impeachment.[14] Lincoln himself, despite all the power he accrued as a war President, was considerably hampered by the party system and might have found it impossible to push through a successful program of Reconstruction.[15]

We must not ignore, moreover, the paradox of weakness in strength, and strength in weakness, which makes it difficult to say whether a slight shift of power away from the President actually weakens the Presidency. The shift might make the President work harder to get along with Congress, which may be a good thing, and also work harder to obtain a congressional majority for his party, which may also be a good thing; so the shift might actually be a *centralizing* force. Besides, the more the President draws power to himself, the more he becomes a focal point for blame.[16] By dispersing power, he can (as Machiavelli recommended to the Prince) shift blame to others for doing the essential dirty work of government, and so enhance his real power. As the political theorist Stephen Holmes emphasizes, liberal states, with their dispersion and limitation of governmental powers, have historically proved more powerful than autocratic ones, and not in spite of, but because of, their rejection of centralized political power.[17] Of course there can be too

[13]Bruce Catton, *U. S. Grant and the American Military Tradition* 153 (1954). Catton writes that Grant subscribed to "the traditional army officer's view that Congress is the boss. Orders may come from the executive branch but it is always Congress that passes appropriation bills, creates or abolishes army posts and functions, confirms or rejects the nominations of higher officers, declares war and ratifies treaties and in general lays down the line which the army has to follow." Id. at 152.

[14]James L. Sundquist, *The Decline and Resurgence of Congress,* ch. 2 (1981).

[15]See Stephen Skowronek, *The Politics Presidents Make: Leadership from John Adams to George Bush* 198–227 (1993).

[16]This point is emphasized by Fitts, note 5 above. Lyndon Johnson's autocratic management of the Vietnam War appears to be a case in point. See Ronald A. Heifetz, *Leadership without Easy Answers* 150–170 (1994). Cf. Richard J. Ellis, *Presidential Lightning Rods: The Politics of Blame Avoidance* 157–158 (1994), contrasting Johnson with Eisenhower.

[17]Stephen Holmes, *Passions and Constraints: On the Theory of Liberal Democracy* 18–22 (1995).

much dispersion, too much limitation. But the pertinent question, which is unanswerable, is whether the impeachment of *this* President on *these* grounds was likely to impair our system of governance.

Thus far I have been tacitly assuming that every loss of power by the President is an equal gain of power for Congress; that the quantum of federal power is unchanged. But this is unrealistic. Because Congress does not have executive capacity, weakening the Presidency is likely to weaken the federal government as a whole. One probable consequence would be to shift power to the states; another, to shift power from the public to the private sector. Would these be good consequences or bad for the nation as a whole? It is a brave soul who would venture a confident answer.

There were, however, other possible downsides to impeaching Clinton besides the speculative one that it might dangerously weaken the Presidency. His impeachment exemplified and encouraged the unlovely form of political combat that Ginsberg and Shefter have dubbed "RIP" (revelation, investigation, and prosecution; see Chapter 3). And if Clinton had been convicted by the Senate and forced from office, this would have meant a change of government—and all the transitional costs entailed by such a change even when the new President is of the same party as the old—with only two years, or less (depending on the length of the trial), before the next Presidential election.

American politics may become further embittered, at least in the near term, by an impeachment cast as this one has been as a partisan ganging-up. Political rivalry, compared to business or even academic rivalry, is often bitter and emotional, because of its zero-sum quality (there are clear winners and clear losers) and because the audience (the electorate) often lacks the information and interest that would enable it to recognize demogoguery for what it is. Democrats may be desperate to find a way to get even with the Republicans for engineering Clinton's impeachment,[18] while Republicans may be desperate to get even with the Democrats for pinning the label of "partisanship" to their back. Here Bruce Ackerman's point about lame-duck impeachment (see Chapter 3), unsound as law, comes back as practical politics. Because the lame-duck House had a larger Republican majority than the newly

---

[18]Remember that the Jeffersonian Republicans' turn to political impeachment was their attempt to get even with the Federalists for trying to crush the Republicans by means of the alien and sedition laws.

elected one, impeachment would have been less likely to pass the new House, though one of the two articles that the lame-duck House voted would probably have passed.[19] Supporters of a President brought low by lame ducks would be likely to think the process unfair and democratic preference flouted.

The force of this point is weakened, however, by the existence of a national consensus, dating from December 11, 1998, when the President expressly invited Congress to censure or otherwise rebuke him, that the President should be punished; the argument was over the form the punishment should take. Given the party balance in the Senate, conviction was so unlikely that the real choice was between impeachment followed by censure and impeachment followed by acquittal and then censure. The difference between these modes of "punishment," though not trivial, may be small. And the cathartic effects of a trial should not be underemphasized. The loser will have the satisfaction of having gotten his "day in court" and will usually, and in this case, have landed some sharp blows on the winner's face.

Other possible consequences of impeachment are also shrouded in doubt. We do not know whether the impeachment (with or without forcible removal) of a criminal President from office would restore a salutary Presidential charisma or weaken it further. We do not even know, to recur to a question raised in Chapter 4, whether the nation *needs* charismatic Presidents other than in times of crisis—but of course crises usually cannot be predicted.

And while it can be argued that allowing President Clinton to get away with obstruction of justice would rend the fabric of the law and undermine conventional morality, it is not clear that he would have gotten away with it even if he hadn't been impeached. He would still have been subject to prosecution in the ordinary course of criminal justice after and perhaps before his term of office expires, though as I have noted the power of Presidential self-pardon may make the prospect of a criminal prosecution illusory. Removing Clinton from office would certainly have been a dramatic affirmation of the nation's commitment to the rule of law and high moral standards—but an affirmation tainted

[19]The Democrats picked up five seats in the new House. With a shift of 5 votes from the Republican to the Democratic column, the vote would have been 223 to 211 to impeach Clinton on the first article of impeachment and 216 to 217 on the third. This is assuming no other changes in votes, or, more plausibly, that any other changes would have canceled out.

by widespread suspicion of the tactics and motives of his opponents. And many people believed that even before he was impeached Clinton's place in history had become so tarnished by the uproar over the Lewinsky business that prosecution or even censure would be supererogatory, would be "piling on."

Other pertinent questions that elude confident answer are whether it would have been lawless to forgo impeachment because the President is popular, or undemocratic to disregard his popularity in deciding whether to impeach him; and what weight in the decision whether to impeach should either the questionable tactics and motives of Clinton's prosecutors and persecutors, or his achievements in office, have had.

Rigorism, Pragmatism, and Populism

Clinton's case raises a nice issue of political philosophy, namely the choice between a pragmatic approach to government and a rigorist, moralistic approach, such as that of Kant and his epigones or that of Catholic natural lawyers. If we can resolve that issue, maybe we'll know whether Clinton should have been forced from office.

A pragmatic decision-maker wants decisions to be based on an assessment of their probable consequences. In legal cases, and *a fortiori* in impeachment, which is only quasi-legal, this is a legitimate or at least common approach when the conventional materials of legal decision-making, such as precedent or a clear statutory or constitutional text, yield no direction. Since it is unknowable whether the good consequences of impeaching and removing Clinton outweigh the bad, the pragmatist would lean against impeachment. A rigorist would want to shift the focus of inquiry to the intrinsic gravity of the President's conduct from a moral and legal standpoint, a shift not helpful to the President. A Catholic natural law theorist would be especially likely to condemn that conduct because of his strong moral disapproval of the sexual relationship out of which it arose.

The rigorist might accuse the pragmatist who believes that it was better on the whole, because of the uncertain balance of costs and benefits, for Clinton to be allowed to complete his term of condoning criminal conduct—even of "licensing" Presidents to commit crimes so long as the crimes do not impair Presidential effectiveness too greatly. Or at least of licensing popular Presidents to commit crimes, since impeachment would be less traumatic the less popular the President was. The pragmatist might be thought to be urging that the popular President be "rewarded" for his popularity by being immunized from criminal prosecution, and thus that legal justice yield to popular justice. Pragmatists are famously skeptical about "truth" and hence, it might seem, ill equipped to take a strong stand against a perjurer. They can thus be accused of lacking an epistemological as well as a moral compass and a staunch, unwavering commitment to the rule of law.[20]

This characterization of the pragmatic position is imprecise. It is a canard that pragmatists disbelieve in "truth" and so are disabled from disapproving of perjury. They are skeptics about Truth in the sense of metaphysical certainty, such "Truths" as that God exists (or does not exist) or that modern physics describes nature as it really is. They are not skeptical about whether the Holocaust really occurred or whether President Clinton stained Monica Lewinsky's dress or lied to the grand jury. And while they doubt that it can be proved that there are universally valid moral principles, they don't doubt that perjury and other obstructions of justice are morally objectionable practices in the United States of today and that criminals should not be acquitted because they are popular.

Impeaching and convicting President Clinton for his obstructions of justice would have demonstrated an impressive commitment, Kantian in its rigidity, to the rule of law and would have sounded a clarion call for the reinvigoration of a traditional morality that condemns adultery, lying, and breaking the law and insists that public officials be role models in the moral as well as the political realm. These may be good consequences, which pragmatists should welcome. But the perceived partisanship of the impeachment of the President, although perhaps mitigated slightly by Robert Livingston's dramatic though soon forgotten renunciation of his claim to the Speakership of the House of Representatives because he had committed adultery,[21] diminished the symbolic value of the impeachment. Anyway a pragmatist does not believe that the rule of law and conventional morality are the only social goods to be considered when deciding whether to impeach a President. And where is the proof that the clarion call would be heeded?

[20]See Richard A. Posner, *Overcoming Law* 155–156 (1995).

[21]I say "slightly" because he may have been forced to resign by Republican Congressmen who believed that his becoming Speaker would undermine the effort to oust Clinton.

The most questionable of the pragmatic considerations bearing on impeachment was the President's popularity and, a related though not identical point, the aversion of a large majority of the public to his being impeached. Roughly two thirds of the public gave him positive approval ratings throughout the entire period of the investigation, impeachment, trial, and verdict. This figure by itself is difficult to evaluate. The respondents in most of the public opinion polls were asked what they thought both of the President's character and of his performance as President. This juxtaposition may have made them think they were being asked about performance divorced from character, even though, as we saw in the last chapter, character can be a dimension of Presidential performance. No matter; from polls that asked specifically whether President Clinton should be impeached, from the exit polls conducted after the November 1998 congressional elections, from the election campaigns and outcomes themselves, from the qualms of a number of Republican members of Congress about impeaching Clinton, and from the efforts of Republican Senators to truncate the Senate trial, it is apparent that a large majority of Americans did not want him impeached; and only about 20 percent disagreed with the Senate's acquitting him.

So what? We would think it monstrous for a murderer or other criminal to be acquitted because public opinion polls showed that most people, perhaps unversed in the intricacies of criminal justice, thought he should be acquitted. Potential victims of Presidential crimes would become outlaws, that is, persons unprotected by law, if popularity were a defense to a criminal prosecution.[22] That would be an illustration of popular justice in a very bad sense (see Chapter 2). And I have emphasized the intent of the framers of the Constitution that an impeachment proceeding be primarily a legal proceeding, akin to a criminal prosecution, rather than a political one.

This argument for disregarding public opinion when deciding whether to impeach and convict the President would be compelling if we were still under the Constitution of 1787, which made the House of Representatives the only branch of the federal government elected directly by the people. The Senate was given the assignment of trying impeachments in part because it was not a democratic body and could

---

[22]This point has been obscured by the fact that Paula Jones, the primary victim of President Clinton's criminal acts, obtained a generous monetary settlement of her claim against him. His efforts to obstruct justice did not succeed.

therefore be trusted (not entirely, or a two-thirds vote to convict would not have been required, but more than the House could be trusted) to act as a judicial tribunal. All is changed. Now directly elected by the people, just like the members of the House, Senators are expected to be responsive—not slavishly responsive, but responsive—to the desires of the voters. Even more important, the President is now in effect directly elected.[23] He is the people's choice, rather than the choice of notables in a College of Electors. The people, or rather the politically interested people—many Americans are apathetic about politics—want a voice in the decision whether to remove him from office before the expiration of his term. They expect their representatives, the members of the House and of the Senate, to hear and heed their voice. Although the legal and evidentiary issues bearing on the question whether President Clinton committed impeachable offenses are technical and even esoteric, the people did not feel incompetent to weigh in on them, because they were flooded with information and opinion by the media. Illustrious figures from the world of law told the people what to think about every issue involved in the proposed impeachment. They told the people different things, but implied by their participation in media events aimed at the general public that the people were competent to choose among competing professional opinions. The implication was strengthened by the televising of the impeachment proceedings in the House and the trial in the Senate.

Although people who are not lawyers or political scientists may have exaggerated their competence to decide whether the President had committed impeachable offenses, they could hardly have deferred in the matter to the professional elite, because the elite was passionately divided, and, moreover, frequently unprofessional. Given that the bodies responsible for making the impeachment decision are now populist organs, and the impeachment target (in the case of Presidential impeachment) a populist figure, and given the disarray in the elite, it is hard to argue that public opinion should have played *no* role in the decision whether to impeach President Clinton.

And remember that the President remains subject to the ordinary processes of the law, whether during or after his term. If he committed torts (civil wrongs) against individuals, he can be sued for damages. If

---

[23]The qualification "in effect" is in recognition that a candidate could have a plurality of votes in the Electoral College without having a plurality of the popular vote.

he committed crimes, he can be prosecuted (unless he pardons himself!). A fundamental tenet of American ideology is preserved: No one is above the law; the President is not above the law, even if he is very difficult to impeach and even more difficult to convict, whether tried by the Senate or by an ordinary court. The Kantian rigorist can take solace in the possibility, theoretical though it may be, that the President can be punished in the regular law courts for any crimes that he committed, and can be punished in history for any other misconduct.

Weighing against these arguments for pragmatic lenity in impeachment is the President's effrontery in denying, right up and into the impeachment debate, that he had broken the law, or even that he had lied. As we saw in Chapter 4, to tell a lie that no one believes can actually be worse than telling a lie that deceives. The liar who hopes to convince with his lie does not deny the reality of truth and falsehood; indeed, truth is the fulcrum that makes his lie effective. The liar who lies not to convince but to save face or to flaunt his power is frightening; he appears to be challenging a fundamental and indispensable value of civilized society.

I said that if we could choose between the pragmatic and the rigorist approach to impeachment, we might be able to answer the question whether President Clinton should have been impeached and convicted. But as usual in debates over moral or political philosophy, there is insufficient common ground among the debaters to enable an objective answer. About all that can be said is that a moral rigorist would be inclined to think that the President committed impeachable offenses, while a pragmatist would lean, though perhaps only slightly, the other way.

Proportionality and Alternative Punishments

There is still to be considered the argument that impeachment was a *disproportionate* response to President Clinton's misconduct, even if that misconduct was far worse than just "lying about sex." The punishment should fit the crime. The crime was serious but maybe not serious enough for *this* punishment. Although there are some mandatory minimum punishments in the criminal law, rarely is the punishment prescribed by a criminal statute a point rather than a range. But in the case of impeachment and conviction, Article II, section 4, of the Constitution leaves no room for reasonable doubt on this score: an impeached and convicted official "shall be removed from Office." The only leeway concerns disqualification from future office-holding. The Senate has discretion as to whether to decree this. This is implicit in the language of Article I, section 3, clause 7—"Judgment in Cases of Impeachment shall not extend further than to removal from Office, and disqualification to hold and enjoy any Office of Honor, Trust or Profit under the United States"—when juxtaposed with the omission from Article II, section 4, of any reference to disqualification.

The words "further than" might seem to imply that removal and disqualification are merely maximum punishments. But this reading would create a contradiction between the "further than" clause and the "shall be removed" clause. The two clauses are easily reconciled. The "further than" clause fixes the maximum punishment and the "shall be removed" clause the minimum. The convicted official must be removed from office, but the only further punishment that the Senate can impose is to bar him from future federal office. It would be excessively paradoxical to convict an official of high crimes or misdemeanors yet allow him to remain in office. It would announce to the world that the United States is content to be governed by criminals, or worse. It would also inject additional uncertainty into the impeachment process. If removal from office (with or without disqualification from holding future office) is merely the maximum punishment for committing high crimes or misdemeanors, this implies—since ten days of house arrest is a lighter punishment than being kicked out of the Presidency—that the Senate could sentence the President to house arrest, or perhaps even to a short jail term, provided that he was allowed to continue in office. Or that it could suspend him from office for a year. Or sentence him to spend a day in the stocks and to wear a Pinocchio nose and a scarlet "A" for a month.

Allowing alternative punishments to removal from office would also have the effect of lowering the impeachment threshold (though we cannot be certain that this would be a bad thing). Making the penalty for an offense very severe, and inflexibly so, is a way of discouraging prosecutions.[24] It is a particularly important way when the offense is vaguely

[24]That is one reason why prosecutors often charge a defendant with a lesser included offense of the main offense with which they are charging him, for example manslaughter as well as murder. The jury may refuse to convict if they are given a choice only between finding the defendant guilty of a very grave crime, which the jury knows carries a very heavy penalty, and acquitting him.

defined. It is a way of saying, and maybe in the case of impeachment the only way of saying because of the difficulty of enumerating the situations in which impeachment of a President is warranted, that prosecution should be confined to the gravest instances of the offense, since the prescribed punishment in the event of conviction would be disproportionate otherwise. Another way to put this is that to authorize light punishments for high crimes and misdemeanors would reduce the minimum gravity required to declare conduct a high crime or misdemeanor.

This objection also applies to the argument that the House of Representatives can properly decline to impeach a President or other official whom it believes to be guilty of high crimes and misdemeanors or that the Senate can properly decline to try, and if it finds him guilty convict, a President who it believes may have committed high crimes and misdemeanors. This would depreciate the gravity of impeachable offenses by making trial and punishment optional.

If I am right so far, the Constitution does not authorize any lighter punishment for an impeached official than removal from office, or any additional punishment except disqualification from holding a federal office in the future. What then to do with a President who commits serious wrongs, but perhaps not quite serious enough to warrant removal from office? Various answers were batted around during the impeachment and trial of President Clinton. The main one was censure, and let us consider its propriety.

Censure is questionable, as we shall see, but some of the arguments made against censure are also questionable. For example, it does not follow *from the impeachment provisions* of the Constitution that Congress cannot enact a resolution expressing its disapproval of a person; it "censured" Andrew Jackson in this manner. This is provided that either the *entire* Congress act—that the censure be expressed in a joint resolution—or that, if only the Senate acts, it be before the Senate convicts or after it acquits. It would be improper for the Senate, after a trial resulting in conviction, to censure the President (or whoever the impeached and convicted official was); censure is not an authorized punishment of an official who is impeached and convicted. The Constitution, and for good practical reasons as we have seen, is specific about the punishments that the Senate can impose on a convicted official.

Another mistaken objection is to suppose that a resolution of censure would lower the threshold to impeachment. Censure is an alternative to impeachment rather than a tepid substitute punishment for the removal of an impeached and convicted official.[25] It was an attractive alternative to people who opposed the removal of Clinton, or realized the Senate would not vote to convict him by the requisite supermajority, but feared that letting him off scot-free would undermine legality and morality. Were congressional censure a generally accepted mode of punishing federal officials, it is less likely that Clinton would have been impeached.

The only deterrent and retributive force of a congressional resolution of censure would, it is true, be a moral force. But given the infrequency with which Presidents have been censured, that force could be considerable—provided that a majority of the President's own party voted for the censure, which would pull the sting of partisanship. By the same token, a practice of censuring Presidents when they misbehave would be unlikely to weaken the Presidency significantly. The public understands the tensions between the branches of government and is unlikely to give a congressional resolution of censure any more weight than it intrinsically deserves.

With the consent of the President, Congress could go further; could for example fine him. This would clearly be a bill of attainder, that is, a legislative punishment, which the Constitution forbids. But the President could hardly complain about Congress's exceeding its powers, for it would be with his consent; and no one else would have standing to challenge Congress's action either. Nevertheless, there are serious questions about such a fine. One is what exactly it means to fine a President who has no net assets[26] and plenty of wealthy friends; the punishment would be in the symbolism rather than to the pocketbook, though symbolic punishments should not be sneezed at, as we are about to see. But is an illegal punishment an appropriate means of expressing the nation's moral outrage at the President's conduct?

Censure can be criticized as at once unnecessary and incomplete. Unnecessary because the President can be prosecuted in the regular

---

[25]This is the theory behind the provision of the Judicial Conduct and Disability Act of 1980 that authorizes circuit judicial councils to issue public or private censures or reprimands of misbehaving federal judges. See 28 U.S.C. §§ 372(c)(6)(B)(v), (vi); Michael J. Gerhardt, *The Federal Impeachment Process: A Constitutional and Historical Analysis* 100–102 (1996). For remember that, like the President, federal judges can be forced from office only by impeachment and conviction.

[26]He has some current assets, but his net worth is negative because of his huge liabilities to his lawyers for fees. No doubt he will quickly recoup after leaving office, however.

courts for the criminal aspects of his misconduct, certainly after his term of office and perhaps during, though the self-pardoning power places a question mark after this argument. Incomplete because Clinton is afraid to confess to having committed any crimes,[27] and so as a humiliation ritual censure would fall short. But it would have been humiliation enough if a majority of Democrats had voted for censure; Clinton could not explain away a censure supported by his own party as a partisan slap. Censure without confession would have the further advantage of being obtainable with lower transaction costs than a censure to which the President consented (and by consenting acknowledged to be a warranted rebuke), since the President would not have to be a party to the negotiation.

The deepest objection to censure lies in the Constitution's prohibition against bills of attainder. Even though no one could challenge such a bill in the courts if the target consented, an illegal punishment is a dubious instrument for expressing authoritative disapproval of illegal conduct. And Clinton might not consent, and might get the courts to void the censure resolution if it was indeed a bill of attainder. It clearly would be if it fined the President. A punitive purpose coupled with a characteristically punitive sanction, such as a fine, would unmistakably mark a censure resolution as a bill of attainder.[28] But what if the fine were omitted? Would a bare resolution of censure, a resolution that deprived the President of nothing but his good name, be a bill of attainder?

This issue is unresolved. Congress has used censure sparingly, and the incentive to challenge a toothless censure is weak. The statutes that have been attacked in the courts as bills of attainder have deprived people of property, salary, pensions, employment, and other readily monetizable goods. The focus of judicial consideration of such challenges has been on the question whether the *aim* of the congressional action

[27]Laurence H. Tribe, in "How to Bring Clinton to Justice without Punishing the Nation," *Boston Globe*, Sept. 16, 1998, p. A27, says that "the president must fully acknowledge his deception and, without necessarily confessing to crimes for which he has not yet been indicted, abandon the off-putting pronouncements of technical legal innocence." But how is such a balancing act possible? A "full" acknowledgment of his deception would involve admitting, at a minimum, all the elements of the crime of perjury.

[28]See generally Nixon v. Administrator of General Services, 433 U.S. 425, 468–484 (1977); Laurence H. Tribe, *American Constitutional Law* 642–643, 646 n. 25, 650–655 (2d ed. 1988).

was punishment, rather than on the hurtful *consequence* of the statute for the target, except insofar as the consequence illuminated Congress's purpose. Illustrative is the *Nixon* case, which happens to be the only case in which an alleged bill of attainder arose from an impeachment inquiry. After Nixon left office, taking as is the custom of Presidents his papers (and the famous tapes) with him, concern was expressed that he might destroy some of these materials and that this would both impede the uncompleted Watergate-related prosecutions and deprive the public of materials of historical importance. So Congress passed a law ordering the General Services Administration to take custody of Nixon's papers and tapes. Nixon contended that the law was a bill of attainder, punishing him by taking his property. The Supreme Court held that it was not because Congress had intended not to punish him but merely to preserve documents of forensic and historical value.[29]

No similar argument could be made with reference to Clinton; if punitive purpose is the test for whether a congressional enactment is a bill of attainder, then a resolution censuring President Clinton would have been a bill of attainder, for the only and the undeniable purpose would have been to punish him. But that leaves the question whether in addition to having a punitive purpose, a law must, to rise to the level of a bill of attainder, impose something like a criminal penalty, or at least a deprivation of something of tangible value. In other words, it is an open question whether pure stigma is enough of a "punishment" to make a resolution of censure a bill of attainder. Justice Hugo Black thought that a blacklist could be a bill of attainder. He quoted Madison's opposition in 1794 to a congressional resolution expressing public disapproval of certain organizations, on the ground that such "censure" would constitute a bill of attainder.[30] A vote of censure would be like a blacklist; it would mark Clinton as a wrongdoer and might deprive him of certain employment opportunities, such as a university presidency.

It could be argued that the wording of the resolution is critical, that if it merely expressed disapproval rather than condemnation it would not rise to the level of punishment. No doubt the resolution could be

---

[29]433 U.S. at 478–480.

[30]Joint Anti-Fascist Refugee Committee v. McGrath, 341 U.S. 123, 144 and n. 1 (1951) (concurring opinion). See also David P. Currie, *The Constitution in Congress: The Federalist Period, 1789–1801* 191 (1997), appearing to agree with Madison.

so watered down as not to count as punishment. Disapproval and punishment are not synonyms. But by the same token, disapproval is not a very good substitute for punishment.

There is renewed interest among students of criminal justice, an interest highly pertinent to the issue of censuring a President, in shaming penalties.[31] Examples are requiring a convicted sex offender to display a poster in his front yard that reads, "I am a convicted sex offender," and a vandal to clean sidewalks while wearing prison garb. No one doubts that these are *penalties;* if Congress imposed them on individual malefactors (as distinct from passing a general law, prospective in operation, that made shaming penalties an authorized or required sanction for some class of offenses), they would be bills of attainder. Proponents of the censure of President Clinton conceived of it as a shaming penalty but failed to consider how it could, if viewed so, be squared with the prohibition against bills of attainder.

Whether censure is constitutional or not, meaningful or not, punishment or not, during the run up to impeachment in the House the possibility of resolving the matter by a vote of censure offered a haven for the Democrats but loomed as a trap for the Republicans. If Clinton stumbled as President and the public turned against him, the Democrats could say that they had known he was bad and therefore had voted to censure him, stopping short of impeachment only because the public didn't want it and it would have disrupted the operations of the government too much. If the Republicans went along with censure, they would become complicit in these arguments. If instead they took the position (as they did in the impeachment debate) that censure is unconstitutional, a mere slap on the wrist, a cop-out, or an unacceptable lowering of the threshold to impeachment—that it was impeachment or nothing—then if the public turned on the President the Republicans could say, "We told you so—he should have been impeached."

Once Clinton was impeached, censure became more attractive even to Republicans. It offered a way of heading off a Senate trial that might so disrupt the business of government that if the nation got into trouble

---

[31]See, for example, Dan M. Kahan, "What Do Alternative Sanctions Mean?" 63 *University of Chicago Law Review* 591 (1996); Kahan, "It's a Shame We Have None," *Wall Street Journal,* Jan. 15, 1997, p. A16; Toni M. Massaro, "The Meanings of Shame: Implications for Legal Reform," 3 *Psychology, Public Policy, and Law* 645 (1997). In the case of shameless malefactors, these penalties are better described as "humiliation penalties."

in the next few years the Democrats would be able to blame the Republicans for having insisted on a trial. Also, while censure viewed in isolation might be viewed as a mere slap on the wrist, the combination of impeachment and censure could not be so viewed, provided that the wording of the censure was strong and unequivocal and that either the President signified his assent or a majority of Democrats in both houses of Congress voted for it. But since the Constitution assigns to the Senate the task of trying an impeached official, once President Clinton was impeached and the venue of the proceeding thus shifted to the Senate it became difficult for the Senators to justify issuing a resolution of censure without first conducting some sort of trial to determine the gravity of the President's offenses.

Censure would have had the pragmatic virtue of reducing the pressure to prosecute the President criminally. One argument against impeachment was that the proper setting for a determination of criminality is a criminal trial. The principle that even the highest officials in the land are subject to the ordinary processes of law is an important component of the idea of corrective justice, which is fundamental to the ideology of the rule of law. But some principles are better left in aspirational than in implemented form. An actual criminal prosecution of Clinton, even if deferred until he left office in 2001, strikes me as a grotesque prospect. I don't think it is monarchical to suggest that a President should be entitled to a uniquely generous exercise of prosecutorial discretion in his favor—so generous, indeed, as to excuse him from being prosecuted for criminal behavior committed before or during his term of office that could not reasonably be described as monstrous. Would not the disgrace of being labeled a criminal by a censure resolution be punishment enough for such a lofty figure? The fall from grace is greater, the higher the altitude from which the fall begins. President Clinton's proven criminal acts, although reprehensible, were not monstrous. He has been disgraced and his place in history tarnished, perhaps indelibly; that, plus censure, even if censure can be no more than an expression of disapproval falling short of actual punishment even symbolic, might have been punishment enough to satisfy all but the most vindictive of his opponents.

The possibility of criminal prosecution would cast a pall over the 2000 Presidential campaign. Candidates would be asked to take a stand pro or con pardoning Clinton if he hadn't already pardoned himself (or even if he had—for there is at least a slight doubt about the validity of self-pardoning). The campaign might turn into a referendum on Clinton, with the Democratic candidate promising to pardon him in order to bring the Clinton-Lewinsky imbroglio to an end at long last and the Republican candidate vowing to allow criminal justice to take its course. The scandal and its aftermath constitute a fascinating chapter in American political, social, and legal history. But enough is enough!

The stricken look on the Clintons' faces when they appeared in the Rose Garden on December 19, 1998,[32] immediately after the President was impeached, is evidence that despite all the charges of undue partisanship leveled against the Republicans, and the many pratfalls that they took on the road to impeachment, impeachment is an effective, powerful, and legitimate form of shaming penalty. All that remained was for Clinton to make a full and frank confession that he had lied and broken the law. After impeachment and confession, a censure resolution, fine, trial, conviction, criminal prosecution—all would have been superfluous. The combination of impeachment and confession would have been a shaming penalty at once constitutional and efficacious, and censure a superfluous addition. It was not to be.

Many people had difficulty seeing the point of a trial if the only sanction likely to emerge from it was censure. It seemed that in that case only enough of a "trial" was needed to avoid insulting the House by refusing to listen to the thirteen Congressmen whom the House had appointed to prosecute Clinton in the Senate. I do not agree. Of course if Clinton had confessed, there would have been no need for a trial; there would also have been no need, I have argued, for a censure resolution. But because he did not confess, there was need for a trial, and this for two reasons. The first is that the articles of impeachment adopted by the House went beyond what the evidence gathered by the Independent Counsel could sustain, at least if proof beyond a reasonable doubt (or by clear and convincing evidence) is the right standard of proof in an impeachment trial. It could be argued that a lesser burden is appropriate when the only sanction to be imposed on the guilty President is censure, but this seems a questionable argument, if only because it would throw a cloud over the entire proceeding. There would be no determination of whether the President had been proved guilty of *any*

[32]Before Clinton started to speak. As soon as he started, he regained his usual composure.

criminal conduct with the certitude that we demand in criminal proceedings.

The second objection to the aborted or truncated trial is similar to the first, and even bears a distant family relationship to the objection to meting out summary punishment to the Nazi leaders, as the British at first urged in lieu of a judicial proceeding. The summary proceeding would leave the facts uncertain and hence contestable. There was no serious doubt about the Nazi leaders' guilt; and there is no serious doubt about Clinton's having committed the criminal acts that I discussed in Chapter 1. But when the legal process is not allowed to run its course, there is an open invitation to historical revisionism. Clintonites could have said, "How do we know that Monica Lewinsky was telling the truth? She was never cross-examined. Nor was Linda Tripp. Nor were Vernon Jordan or Betty Currie allowed to tell their stories to sympathetic interrogators, as they would have been in a trial in which they testified for the defense. Paula Jones's lawyers were not questioned, and so the tentacular and insidious scheming of the vast right-wing conspiracy was never adequately explored." A full trial would have laid most of these questions to rest; the partial trial that was conducted laid some of them to rest (Clinton's lawyers decided not to cross-examine Lewinsky). It would not have mattered greatly if a full trial had ended in an acquittal with no censure and no confession; given the inevitable politicization of the Presidential impeachment process under current conditions, neither conviction nor acquittal would be a reliable indication of which side truth and justice lay on. Regardless of outcome, the President's misconduct would have been fully aired before the nation. As it was, a rather bobtailed trial ended in acquittal without either a confession or censure; but perhaps, considering the alternatives, this was the best that could be expected.

Another alternative to a "clean" conviction or acquittal was proposed. This was for the Senate's verdict to have two parts. The first would be a finding on whether Clinton engaged in the misconduct charged in the articles of impeachment. The second would be a finding on whether, if so, the misconduct rose to the level of a high crime or misdemeanor. Democrats who had argued that censure was constitutional argued that the two-stage verdict would be unconstitutional because not provided for in the impeachment provisions of the Constitution. The two arguments cannot be reconciled. The motives for each were political. If the Senate found that Clinton had committed perjury and other obstructions of justice, but acquitted him because Democrats voted en bloc for acquittal, they would have some explaining to do to their constituents (how could you let an *adjudicated* perjurer and obstructer of justice remain in office?), and the obloquy of a criminal Democratic President might rub off on them. Censure would allow Democrats to express disapproval of the President's behavior without committing themselves to any particular description of what they were disapproving of.

The argument against the constitutionality of the two-stage verdict is that the first stage would be a bill of attainder if condemnation, as in a strongly worded resolution of censure, is an "attainder" even if no tangible punishment—nothing beyond the condemnation itself—is imposed. This would be a powerful argument if there were no trial and all the Senate did was declare that the President had engaged in misconduct. But since the finding would be made as part of the trial process itself, in which the Senate was acting in a judicial rather than a legislative capacity, it could not be regarded as merely a bill of attainder. Findings are a common part of the judicial process. In a federal civil nonjury trial, the judge is required to issue findings of fact and conclusions of law en route to announcing his judgment.[33] If it is a jury trial, the judge can require the jury to answer specific questions of fact.[34] And in a federal criminal nonjury trial the judge is required, upon request by either party, to make findings of fact.[35] Employing such a procedure in an impeachment trial would make the outcome a more helpful precedent. The blind acquittal of President Clinton has left unclear whether the misconduct alleged in the articles of impeachment did not rise to the level of high crimes or misdemeanors or whether the evidence simply failed to support the allegations to a sufficient degree of certitude. The two-stage verdict would have eliminated that uncertainty.

The President would be entitled to insist that a finding against him in the first as well as (of course) the second stage be supported by two thirds of the Senators. For given that the finding would operate as a kind of punishment, any dilution of the two-thirds requirement would

[33]Fed. R. Civ. P. 52(a).
[34]Fed. R. Civ. P. 49.
[35]Fed. R. Crim. P. 23(c).

enable a bare majority of the Senate to punish the President by finding him guilty of misconduct and then adjourning the trial to prevent him from winning an acquittal.

With this safeguard in place, the two-stage verdict would be constitutional and it would have the advantage I mentioned of making the judgment, whether acquittal or conviction, a more useful precedent for future impeachment controversies. But it would be unwise, and was properly rejected. The Senate, even when it is trying impeachments, is not, in fact, a judicial body. Any doubts on this score were dispelled by the behavior of the Senators in Clinton's trial. As I pointed out in Chapter 3, almost all of them would have been disqualified, and for compelling reasons of bias, as jurors in a real trial of the President before the trial began, and doubly disqualified later because of the public statements and *ex parte* contacts that they made during the trial. And besides being the jurors in an impeachment trial, the Senators are also the judges (and both trial and appellate judges rolled into one), offices that few of them are qualified by temperament or experience to fill. A Senate trial is too close to popular as opposed to legal justice to be taken seriously as a process for determining facts. A finding by the Senate that the President had or had not committed the acts alleged in the articles of impeachment would be unreliable. It would be censure dressed up as adjudication.

CHAPTER 6

The *Kulturkampf*

Clinton has become a polarizing figure in American politics and culture as a result of the Lewinsky affair and its aftermath. I am particularly struck by how the "intelligentsia"—a word I'll use to denote highly educated people, in this country mainly academics and journalists, who write books or articles dealing with matters of social or political significance—became passionately divided over the question of impeachment and more broadly over the proper evaluation of the entire business.

It is important to distinguish polarization from disagreement. One should not be surprised that people disagree over how harshly to judge Clinton's behavior, and that of Starr and the other supporting players, and over whether impeachment was the proper response. These are difficult questions. What is surprising, or at least calls for explanation, is the *emotionality* of the disagreement. The tone in which the issue has been debated, and the recklessness with which many intelligent people, including many academics,[1] took sides passionately and dogmatically before it was possible to know what the facts were, their refusal to face the facts when they became known, their unwillingness to concede any merit to points made by opponents, their proneness to exaggeration, distortion, and oversimplification, and the sheer unreason demonstrated by so many of the people who became caught up in the public debate—all these were signs of the emotionality that the issue aroused.

---

[1] I give additional examples of academic "loss of cool" over the Clinton-Lewinsky mess in the next chapter.

So impassioned a polarization of public opinion regarding allegations of criminal and immoral behavior that are for the most part demonstrably true, yet denied, suggests an analogy to the Dreyfus case, though there the allegations were as demonstrably false, making Clinton's case the inverse of Dreyfus's.

The spectrum of public opinion about Clinton is broad. At one end is found the Clinton haters, and next to them the Religious Right or, as it used to be called, the Moral Majority. This group includes not only southern evangelical Protestants, the traditional core of the Religious Right, but also, by a slight stretch, conservative Catholics such as William Bennett and Richard John Neuhaus. Nearby are social conservatives of primarily secular bent (such as Robert Bork, Irving Kristol, and William Kristol, and the editorial-page writers of the *Wall Street Journal*), who nowadays are closely allied to the Religious Right; for most purposes, the Religious Right and the secular social conservatives can be lumped together as moralistic conservatives.[2] We also find in this part of the spectrum Republican congressional leaders, who pressed for impeachment partly for political gain and partly out of conviction. In the initial stages of the crisis, many journalists, editorial-page writers, and Common Cause–type "good government" reform advocates, not noted for partisanship[3] (unlike the *Wall Street Journal*'s editorial-page writers, who had been conducting a vendetta against Clinton since his inauguration),[4] joined the chorus demanding that Clinton resign or be

[2] For an unkind but penetrating anatomizing of this group, focusing naturally on the most extreme statements of its most extreme members, see Andrew Sullivan, "Going Down Screaming," *New York Times Magazine,* Oct. 11, 1998, p. 46. If they had a philosophical guru, it would be Alasdair MacIntyre, whose "soft antiliberalism" is caustically described in Stephen Holmes, *The Anatomy of Antiliberalism,* ch. 4 (1993). Of course there is quite a bit of space between MacIntyre and, say, Jerry Falwell; the group I am calling the moralistic conservatives is heterogeneous, and so my characterization of it is not accurate for all its members. I call them "moralistic conservatives" rather than "moral conservatives" because my interest is in attitudes, not behavior; it is well known that these often do not coincide.

[3] They were scandalized not only by Clinton's lies but also by his possibly culpable participation in campaign-finance irregularities during his reelection campaign in 1996. They later backed off from calling for his resignation or impeachment.

[4] There are now four volumes (*A Journal Briefing—Whitewater*) of editorials and editorial-page articles attacking Clinton, available for purchase from the *Wall Street Journal*. It is impossible to assess the soundness of the *Journal*'s charges. Some clearly are exaggerated and many are highly speculative, but others, even those unrelated to the Clinton-Lewinsky mess, may ultimately be proved correct. For a harsh but not un-

forced from office. At the other end of the spectrum could be found blacks,[5] feminists, Democrats, environmentalists, and the academic Left (ranging from "left liberals" who are slightly to the left of Clinton to Marxists and other radicals). I am painting with a broad brush, not only because there are overlaps among the various groups but also because not all members of each group subscribe to the group's dominant or defining views. But a crude taxonomy will suffice for my purposes.

I want to examine why these groups, these tendencies really, have lined up as they have, because this will provide a clue to the emotional intensity of the debate. Originally it seemed that the Republican congressional leaders had fanned the scandal flames purely for political advantage; for when the advantage seemed to evaporate with the November 1998 elections, they backed away. They had overplayed their hand, presumably through miscalculation rather than under the distracting pressure of strong emotion. And yet, partly perhaps in reaction to Clinton's continued stonewalling, the leadership pressed on to impeachment despite the palpable political risks.

The Clinton haters had formed up long before the Lewinsky scandal hit the press; it was just more grist for their mill. Still, the phenomenon of Clinton hating cries out for explanation. Some Clinton haters may be paranoid in the clinical sense. Rumors had long swirled around Clinton, and mentally unstable people are sometimes irresistibly and uncritically drawn to rumors about skullduggery in high places. Much Clinton hatred, however, blends insensibly into the moralistic conservatives' intense but certainly not insane antipathy toward Clinton.

Why conservatives should dislike Clinton so is a great mystery;[6] and part of the explanation is that not all do. Although moralistic conservatives get most of the media attention, probably a majority of American conservatives are libertarian rather than moralistic. They are closer to John Stuart Mill (whether they know it or not) than they are to William Buckley and Jerry Falwell. They support free markets and limited government. They want government to concentrate on national defense and the repression of serious crimes and to go easy on redis-

grounded assessment of the full range of Clinton's conduct, see Ann H. Coulter, *High Crimes and Misdemeanors: The Case against Bill Clinton* (1998).

[5]See Jay Nordlinger, "Clinton's Last Friends," *Weekly Standard*, Sept. 28, 1998, p. 12.

[6]See, for a brief but illuminating discussion of the puzzle, David Maraniss, *The Clinton Enigma: A Four-and-a-Half-Minute Speech Reveals This President's Entire Life* 92 (1998).

tributing income and wealth. They don't worry a lot about the "moral tone" of society and hence about homosexuality, abortion, pornography, and recreational drug use. They don't want either a socialist or a puritan commonwealth; they want a strong, prosperous, free society. These people have no reason to be violently antipathetic toward President Clinton. They don't agree with all his policies or appointments. They don't like his opposition to school vouchers, his cozying up to unions, or his continued support of racial preferences labeled "affirmative action." And they are beginning to worry that he may have a screw seriously loose. But they like his strong support of free trade, his reform of welfare, his success in balancing the budget, the tough line he takes on crime, his retention of Alan Greenspan as Chairman of the Federal Reserve Board, his appointment of Robert Rubin as Secretary of the Treasury, his unconcern with the enormous expansion of personal fortunes in the 1990s, his willingness to compromise with the congressional Republicans, his desire to reform entitlement programs, and most recently his preference for using annual federal budget surpluses mostly to reduce the national debt (the essence of his program to "save Social Security") rather than to fund new government programs. They like the way he has shifted the center of the political spectrum to the right. He has consolidated the Reagan revolution; no longer do you hear people calling the 1980s "the decade of greed" or decrying income inequality. The rental of the Lincoln Bedroom in the White House to wealthy campaign contributors opens a new front in the war for the commodification of everything, a libertarian project. Lately Clinton has been taking a very tough line on national defense. From the standpoint of policy, Clinton is pretty indistinguishable from a Nelson Rockfeller Republican, even a George Bush, Bob Dole, or Gerald Ford Republican. It is a little as if the Democratic Party had disappeared and the Republican Party had fissioned into a left (Nelson Rockefeller, William Weld) wing led by Clinton and a right (Dan Quayle, Jesse Helms) wing led by Trent Lott and Tom DeLay.

Libertarian conservatives remain wary of Clinton because they know he would have been happy to govern from the left—witness his socialistic health plan. But ever since the Republicans took control of Congress, after the 1994 midterm elections, that option has been denied Clinton; and with good grace, or at least considerable alacrity (some would say with an alacrity indicative of a lack of principles), he has tacked to the right. Libertarian conservatives doubt that President Bush in a second term, or a President Dole, would have been markedly to the right of Clinton on issues of importance to them. Some feel that Clinton's being a Democrat has actually enabled him to govern to the right of a Dole or a Bush; and some that his politics of inclusion, though largely symbolic, has value in maintaining social peace—that it has contributed to a long-overdue mainstreaming of blacks and other disaffected minorities. It is true that as soon as he was impeached, and accelerating with and after the 1999 State of the Union address delivered while the Senate trial was being conducted, the President shot off a veritable Gatling gun of expensive policy proposals, some of a socialist hue. But it was understood that he was merely throwing sand in the eyes of the public, that no ambitious socialistic proposal of a lame-duck President would be enacted by the Republican Congress.

Moralistic conservatives actually agree with libertarian conservatives on many issues;[7] otherwise the Republican Party would fly apart completely. In particular they agree on the importance of personal responsibility. They believe in free markets (though less enthusiastically than the libertarians), because they think it is right that people should shoulder responsibility for their own economic choices and performance. They believe, as do most libertarian conservatives, in strict enforcement of the criminal laws because they believe that criminals are morally responsible for their conduct and therefore answerable for its consequences. They believe, in short, that with rights come responsibilities. This belief, which incidentally need have no grounding in a metaphysics of "free will"[8]—which can be entirely pragmatic—creates a gulf between all conservatives, on the one hand, and liberals on the other, who tend to believe that people are not fully responsible for their economic successes or failures or fully culpable for their antisocial behavior. It is not only Clinton's illegalities that offend conservatives; it is his refusal to take responsibility for them—his insistence on being allowed to

[7]This is evident in the remarks of Norman Podhoretz in "Clinton, the Country, and the Political Culture: A Symposium," *Commentary,* Jan. 1999, pp. 20, 39–41. Podhoretz is a leading neoconservative, a group increasingly allied with the moralistic conservatives, and *Commentary* is the leading journal of the neoconservative movement. The symposium in which his remarks appear, along with those of a number of other neoconservatives and moralistic conservatives, is notable for its sobriety; one senses the chastening effect of the November 1998 elections.

[8]See, for example, W. V. Quine, "Things and Their Place in Theories," in Quine, *Theories and Things* 1, 11 (1981); Richard A. Posner, *The Problems of Jurisprudence* 171–179 (1990).

apologize and "move on" without having to pay a price for his irresponsibility, as if he were a child. Liberals rather like treating adults as children; that is what paternalism means, and liberal policies tend to be paternalistic.

But it is not the libertarian conservatives who are fierce on the subject of Clinton. Their hostility to him for his irresponsibility is tempered by a broad agreement with his policies. It is the moralistic conservatives who are fierce, and the reason is that they feel most intensely about just those issues on which Clinton differs with them: homosexuality, premarital and extramarital sex, feminism, and abortion.[9] Yet even these disagreements, disagreements that moralistic conservatives would be likely to have with any Democratic President, cannot explain the intensity of the hostility to Clinton of moralistic conservatives (and hence, by a process to be explained, the intensity of the support for him at the other end of the political spectrum). It is not what Clinton says or does, but what he is, that is the provocation. David Bell compares Clinton to Nixon in this respect:

> Each, in the eyes of the winning side in these ideological shifts [liberals, in the case of Nixon, who became the conservator of the Great Society, and conservatives, in the case of Clinton, who became the conservator of the Reagan revolution], nonetheless became the symbol of what was most despised about the losing side. To 1960s liberals, Nixon symbolized the dark side of the America of the 1950s: paranoid, resentful, parochial, untrustworthy, and mean. He was the alter ego of Joe McCarthy. To 1990s conservatives, Clinton symbolizes the dark side of the America of the 1960s: irresponsible, amoral, unpatriotic, untrustworthy, and profligate. He is the alter ego of Jane Fonda. In each case, the men's repeated ability to bounce back from adversity has only intensified the hatred.[10]

Clinton is part of the generation of the 1960s. He smoked marijuana as a student. He dodged the draft during the Vietnam War. He's an adulterer. He's a Yale Law School wiseguy. He lacks *gravitas;* he even

---

[9]The difference can be given a name: John Stuart Mill. He is anathema to moral conservatives. See, for example, Robert H. Bork, *Slouching towards Gomorrah: Modern Liberalism and American Decline* 59–61 (1996).

[10]David A. Bell, "Richard Milhous Clinton," *New Republic,* Jan. 18, 1999, p. 18. See also Stephen Skowronek, "President Clinton and the Risks of 'Third-Way' Politics," *Extensions,* Spring 1996, p. 10, discussed more fully below.

talks about his *underwear* in public. He is Hollywood-star-struck. He is "politically correct" and appoints openly gay men and lesbians to high federal office. His wife is a strong, assertive professional woman who makes him look weak. Now he tops it all off with "deviant" sex in the White House office complex and a cascade of lies to cover it up. To the moralistic Right he is a carnivalesque roisterer, a scapegrace, a Prince of Disorder, a value-free postmodernist—and such an accomplished con artist that the American people can't find it in their hearts to hate him for his hateful acts. To anyone whose sense of morality and decorum assumed its permanent form before 1968 and who thinks the nation has undergone a precipitous moral decline since, this man is a scandal whatever his policies.[11]

Writing presciently in 1996, the political scientist Stephen Skowronek grouped Clinton together with Nixon and Woodrow Wilson as exemplars of "third-way politics."[12] "Third-way leaders like Clinton have sought . . . to occupy a new middle ground largely defined by their opponents." Because they "threaten to appropriate much of the field of action carved out by their opponents and to attract disaffected elements within the dominant coalition," the political contest is "framed by the president's purposeful blurring of received identities and his opponents' stake in keeping those established identities intact" (p. 11). It is therefore in the nature of "third-way politics" to raise questions about a President's "authenticity and credibility" and sometimes, because of the precariousness of the third-way President's balancing act, to "bring [about] a colossal collapse of presidential authority" (p. 12). Skowronek instances Andrew Johnson, Wilson, and Nixon; now he can add Clinton. Because of these questions of authenticity and credibility, because "third-way programs are apt to be portrayed as clever tricks masking rear-guard resistance to real reform," and because opponents therefore seek "some account of how a man could use the presidency to deny the truth about himself and pose as something else," "no asset will prove more valuable to incumbents than an unimpeachable character" (pp. 13–14)—a lesson Clinton learned too late.

The sharpest difference between libertarian and moralistic conservatives is that, at present anyway, the former are optimistic and the latter pessimistic. The libertarians revel in the fall of communism, the

[11]See, for example, Bork, note 9 above, at 341.
[12]Skowronek, note 10 above.

triumph of the free market, the rush of prosperity, the technological revolution, and the abatement of our social problems. For moralistic conservatives, the fall of communism is a downer, because by depriving us of a diabolical enemy it has made us soft; the abatement of our social problems is a meaningless blip; wealth and technology are sapping our moral values. "The decline runs across our entire culture . . . As we approach its desolate and sordid precincts, the pessimism of the intellect tells us that Gomorrah is our probable destination."[13] Since it would cheer up the people who think this way to see Clinton impeached, it becomes easier to understand the ferocity of the Left's resistance to impeachment.

The hatred of moralistic conservatives for Clinton is uncannily mirrored by the love of many (though probably not most) liberals for him. This is a new thing, at least in scale and intensity. Until the Lewinsky scandal broke, many liberals were either tepid about Clinton or actually disliked him. And this for the same reasons that many libertarian conservatives rather liked him—his centrist, broadly libertarian policies and major appointments. Blacks and feminists liked him a lot, mainly I think because of his skill in practicing a politics of inclusion that involves combining empathetic rhetoric with high-profile appointments.[14] It is a politics that, not incidentally, favors the better-off, more articulate, and politically more active members of the favored interest group, for it is they who get to hobnob with the President and receive prestigious appointments. Some academic liberals liked Clinton because of his intelligence and his genuine interest in issues of policy. Others—the mirror image of the moralistic conservatives—liked him because he stands for the kind of mild bohemianism which is so common a style of life in American universities, although his private behavior with women is more that of an old-fashioned philanderer. The Democratic establishment, however, was distinctly cool to Clinton because of his lack of commitment to the traditional liberal pieties and his evident

---

[13]Bork, note 9 above, at 342–343. The "desolate and sordid precincts" are apparently "America's intellectual and moral capital" after its "torching" by "the barbarians of modern liberalism." Id. Bork later wrote that if Clinton was not removed from office, "it will be a clear sign that we have turned a corner, that American morality, including but not limited to our political morality, is in free fall." Robert H. Bork, "Counting the Costs of Clintonism," *American Spectator,* Nov. 1998, p. 55.

[14]And he has always had a remarkable rapport with blacks. See, for example, David Maraniss, *First in His Class: The Biography of Bill Clinton* 293–294 (1995).

contentment with the modus vivendi that he had worked out with congressional Republicans, leaving congressional Democrats and such major constituent groups as the labor unions out in the cold.

As the Independent Counsel's investigation of the criminal aftermath of Clinton's affair with Lewinsky gathered steam and merged with Republican calls for impeachment, a remarkable unification and intensification of Clinton's support occurred. Almost all shades of liberal and left opinion rallied to his defense,[15] often losing all sense of proportion and in the process producing a weird convergence between liberal and conservative characterizations of what was at stake in Clinton's struggle to survive. For David Frum, moralistic conservative, "what's at stake in the Lewinsky scandal . . . [is] the central dogma of the baby boomers: the belief that sex, so long as it's consensual, ought never to be subject to moral scrutiny at all."[16] From the other side of the aisle we hear Arthur Schlesinger, Jr., intoning: "All the Independent Counsel's charges thus far derive entirely from a President's lies about his own sex life . . . Lying about one's sex life is not a monstrous crime . . . Gentlemen always lie about their sex lives. Only a cad tells the truth about his love affairs."[17] For Frum, Clinton is a sexual immoralist; for Schlesinger, he is a gentleman. He is neither; he is *l'homme moyen sensuel.*

Both Frum and Schlesinger allowed their disagreement over sexual morality to obscure the conduct at issue, conduct to which sex is almost incidental.

> The sex was little but the lies were big. As was his [Clinton's] disrespect for, and damage to, the rule of law and a judicial process which depends for its effective functioning upon truthful testimony of witnesses. In rapid succession came repeated lying in court, encouraging others to join and support his lies, perjury and subornation of perjury; obstruction of jus-

[15]For a rare exception—a sharp attack on Clinton from what passes as the far Left today, published in, of all places, the *Wall Street Journal*—see Patrick H. Caddell and Marc Cooper, "The Death of Liberal Outrage," *Wall Street Journal,* Dec. 23, 1998, p. A14. See also Walter Shapiro, "Blind Faith: Why Liberals Stick with Clinton," *New Republic,* Feb. 1, 1999, pp. 12, 13, asking why "liberals [have] rushed to mortgage their own integrity in their zealous defense of Clinton's loathsome legalisms," and remarking that "there is something that smacks of Bonapartism in the Democrats' confusion of personal fealty with political principle . . . Democrats insist on lionizing a president who is, at his core, an old-style moderate Republican."

[16]David Frum, "A Generation on Trial," *Weekly Standard,* Feb. 16, 1998, pp. 19, 23.

[17]Arthur Schlesinger, Jr., "The Background and History of Impeachment," statement before the House Judiciary Committee, Nov. 9, 1998.

tice; use of government officials and employees under his direction—his personal secretary and the White House press officer and other staff aides, members of the Cabinet and Congress—all paid by the taxpayers—to spread and support his lies; his casual contempt for judicial oaths; his frivolous and unprecedented invocation of executive privilege to shield subordinates from giving truthful testimony in court; his use of the presidential "bully pulpit" to hoodwink the American people; the scorched-earth, take-no-prisoners attack on his accusers to divert attention from his misdeeds in a desperate and unlawful, but in the end unsuccessful, effort to conceal the embarrassing escapades in the Oval Office.[18]

That is the conduct on which the debate should have focused. But if the core of the opposition to Clinton is not that he is a liar or even a criminal (for the Right displayed little indignation over the crimes committed by participants in the Iran-Contra affair),[19] but that his personal conduct and attitudes are revolting, then the claim of his defenders to be warding off a puritan assault on sexual liberty cannot be dismissed as sheer demagoguery.

Writing in the *Times Literary Supplement* in the summer of 1998, the liberal philosopher Thomas Nagel denounced "the shameful farce now being played out in Washington." He singled out for criticism "the sinister and obsessionally puritanical Starr," "the lurid and poisonous Linda Tripp," and "the fetishistic and infantile Monica Lewinsky."[20] These characterizations, for which no proof is or, save possibly in the case of Linda Tripp,[21] could be offered, introduce an article on privacy

[18]Philip Elman, "An Argument for Lowering Voices—Clinton's 'Private Moral Wrongs' and Starr's 'Torquemada Inquisition' " 3 (Oct. 15, 1998, unpublished). Elman, now retired, was formerly an assistant to the Solicitor General, member of the Federal Trade Commission (appointed and reappointed by Kennedy), law professor, and Washington lawyer.

[19]This is to put it mildly, when one considers Henry Hyde's public defense of Oliver North's obstructions of justice (quoted against him during the Clinton impeachment proceeding), President Bush's pardon of Casper Weinberger, and the Republican condemnation of Independent Counsel Lawrence Walsh's rule of law denunciations of the participants in the affair and its cover-up. See Lawrence E. Walsh, *Final Report of the Independent Counsel for Iran/Contra Matters,* vol. 1: *Investigations and Prosecutions* 559–566 (Aug. 4, 1993).

[20]Thomas Nagel, "The Shredding of Public Privacy: Reflections on Recent Events in Washington," *Times Literary Supplement,* Aug. 14, 1998, p. 15.

[21]Though when Nagel characterized her as "lurid and poisonous," not enough of the

excerpted from a much longer article that Nagel had published in an academic journal before the Clinton-Lewinsky affair came to light.[22] In that article, as in the *Times Literary Supplement* condensation, Nagel argues unexceptionably that people are entitled to a private sex life. But by juxtaposing the argument with references to the investigation of the Clinton-Lewinsky affair, Nagel, like Frum, like Schlesinger, draws attention away from the issue that precipitated the investigation and the impeachment inquiry: the issue of obstruction of justice. Nagel forgets, moreover, an important point that he had made in the longer article. This is that privacy is a duty as well as a right. The precondition of freedom to behave unconventionally in private is to avoid flaunting one's unconventionality; flaunting makes it a public issue (pp. 12–17, 26–30). Clinton did not want his affair with Lewinsky to become public. But he took an enormous risk that it would. The risk materialized and the result, as Nagel would have predicted, was to create a public issue of what Nagel rightly argues should be private conduct.

American sexual morality is pluralistic. An enormous variety of attitudes toward adultery, oral sex, phone sex, sex between a young woman and a middle-aged man, between employee and employer, co-exist; and they coexist in part because of tacit agreement that these are (the last least securely) private matters. By forcing these attitudes into articulate competition, Clinton precipitated the rancorous *Kulturkampf* that is the subject of this chapter. One would expect Nagel to call him to account for this, and also to attempt to reconcile his own condemnation of the Clinton-Lewinsky investigation with his statement in the longer article that "it is a good thing that sexual coercion of an employee or a student should be legally actionable" (p. 27). Paula Jones was charging sexual coercion by an employer, and Clinton resorted to illegal tactics to thwart her effort to prove it. How can Nagel condone those tactics while approving sexual harassment litigation?

Kant famously took a very hard line both against lying[23] and in favor

---

tapes of her conversations with Monica Lewinsky had been published to sustain the characterization.

[22]Thomas Nagel, "Concealment and Exposure," 27 *Philosophy and Public Affairs* 3 (1998).

[23]For example, "To be truthful (honest) in all declarations is, therefore, a sacred and unconditionally commanding law of reason that admits of no expediency whatsoever." Immanuel Kant, "On a Supposed Right to Lie Because of Philanthropic Concerns," in Kant, *Grounding for the Metaphysics of Morals with On a Supposed Right to Lie Because of Philanthropic Concerns* 63, 65 (James W. Ellington trans., 3d ed. 1993). For

of compliance with legal norms,[24] and these positions retain a following in modern philosophy.[25] I would have expected a moral philosopher like Nagel, writing about a lying scofflaw of a President, either to criticize the President forthrightly or to explain why lying and illegality aren't serious moral lapses either generally or in the case of President Clinton. I would have expected Nagel to reflect on the validity and pertinence of the observation by the philosopher Sissela Bok that "few lies are solitary ones . . . More and more lies may come to be needed; the liar always has more mending to do . . . The sheer energy the liar has to devote to shoring them up is energy the honest man can dispose of freely."[26]

Neither Nagel nor Schlesinger argues that sexual privacy is so transcendent a value that it should be accorded an absolute privilege in the courts. If it were, the tort of sexual harassment would have to be abolished, and the laws governing rape, incest, paternity, child pornography, child molestation, spousal abuse, military and prison discipline, and the transmission of sexually transmitted diseases curtailed. Judge Wright in the Paula Jones case may have made a mistake in allowing Clinton to be questioned about Monica Lewinsky, but she had the difficult task of balancing a claim of sexual privacy against a claim of sexual harassment. All sorts of bad things happen in private.

What is more worrisome to many people is the erosion of privacy by technology that the investigation of Clinton dramatized. Without tape recordings and DNA tests, without television and the Internet, without e-mail messages that are difficult to erase, the world would not have become intimate with the details not only of President Clinton's sex life but also of Monica Lewinsky's sex life and that of her friends and ex-lovers. People are afraid of the combination of old-fashioned Com-

---

a possible qualification, misunderstood however by Clinton's defenders, see the next chapter.

[24]"The moral requirement of obedience to actually existing law, Kant concluded, is 'absolute.' " Jeremy Waldron, "Kant's Legal Positivism," 109 *Harvard Law Review* 1535, 1545 (1996).

[25]On lying, see, for example, Sissela Bok, *Lying: Moral Choice in Public and Private Life* (1978) (though she does not go as far as Kant). On compliance with legal norms, see, for example, Jürgen Habermas, *Between Facts and Norms: Contributions to a Discourse Theory of Law and Democracy* (1996); Ernest J. Weinrib, "Law as a Kantian Idea of Reason," 87 *Columbia Law Review* 472 (1987).

[26]Bok, note 25 above, at 25.

stockery with new-fangled electronics. (At the same time, they are rightly fearful of the dangerous privacy that the Internet enables for the hatching of schemes of violence.)

If the Right had been content to criticize Clinton's conduct, even his sexual conduct, the Left would not have reacted so fiercely. The Right wished instead to label and condemn him as a representative of a style of life that is common to many liberal academics, urban sophisticates, and unregenerate members of the generation of the 1960s. This made the attack of the Right on Clinton a personal attack on *them,* a questioning of their legitimacy, their entitlement to think of themselves as full citizens and real Americans. It was not just the self-identified Left that reacted this way to the campaign to impeach Clinton. Black people who watched southern Congressmen denouncing Clinton's sexual immorality were reminded of a long history of white criticism of blacks as sexually incontinent. Two blacks, Vernon Jordan and Betty Currie, figured prominently as implied targets of Starr's investigation. Homosexuals were alarmed to see members of Congress thundering sexual orthodoxy from political pulpits. And as the members of these groups locked arms in defense of Clinton, they confirmed the worst fears of the moralistic conservatives by making him appear continuous with the homosexuals, the radical feminists, the Hollywood bohemians, the libertines; and so the conflict escalated in intensity.

It is bracing to have an enemy. Indeed, without an enemy to inspire enough fear to submerge differences on lesser issues, it is difficult to hold a coalition together. The Right used to have communism to rally against. Communism has died, and Clinton has coopted a number of traditional conservative issues, such as capital punishment, welfare reform, sound money, a balanced budget, entitlement reform, and now a quick-on-the-trigger military posture that has arguably led to repeated violations of the War Powers Resolution[27]—that Democratic icon that Republicans loved to denounce during Republican Presidencies and that Democrats accused Presidents Reagan and Bush of repeatedly violating.

All that remains, in light of Clinton's flagrant appropriation of Republican policies, to fill the indispensable role of the enemy is—Clinton himself. His conduct in the Lewinsky matter has made him a plausible

---

[27]50 U.S.C. §§ 1541–1548. See generally John H. Ely, *War and Responsibility: Constitutional Lessons of Vietnam and Its Aftermath* (1994); Harold Hongju Koh, *The National Security Constitution: Sharing Power after the Iran-Contra Affair* (1990).

personification of a nameless, insidious, vaguely but unmistakably left-ist threat to American values. The Left, demoralized by the triumph of capitalism and the discrediting of big government, now unites against a deliciously sinister menace—the vast right-wing conspiracy that is bent on doing in Clinton en route to restoring sexual repression and engineering a social counterrevolution that will take us back to the 1950s. That is, indeed, where some moralistic conservatives would like to take us: "It would be difficult to contend that, the end of racial segregation aside, American culture today is as healthy as the culture of the 1950s."[28]

The enemy of my enemy is my friend. Feminists know that the Right doesn't mean it when it says that victims of alleged sexual harassment such as Paula Jones deserve a legal remedy. Where was the Right when Anita Hill accused Clarence Thomas of sexual harassment? The Right is the feminists' enemy, the American Taliban. Clinton is the enemy's enemy. He is also a dependable ally of the feminists except when it comes to his personal behavior, since sex with a subordinate is on the list of behaviors that feminists want to interdict. Like any politician, the feminist politician prefers inconsistency to defeat.[29] And radical feminists could take comfort in the role reversal in Clinton's affair with Lewinsky (with Clinton playing the pursued, the coy "girl" who refuses the "boy's"—Lewinsky's—repeated importunings to "go all the way"), in his decentering of vaginal intercourse, and in his implicit endorse-ment of the dildo (in the cigar incident).

There is also a "choice of evils" question. Feminists and union leaders may not have been—may still not be—enthusiastic about Clinton. But the choice they saw with the 1998 midterm elections approaching was between Clinton and a Republican landslide. And if they saved him maybe he would pay them back, though he is not famous for expressing gratitude. In January 1998, when the scandal first broke, they might have preferred a quick exit by Clinton, giving Vice President Al Gore a chance to solidify his position in advance of the Presidential election in 2000. But as the months wore on, it became clear that resignation or impeachment held such danger for Gore (because he is so closely paired

---

[28]Bork, note 9 above, at 342.

[29]Some feminists who are not politicians have been forthright in condemning the Pres-ident for lying under oath. See, for example, Jean Bethke Elshtain, "Going Public," *New Republic,* March 23, 1998, p. 12; Linda Silberman, Letter to the Editor, *New York Times* (late ed.), Aug. 24, 1998, p. A16.

with Clinton in the public mind) and the Democrats that the only sensible choice was to fight wholeheartedly for Clinton's survival.

Realpolitik has its risks. Statements by feminists belittling Clinton's sexual involvement with a subordinate and his resort to perjury and other obstructions of justice in fending off a suit for sexual harassment will be thrown back at feminists by future politicians accused of similar wrongdoing, and perhaps by defendants in run-of-the-mill sexual harassment cases. Feminists will be ridiculed for having been allied, however temporarily and adventitiously, with Larry Flynt. They will be—they are being—accused of confusing gender equality with class privilege.[30] To the extent that the Left is made to seem cynical and opportunistic by supporting Clinton, its moral authority will erode.[31] To the extent that it seeks to deflect charges of cynicism by offering neutral reasons for its defense of Clinton, for example that "boys will be boys" or that protecting privacy is more important than stamping out sexual harassment in the workplace, the Left may be illustrating Habermas's dictum that "concealing publicly indefensible interests behind pretended moral or ethical reasons necessitates self-bindings that . . . lead to the inclusion of others' interests,"[32] the others here being the boys.[33]

From the beginning, the main line of defense for Clinton was that the scandal and the ensuing investigation by the Independent Counsel were just about sex. They were not; but the point was obscured by the fact that conservatives like David Frum wrote that Clinton's attitude toward sex was indeed the issue, that the Republican leaders in Congress were understood to be threatening impeachment because they

---

[30]"Clinton has done his illegal best to ensure that one law applies to 'white trailer trash' like Jones and another to the self-conceived Überclass represented by the Friends of Bill and Hillary . . . When Paula Jones and her conservative lawyers had the effrontery to assume that they, too, might use the same tactics—those perfected by the Friends of Bill and Hillary for the sake of 'deserving' women—it became clear that, in the view of the Clinton elites, this law was reserved exclusively for them—for Jones's betters—and their political clients." Kenneth Anderson, "The American Inquisition: How the Religious Right and the Secular Left Collude in the Growth of the Prosecutorial State," *Times Literary Supplement,* Jan. 29, 1999, p. 12.

[31]As Caddell and Cooper, note 15 above, put it, "The last supper of his [Clinton's] presidency is being paid for with the bankrupting of the liberal moral treasury."

[32]Habermas, note 25 above, at 340.

[33]See Peter Beinart, "Private Matters: How the Personal Became Political," *New Republic,* Feb. 15, 1999, pp. 21, 22–23.

thought it would play well with their morally conservative constituents, and that the Starr Report place great emphasis on the details of Clinton's sexual contacts with Lewinsky. Nowadays virtually the only issues (other than euthanasia) that separate religious enthusiasts from people who are indifferent to religion are issues relating to sex, and specifically the propriety of abortion, homosexuality, fornication, adultery, and pornography. Despite Clinton's ostentatious religiosity, his now well-publicized extramarital sexual escapades have aligned him, in the minds of the most intensely religious people in this country, with the enemies of religion. This in turn has made people who think of themselves as being a little more like Clinton (or Mrs. Clinton) than like Jerry Falwell or Trent Lott feel that the pursuit of Clinton by Starr and the congressional Republicans had the flavor of a witch hunt—while for the pursuers it had the flavor of a crusade.

Another thing that helps to explain the polarization of opinion over Clinton is the difficulty people have in liking and disliking the same person (or group, or movement) at the same time. The enemy of my enemy who is therefore my friend need not be my *good* friend, as Churchill had no difficulty seeing when he found himelf allied with Stalin. But this kind of ambivalence is difficult for many people to sustain, especially in emotional settings, such as war, or the political struggles that war resembles (more on that resemblance in the next chapter). It is difficult to dislike Clinton *and* the Religious Right, because if you dislike the latter *very* much, you will find it hard not to feel gratitude and affection toward Clinton for fighting with all his might to deny them victory. Some people have a related difficulty of separating Clinton's executive from his exemplary moral characteristics. They can't really see him as a Jekyll and Hyde figure; they want him to be all one or all the other,[34] and since they disagree on which he is, they find themselves in mutually uncomprehending warring camps. One is put in mind of the posthumous division of another complex political figure, John F. Kennedy, into two inconsistent symbols:

---

[34]George Orwell pointed to a corresponding problem in art: "One ought to be able to hold in one's head simultaneously the two facts that [Salvador] Dali is a good draughtsman and a disgusting human being. The one does not invalidate or, in a sense, affect the other." "Benefit of Clergy: Some Notes on Salvador Dali," in *The Collected Essays, Journalism and Letters of George Orwell*, vol. 3: *As I Please, 1943–1945* 156, 161 (Sonia Orwell and Ian Angus eds. 1968). In making this argument, Orwell was swimming upstream.

To those who yearn for a new age of public activism and commitment, the heroic Kennedy remains a bright and beckoning symbol of the world they have lost. But to many others, disillusioned with idealism and mission and, above all, active government, Kennedy has become a symbol of a heedless, action-oriented impetuosity that led the nation into a series of catastrophes and frustrations from which it has not yet wholly recovered.[35]

Recent studies of signaling and social norms help to explain the rapidity and intensity with which the nation became polarized over the Clinton-Lewinsky affair.[36] Moralistic conservatives seized on the affair to signal their rejection of adultery, lying, lawbreaking, and other forms of moral laxity. That the President should have exhibited such behavior was the clearest sign yet of the moral degeneracy that these conservatives believed was engulfing the country, and so by denouncing the President they were sending a signal of enormous strength and clarity. Any like-thinking person could be expected to signify agreement; anyone who failed to do so would invite suspicion of being morally lax. No doubt the signalers hoped that, much as with appeals to patriotic symbols such as the American flag, even people who did not in their heart of hearts think that ill of adultery, lying, and lawbreaking would signal agreement lest they be ostracized as dishonest, immoral, and untrustworthy. The result would be an impression of unanimity, which would magnify the political strength of the conservative movement. But it turned out that many people were concerned that, just as patriotic appeals had sometimes led to jingoism and the stifling of dissent, the denunciation of moral laxity in the specific forms displayed by President Clinton might lead to the adoption of a much longer list of moral "reforms" that would leave little room for dissenters from the moral orthodoxy of the Religious Right. The norm entrepreneurs among the people who were worried about this possibility therefore propagated a contrary signal, that of liberalism or tolerance. Like-thinking people flocked to signify their assent lest they be taken to be puritanical, rigorist, extreme, and so, again, untrustworthy. The country became divided into camps, each seeming more homogeneous than it really was,

---

[35] Alan Brinkley, *Liberalism and Its Discontents* 221 (1998).

[36] See, for example, Timur Kuran, "Ethnic Norms and Their Transformation through Reputational Cascades," 27 *Journal of Legal Studies* 623 (1998); Eric A. Posner, "Symbols, Signals, and Social Norms in Politics and the Law," 27 *Journal of Legal Studies* 765 (1998).

the two seeming farther apart than they really were. The *reductio ad absurdum* was Alan Dershowitz's statement that "a vote against impeachment is not a vote for Bill Clinton. It is a vote against bigotry. It's a vote against fundamentalism. It's a vote against anti-environmentalism. It's a vote against the right-to-life movement."[37]

The competing signals induced people to choose sides—to stand up and be counted—because failure to do so might invite ostracism by both sides in the dispute. If you leaned toward moral conservativism, and especially if many of your personal or professional associations were with hard-core moralistic conservatives, you would hesitate to express whatever reservations you felt about anathematizing Clinton, because your hesitations would mark you as untrustworthy by the group that you valued belonging to. If you were a member of the liberal intelligentsia, you would hesitate to express whatever reservations you might feel about letting Clinton off lightly because that would mark you among the members of your reference group as untrustworthy.[38] For example, they might think you insensitive to the rights of homosexuals, some of whom feel that if Clinton goes they may be next on the Right's hit list. And thinking this, your fellow liberals would have less regard for you and as a result your transactional or associational opportunities might suffer. In this fashion, a number of people who might have been more comfortable in the middle were tugged toward one pole or the other in order to preserve the trust of the members of their social or professional set.

Once you take a position, moreover, you are apt to feel a sense of commitment to it. Cognitive psychologists affix the label "confirmation bias" to the tendency to interpret subsequent evidence bearing on a controversy as supportive of the position to which at first you were only tentatively committed.[39] As the supportive evidence accumulates, the commitment rigidifies. Mounting conviction makes the position of opponents increasingly difficult to accept as held in good faith. Disagreement becomes antagonism. The opponents stop listening to each other. At this point the debate has become polarized, and the debaters have become partisans.

[37]Alan Dershowitz on *Rivera Live*, CNBC News Transcripts, Dec. 14, 1998.

[38]On the clumpiness and conformism of intellectuals, especially academic ones, see Richard A. Posner, *The Problematics of Moral and Legal Theory* 75–81, 90 (1999).

[39]See Matthew Rabin, "Psychology and Economics, 36 *Journal of Economic Literature* 11, 26–28 (1998), and references cited there.

———————•———————

CHAPTER 7

Lessons for the Future

The year-long politico-legal struggle that welled out of President Clinton's affair with Monica Lewinsky is a potentially rich source of insights about the present and lessons for the future. Some I have mentioned already, such as the change that the crisis has revealed in Americans' conception of political leadership and in the forms of political combat, and the need of both houses of Congress for sensible and detailed rules to govern impeachment proceedings. I focus in this chapter on two other points, which turn out to be related to each other. One is the inadequacy of certain kinds of professional thinking to deal with novel issues of social policy—indeed with novelty, period. The other is the unpredictability of struggle—of war above all but in this case of a political struggle isomorphic with war.

The Failure of Legal Reasoning

Three kinds of professional thinking or practice have been shown up as failures. One is the kind of narrowly "legalistic" reasoning that the current Supreme Court employs in deciding even politically momentous cases. The pertinent examples are the two cases—*Morrison v. Olson,*[1] upholding the independent counsel law, and *Clinton v. Jones,*[2] allowing Paula Jones's suit against Clinton to go ahead while Clinton was still in office—that enabled Clinton's affair with Lewinsky to mushroom

[1] 487 U.S. 654 (1988).
[2] 117 S. Ct. 1636 (1997).

into a political crisis. The second body of professional thinking that the crisis has shown up is moral, political, and legal theory as deployed by "public intellectuals," a category that includes those law school professors and law school deans who speak out on current issues. Third is legal thinking at the practice as distinct from the academic level.

The investigation and everything that followed from it had many causes, notably the sexual affair itself and Clinton's failure to settle the Paula Jones case in 1997. One other cause, for sure, was the Supreme Court's decision to allow the Paula Jones case to go forward. Clinton's lawyers had argued that all proceedings in it should be suspended until he left office. Had this argument prevailed, Lewinsky would not have been brought into the Paula Jones suit until the year 2001 and there would have been no occasion for President Clinton to obstruct justice while he was President.

It is less certain that the Supreme Court's decision upholding the constitutionality of the independent counsel law played a causal role in the investigation. The law had expired when Robert Fiske was appointed independent counsel. Had the law not been reenacted, he would have remained the independent counsel. The question then becomes whether, like Starr, he would have sought to expand his investigation of Whitewater to cover Clinton's lying under oath and related misconduct in the Paula Jones case, or, if not, whether another independent counsel would have been appointed to do so and would have followed essentially the course that Starr followed. For the reasons that I gave in Chapter 2, it is unlikely that investigation of Clinton's affair with Lewinsky by an independent counsel could have been averted. But suppose that the independent counsel law had been invalidated back in 1988, the date of the *Morrison* decision, or at least that the Court had made clear that it was not passing on the constitutionality of applying the law to the President. Then Attorney General Janet Reno might not have appointed an independent counsel to investigate Clinton's involvement in Whitewater, a matter involving alleged wrongdoing many years before Clinton became President. Although the independent counsel law had expired when Reno appointed Fiske, it was expected to be, and soon was, reenacted, and the expectation may have played a decisive role in her decision to appoint an independent counsel. Had there been no Whitewater independent counsel, Linda Tripp would have been less likely to disclose her tapes, given the risk she faced of being prosecuted for violating state law in making them. Even if she would have handed them over to the Justice Department (or to Paula Jones's lawyers, who might have handed them over to the Department), the Attorney General might have declined either to appoint an independent counsel to investigate a matter seemingly so remote from the President's official conduct or even to conduct an investigation "in house." And if the Department had done such an investigation, it would have been unlikely to do so as assiduously and pertinaciously as an independent counsel or to refer the results of its investigation to the House of Representatives for possible impeachment.

Even if an investigation of the Clinton-Lewinsky mess by an independent counsel was inevitable with or without an independent counsel law, the ensuing ordeal might have been less acute had there been no law. Although designed to give independent counsels more credibility than prosecutors employed or appointed by the Department of Justice, the law has had the effect, at least in the case of Starr's investigation of President Clinton, of giving them less credibility. Starr was seen as an agent of a judiciary that is politically hostile to Clinton, in much the same way that Federalist judges like Samuel Chase were seen (correctly, as it happened) to be politically hostile to President Jefferson. Fiske, owing his appointment solely to Clinton's Attorney General, and, though a Republican, not as closely identified with the previous Republican Administration as Starr, and with no ties, direct or indirect, to Paula Jones's lawyers, would not have labored under the same suspicion of being out to "get" the President.

The fact that an independent counsel was appointed at a time when the independent counsel law was not in effect is the first clue that there is something wrong with that law, first enacted in 1978.[3] There is a long history of independent counsels, that is, of nongovernment lawyers being hired by the Department of Justice to investigate government officials because the Department itself would have a conflict of interest.[4] When a credible accusation of serious misconduct is leveled at senior officials of the executive branch, the Department comes under political pressure to take measures to assure the public that the accusation will

---

[3]Title VI of the Ethics in Government Act of 1978, 28 U.S.C. §§ 591–599. The current version of Title VI was enacted in 1994; for a history and summary of Title VI, see (besides the opinions in the *Morrison* case) Niles L. Godes and Ty E. Howard, "Independent Counsel Investigations," 35 *American Criminal Law Review* 875 (1998).

[4]This history is recounted in Donald C. Smaltz, "The Independent Counsel: A View from Inside," 86 *Georgetown Law Journal* 2307, 2311–2321 (1998).

be investigated thoroughly.[5] It was pressure of this sort that led to the appointment of independent counsels (first Archibald Cox and then Leon Jaworski) to investigate Nixon in connection with the Watergate affair. And Nixon was brought down. In light of this dénouement, it is puzzling that Congress thought it necessary to enact an independent counsel law. Maybe Benjamin Ginsberg and Martin Shefter are right that it was a Democratic initiative to shift power from a Presidency expected to be durably Republican (though the law was enacted while a Democrat was President) to a Congress expected to be durably Democratic.[6]

The law requires the appointment of an independent counsel whenever there are reasonable grounds to believe that a senior official of the executive branch may have violated a federal criminal statute; shifts the power to pick the independent counsel from the Attorney General to the judiciary; forbids the Attorney General to fire an independent counsel without cause; and, as we know, requires the independent counsel to inform the House of Representatives of any substantial and credible evidence of a ground for impeaching the President. The law led to a big increase in the number of independent counsel appointments, resulting in many convictions but often of offenses that an ordinary prosecutor, operating under a budget constraint, would have overlooked because they were minor or difficult to prove. Until the appointment of Fiske to investigate Clinton's involvement in Whitewater crimes, no independent counsel had been appointed specifically to investigate a President, although an independent counsel's investigation of the Iran-Contra affair had brushed President Reagan.

MORRISON V. OLSON

The *Morrison* case grew out of an investigation by Independent Counsel Alexia Morrison of an assistant attorney general, Theodore Olson, in

---

[5]Though, to repeat an earlier point, the pressure on Attorney General Reno to appoint an independent counsel to investigate the Whitewater matter may have stemmed in part from expectations that the independent counsel law would soon be reenacted.

[6]Benjamin Ginsberg and Martin Shefter, *Politics by Other Means: The Declining Importance of Elections in America* 28–29 (1990). Not that Congress would appoint or control the independent counsel. But it could feed charges against the President or his appointees to the independent counsel with greater confidence that they would be followed up, rather than bottled up in the office of the Attorney General, himself (or herself) a Presidential appointee.

the Reagan Justice Department. The Court's opinion, written by Chief Justice Rehnquist, is notably dry and legalistic. After the sort of preliminaries that pad out most judicial opinions, the Court asks whether placing the power of appointing independent counsels in the judiciary violates the provision of the Constitution that vests the power to appoint executive branch officials in the President.[7] The provision allows Congress to vest the power to appoint "inferior Officers" in the courts rather than in the President, and so the question becomes whether an independent counsel is an inferior officer. The Court answers "yes" because an independent counsel exercises a limited jurisdiction and can be removed by the Attorney General[8] and because there is nothing incongruous about judges' appointing prosecutors since judges know a lot about prosecution. The Court next considers whether the independent counsel law might violate Article III of the Constitution, the judiciary article, by giving nonjudicial functions to the judiciary other than the appointive power itself, which the Court had just ruled was authorized by the appointments clause of Article II. The Court answers "no," since the other powers given to the judiciary in relation to the independent counsel are minor.

Next the Court asks whether the independent counsel law infringes Article II's grant to the President of the power to take care that the laws be faithfully executed, by preventing him (or his Attorney General) from firing an independent counsel at will. The answer given is again "no," because the President can fire an independent counsel for cause, and cause would include the independent counsel's careless or faithless execution of the independent counsel law or of the laws whose possible violation he was investigating. Finally, the Court asks whether the law upsets the balance of powers among the branches of the federal government, either by being a congressional "power grab" or by enabling the judiciary to usurp executive functions. The Court answers "no" to both questions. The law is not a congressional power grab, because it delegates power to the independent counsel rather than vesting investigative or enforcement powers in Congress. And it avoids judicial usurpation of executive functions by strictly limiting the responsibilities that it assigns to the judiciary.

The lone dissent, by Justice Scalia, argues that the independent coun-

---

[7] U.S. Const., art. II, § 2, cl. 2.
[8] See also Edmond v. United States, 117 S. Ct. 1473, 1580 (1997).

sel law disturbs the equilibrium that the Constitution created among the three branches of the federal government.[9] Scalia points out that "by the application of the statute in the present case, Congress has effectively compelled a criminal investigation of a high-level appointee of the President in connection with his actions arising out of a bitter power dispute between the President and the Legislative Branch."[10] He warns "how much easier it is for Congress, instead of accepting the political damage attendant to the commencement of impeachment proceedings against the President on trivial grounds—or, for that matter, how easy it is for one of the President's political foes outside of Congress—simply to trigger a debilitating criminal investigation of the Chief Executive under this Law" (p. 713). On the same page he warns that the law might erode the President's public support: "Nothing is so politically effective as the ability to charge that one's opponent and his associates are not merely wrongheaded, naive, ineffective, but, in all probability, 'crooks.' " Concerning the panel of judges who appoint the independent counsel, Scalia asks: "What if they are politically partisan, as judges have been known to be, and select a prosecutor antagonistic to the administration?" (p. 730).

Scalia quotes a warning by Robert Jackson, Roosevelt's Attorney General and later a distinguished Justice of the Supreme Court, against the power of a prosecutor to intimidate. The power is held in check, Scalia argues, when prosecutors serve at the pleasure of the President—the President will be blamed for their misconduct—but not when the prosecutor is independent of Presidential control. True, the prosecutor is in principle only quasi-independent, because the President retains, as the majority had emphasized, the power to remove the independent counsel for cause. But practical politics makes the power illusory. The President or the Attorney General would be accused of a cover-up, and,

---

[9]There has been a great deal of academic criticism of the law as well. See, for example, Julie O'Sullivan, "The Independent Counsel Statute: Bad Law, Bad Policy," 33 *American Criminal Law Review* 463 (1998); Cass R. Sunstein, "Unchecked and Unbalanced; Why the Independent Counsel Act Must Go," *American Prospect,* May-June 1998, p. 20. For arguments both pro and con and much useful background information, see Symposium, "The Independent Counsel Act: From Watergate to Whitewater and Beyond," 86 *Georgetown Law Journal* 2011 (1998). There have been many proposals for patching it, see, for example, Ken Gormley, "An Original Model of the Independent Counsel Statute," 97 *Michigan Law Review* 601 (1998), but it hardly seems worth the bother.

[10]487 U.S. at 703.

thinking back to Nixon's order to fire Archibald Cox, everyone would believe the accusation.

Both the majority and the dissenting opinion in *Morrison* are heavily larded with citations to previous Supreme Court decisions, and to historical materials, but this part of the debate between majority and dissent is a standoff. Scalia's argument that the framers of the Constitution intended a unitary executive has been strongly questioned.[11]

What is most striking about the majority opinion is its failure to engage with the *Realpolitik* considerations advanced in Scalia's dissent. The majority's implicit rationale can be reduced to a sentence: as long as the President can remove a prosecutor for cause, the independent counsel law is harmless, for why would a President, unless he was wicked, want to remove a prosecutor if he had no cause to do so? The majority evinces no interest in how the independent counsel law had worked in the past (when the Court decided the *Morrison* case there had been nine investigations under the law) or how it might work in the future, despite the careful attention paid to these issues by the dissent. The majority opinion is "legalistic" in a bad sense in pitching its analysis at a high level of abstraction, where the formal power of removal of the independent counsel for cause is allowed to dissolve the practical objections marshaled by the dissent.

Justice Scalia was prescient. Whether or not the panel that removed Fiske and appointed Starr in his place was antagonistic to the Clinton Administration, there was a sufficient appearance of improper motivation to enable Clinton's defenders to "trash" Starr; and certainly Starr's investigation of Clinton was debilitating for the Administration and touched off an ugly and bitter interbranch power struggle. How ironic that the author of the dissent in *Morrison* should be the Supreme Court's leading formalist!

In hindsight a striking feature of both opinions is that, apart from one sentence that I quoted from the dissent, there is no discussion of independent counsel investigations of the President. On the one hand, the majority opinion is indifferent to the actual circumstances of Morrison's investigation of Olson, on which the dissent dwells at such length, but on the other hand it is oblivious to the possibility that the independent counsel law might be invoked in circumstances far more

[11]See Lawrence Lessig and Cass R. Sunstein, "The President and the Administration," 94 *Columbia Law Review* 1, 15–22 (1994).

questionable than a probe of an assistant attorney general. One might have expected the majority opinion at least to reserve the question of the constitutionality of the law as applied to investigations of the President, and the dissent to draw attention to the point. Neither did. Perhaps as a result of these silences, it has been assumed that *Morrison* settled the question of the constitutionality of the Independent Counsel's investigation of President Clinton. It did not; and I am surprised that during Starr's investigation the President's lawyers did not urge that *Morrison* be read narrowly and question the constitutionality of the investigation.

What the Justices in the majority in *Morrison* did not foresee, perhaps because the President was not the target of the independent counsel's investigation in that case, was that if an independent counsel were appointed to investigate the President, the machinery of government might be thrown out of whack. An individual having no political legitimacy, because appointed by a panel of judges and thus at two removes from an elected official (the President who had appointed the judges and the Senators who had voted to confirm the appointments),[12] would all of a sudden become one of the most powerful people in the United States. Operating essentially without political check or budgetary constraint, wielding the immense powers that federal law vests in prosecutors, the independent counsel would be empowered, as Starr demonstrated, to tie the President in knots. For almost a year, the Independent Counsel thrashed about, a bull in a political china shop. It was not his fault that he broke so much crockery; neither he nor the judges who appointed him claim to be richly endowed with political acumen or sensitivity. But in the course of his turnings, and surely without envisaging any of the consequences that ensued, he brought about the public exposure of the sex lives of several prominent Republicans, the downfall of Newt Gingrich from the Speakership of the House of Representatives and of his designated successor, the defeat of Republican electoral hopes in the 1998 midterm elections, the resolution of budget disputes on President Clinton's terms, the political rehabilitation of Mrs. Clinton, the deferral

---

[12]Really at three removes, since the Chief Justice appoints the members of the panel that appoints the special prosecutor. The people elect the President, who appoints the Chief Justice, who appoints the members of the Special Division of the D.C. Circuit, who appoint the independent counsel.

of congressional action on a number of policy issues, the impeachment of the President for crimes that he would not have committed had there not been an independent counsel investigation,[13] and even the firing of the editor of the *Journal of the American Medical Association*.[14]

A private citizen clothed with the powers that Starr deployed is an anomaly in our constitutional system. The investigation of the Clinton-Lewinsky mess teaches that it is a mischievous anomaly.

CLINTON V. JONES

One way to describe the weakness of the *Morrison* decision is as an inability of judges, committed as they are to a rhetoric of general principles, precedent, and history, to make practical distinctions, in *Morrison* between the use of the independent counsel law against the President and its use against subordinate officials of the executive branch. The same weakness is at the root of the Court's unanimous decision in Paula Jones's case. This decision has come in for a good deal of ridicule because of the Justices' failure (the decision was unanimous) to foresee that allowing the case to proceed could disrupt the Presidency. The Justices' lack of realism and their inability to differentiate among types of lawsuit to which a President might be subjected are the most disturbing features of the decision.

Part I of the main opinion begins, absurdly to a layperson, with the statement that "Petitioner, William Jefferson Clinton, was elected to the Presidency in 1992, and re-elected in 1996."[15] Anyone who doesn't know these things has no business reading the opinion. The danger, when a judge pads an opinion with sentence after sentence that does no work, that merely labors the obvious, is that he will run out of steam before he gets to the hard part of writing an opinion, which is analyzing the issues. After telling us who Clinton is, the opinion summarizes the allegations of Jones's complaint, and this is unnecessary too because nothing in the Court's reasoning turns on the nature of Jones's com-

[13]Remember that the House declined to impeach Clinton for having lied in his deposition in the Paula Jones case.

[14]He was fired because of his decision to rush into print an article on whether young Americans consider oral sex "having sex." Gina Kolata, "A.M.A. Drops Journal Editor over Sex Paper," *New York Times* (national ed.), Jan. 16, 1999, p. A1.

[15]117 S. Ct. at 1639.

plaint; it might as well have been a personal-injury complaint arising from a traffic accident.[16]

After further preliminaries, the Court finally arrives at the issue, which is whether, as Clinton argued, the Constitution should be interpreted to give the President immunity from damages suits arising out of events that occurred before he became President. (His immunity from damages suits arising out of his official acts as President was conceded.)[17] The Court points out that the purpose of that immunity is to make the President fearless in his performance of official duties, a purpose inapplicable to suits that are based on acts committed before he became President or on purely personal acts whenever committed.

After skirmishing inconclusively with the as-usual inconclusive historical materials, the Court takes up the question whether the immunity sought by the President might be justified by the public interest in his being able to "devote his undivided time and attention to his public duties" (p. 1646). The Court naively grants the premise of the argument, quoting Lyndon Johnson's self-serving declaration that he didn't get enough sleep as President and so buying into the erroneous idea that the more important the job, the longer the hours. But, says the Court, with stunning inconsequence,

> In the more than 200-year history of the Republic, only three sitting Presidents have been subjected to suits for their private actions. If the past is any indicator, it seems unlikely that a deluge of such litigation will ever engulf the Presidency. As for the case at hand, if properly managed by the District Court, it appears to us highly unlikely to occupy any substantial amount of petitioner's time. (p. 1648, footnote omitted)

The Court does not ask whether the past is likely to be predictive of the future in our litigious age, or assess the likelihood that a sex case against the President of the United States will be "properly managed" by a district judge picked at random to preside over the case, or remark that its decision will encourage such suits by removing an obstacle to them—the possibility that the President is immune from suit during his term of office. Justice Breyer's concurring opinion called the majority opinion on the first point (the past as predictive of the future) but im-

[16]As the Court later points out, President Kennedy was in fact sued on such a charge but the suit was settled before any testimony was taken.

[17]See Nixon v. Fitzgerald, 457 U.S. 731 (1982).

plicitly conceded the majority's assumption that the only important consequence of a suit against the President is to take up his time. Both opinions mean the time actually involved in the litigation, though in a footnote the majority does acknowledge, but then lets drop, the possibility that the President "may become distracted or preoccupied by pending litigation" (p. 1650 n. 40).[18] (But that is not the point either.) As in *Morrison*, both opinions in *Clinton v. Jones* are largely given over to discussions of precedent that do no work.

Missing from either opinion is any consideration of the significance of the fact that the Paula Jones case was about sex. This fact should have been as central to the Supreme Court's consideration of the *Jones* case as the fact that Theodore Olson was *not* the President should have been central to the Court's analysis of the *Morrison* case. None of the Justices could have foreseen the injection of Lewinsky into the Jones case, but it should have been apparent to them that depositions and a trial in a case in which the President was alleged to have solicited a woman for oral sex were likely to bring details of the President's sex life into public view. It is not as if Paula Jones had been the first woman other than his wife whom Clinton had been rumored to have been sexually involved with during his political career, or even the first such woman who worked under him in government. Even Supreme Court Justices hear these rumors, and by 1997 no intelligent person thought them wholly devoid of truth. And it should have been apparent to the Justices that public exposure of the details of the President's sex life could undermine the President's authority and effectiveness.

It would, though, have required great skill to write an opinion that gave the President immunity from being sued over sex without making the plaintiffs in sexual harassment suits seem like second-class legal citizens. Either Justices lack that skill[19] or they just did not understand the mischievous potential of the case. It didn't help that the brief for President Clinton did not suggest that the scope of the immunity for which he was contending might vary with the nature of the case, and specifically with its potential for humiliating the President and by doing so disrupting the government and damaging the Presidency.

---

[18]The point is also made in the concurrence. See id. at 1657.

[19]The Supreme Court has not shown a deft hand in dealing with cases involving sex. See Richard A. Posner, *Sex and Reason*, ch. 12 (1992).

At the very least, the Court could have instructed the district judge to manage the litigation in a manner designed to minimize embarrassment to the President. The Justices could have reminded the judge that the soft spot in Paula Jones's suit was the question of injury and that the judge could decide that question before subjecting the President to the indignity of being deposed. (Again, they got no help from the President's lawyers, who did not suggest this alternative to an outright reversal.) In the end, the judge dismissed Paula Jones's suit on just that ground; she could have done so without requiring the President to submit to being deposed.

In both cases that I have been discussing, a closer engagement with the particulars of the case—a descent from the plane of abstract rules on which judges are happiest—might have saved the Supreme Court from committing errors harmful both to the nation and to the Court's reputation. It did not have to decide that the independent counsel law is constitutional as applied to the President; it did not have to allow Jones's case to proceed before the President's term expired; it did not have to allow the President to be deposed, other than as a last resort, if the case did proceed. What is missing from the Court's performance in these cases is an intellectual suppleness, a practicality, and a realism that judges and lawyers ought to have in a society in which disputes of high political moment are routinely submitted to courts for resolution.

I entitled this chapter "Lessons for the Future," and just taking pot shots at the Court with the arrows forged by the facile wisdom of hindsight will not prevent similar blunders in the future. The Court should not be criticized too harshly for not foreseeing the consequences of its decisions. None of the Justices has substantial political experience. Most of them are professional judges (only the Chief Justice has no prior judicial experience—but he has been a member of the Court for more than a quarter of a century), and there is nothing in the training or experience of a judge calculated to impart political savvy. Considering all the blunders that professional politicians, political commentators, and practicing lawyers made in the course of the Clinton-Lewinsky imbroglio, we should not judge judges too harshly for failures of political insight. But the beginning of wisdom is to know that you don't know. The Justices should have known that they could not base their decision in *Morrison* or in *Jones* on political insight (let alone on conventional materials for judicial decision-making—previous decisions, and historical materials, none of which spoke to the case at hand), because they don't have any; yet the cases could not be ducked.

What is the sensible approach to judicial decision-making in areas where judges are more than usually ignorant of the consequences of their decisions? It is to decide as little as possible. In *Morrison* that meant explicitly leaving the decision of the constitutionality of the independent counsel law as applied to the President for another day, rather than striking down the law in its entirety, as urged by Scalia, or upholding it in its entirety, as the Court appeared to do. Scalia had the better of the argument over the probable consequences of the law, but experience under it (the law was only ten years old when *Morrison* was decided) was not yet so conclusive against the law as to warrant a confident belief that it was on balance a bad innovation in constitutional design. Judges should hesitate to stifle innovation by declaring a novel measure unconstitutional. In *Jones,* the path of prudence would have been to grant the President immunity against having during his term of office to defend against (or at the very least, having to submit to being deposed in) a sex case, while leaving open the possibility that the immunity might not extend to types of case less likely to humiliate and confound the President.

If the text of the Constitution or the cases construing that text pointed clearly to one outcome or another in these cases, the Court would have been entitled to decide them in accordance with these conventional materials of judicial decision-making. But since they were cases in which the conventional materials did not indicate what the right decision was, the Court should have faced up to the fact that it could do no better than to decide pragmatically. Had the Justices realized this, they might in each case have decided as I have suggested, rendering what might be called a "Hippocratic" decision, a decision based on the principle of "do no harm." And maybe it would be a good idea, when there is next a vacancy on the Supreme Court, to fill it with someone who has held high-level elective office or otherwise participated in high-level political affairs, as have a number of notable Supreme Court Justices in our history, including John Marshall, Charles Evans Hughes, William Howard Taft, Robert Jackson, Hugo Black, and Earl Warren. The present Supreme Court is notable for its high professional sheen—and lack of political experience.[20]

[20]See Robert G. McCloskey, *The American Supreme Court* 219–221 (2d ed., Sanford Levinson ed. 1994).

I do not wish to disparage rules or commend political judging. That would be unpragmatic. Rules are an important tool of governance, and legal justice must be kept separate from popular justice and political preference. What is unpragmatic is to deny the appropriateness of eschewing generality, of hewing close to the particulars of a case, in areas where precedent gives out and the untoward consequences of premature generalization may be great.

The formalism of the Supreme Court in the *Morrison* and *Jones* cases was paralleled in the impeachment controversy by the formalism of Clinton's attackers. For them the mantra was that no man is above the law, no felony shall go unpunished, prosecutorial excess should not mitigate the defendant's punishment but should instead result in two punishments (of the defendant and of the prosecutor), and expediency should have no weight in the decision whether to impeach and convict the President. A large majority of the public, it turned out to the surprise of Clinton's attackers, does not take such an austere, rigid, Kantian view of the rule of law. It is prepared to allow that a President may be a little above the law, that felonies can be excused when they seem the harmless consequence of human weaknesses that should never have been a subject of legal proceedings, that prosecutorial excess can mitigate a defendant's guilt, and that pragmatic considerations should bear heavily on the decision whether to force a President from office. Or perhaps it would be more accurate to say, given widespread public opinion that the President should incur *some* punishment for his actions, that the American public wants a balance between the kind of legal rigorism advocated by the Republican critics of the President and the alarmingly free-wheeling "equitable" or even populist concept of justice advocated by the most extreme of his defenders. We might call that balance "pragmatism."

Theory's Debacle

Another body of thought besides "legal reasoning" in the conventional sense took a beating as a result of the Clinton-Lewinsky investigation and its aftermath. That is the medley of approaches ("theory" for short, though some of these approaches are subtheoretical) that academic practitioners of "soft" subjects in the humanities and social sciences—

subjects such as moral and political philosophy, history, and law—apply to issues of public policy. I have argued elsewhere that moral theory, broadly defined to include types of political and legal theory that resemble moral theory in form or content, lacks the resources for solving such problems.[21] My skepticism is reinforced by the reactions to Clinton's crisis of the intellectual community, specifically of "public intellectuals," who claim to be able to speak constructively to public issues and not just tend the academic vineyard. Those reactions have been a surprising combination of reticence and stridency. Although Clinton's behavior raised fascinating and important issues concerning the juncture of law and morality, the overlap between private and public morality, the current understanding of sexual morality, the ethics of lying, the trade-off between rule of law virtues and pragmatic considerations, the meaning of contrition, and the appropriate scope and limitations of privacy, very little commentary was forthcoming from public intellectuals, even those who write regularly about current events and so have access to journals of opinion, and in some cases to the ubiquitous cable television talk shows. Their silence may have been due in part to an internal war between their professed values, which tend toward the rigorist, and their politics, which for most of them are pro-Clinton and, especially, anti-anti-Clinton. Those who did sound off, like David Frum, Thomas Nagel, and Arthur Schlesinger, Jr., had, as it seems to me at any rate (see Chapter 6), rather little to say that was worthwhile. Let me give one more example.

In an article written shortly after the scandal broke, the political philosopher Michael Sandel opined that President Clinton might have been "justified" in denying that he was sexually involved with Monica Lewinsky. Sandel cited Kant—rather unexpectedly, in light of Kant's reputation as an uncompromising foe of liars (see Chapter 6)—for the proposition that there is "a sharp distinction between lies and statements that are misleading but not, in the formal sense, untrue."[22] Kant refused to equate the duty not to lie to a duty to tell the truth on all occasions—a duty of complete candor. He recognized that some reticences are not deceptive and that some deceptions created by reticence (what the law

[21]Richard A. Posner, *The Problematics of Moral and Legal Theory* (1998), esp. pts. 1–2.
[22]Michael J. Sandel, "White Lies," *New Republic*, March 2, 1998, p. 10.

calls "misleading omissions") are prudentially justified.[23] But as Sandel neglects to mention, Kant believed that "we may *never* state outright that we *will* tell the truth when we have no intention of doing so. Oaths, for example, must be taken and kept with the utmost seriousness."[24] Clinton had denied his relationship with Lewinsky under oath.

Some of the intellectuals' commentary on the Clinton-Lewinsky matter was recklessly in advance of the evidence, as when former judge Abner Mikva called Starr "sick" or John Judis denounced the media for reporting "the entirely unsubstantiated rumor about Lewinsky's semenstained dress."[25] An honorable exception is Jean Bethke Elshtain,[26] but more typical was the quality of thought displayed by the sociologist (and prolific writer for the *New Republic* and other intellectual but nonacademic magazines) Alan Wolfe. He said:

> The American people are forgiving. We like to give people a second chance, and Clinton will get one because he's been a naughty boy, and you have to forgive naughty boys . . . No one really knows the limits of our tolerance. When this all started, I thought we were living in Nathaniel Hawthorne's Massachusetts.[27]

Although it is impossible to believe that Clinton is as depraved as his worst detractors (even this side of lunacy) claim, his crimes are not the

---

[23]Roger G. Sullivan, *Immanuel Kant's Moral Theory* 170–173 (1989).

[24]Id. at 173 (emphasis in original).

[25]John B. Judis, "Irresponsible Elites," *American Prospect,* May-June 1998, pp. 14, 15. In hindsight, it is apparent that Judis's article failed to identify *any* errors in the media coverage of the Clinton-Lewinsky affair. Particularly amusing is Judis's criticism of *Time* for having "fun with fellatio" by placing the following asterisked comment (in effect a footnote) after the word "sex": "It was only oral. It was passive. So that does not count." This turns out to have been an uncannily accurate prediction of how months later, in his grand jury testimony, Clinton would distinguish his conduct with Lewinsky from sex.

[26]See, for example, Jean Bethke Elshtain, "Politics and Forgiveness: The Clinton Case," in *Judgment Day at the White House: A Critical Declaration Exploring Moral Issues and the Political Use and Abuse of Religion* 11 (Gabriel Fackre ed. 1999); Elshtain, "Going Public," *New Republic,* March 23, 1998, p. 12; Karen R. Long, "Ethicist Decries Clinton's 'Cavalier Disdain' for Rules," *Cleveland Plain Dealer,* Sept. 19, 1998, p. 1F. Long's article also reports Elshtain's apt quip that "the problem with being a public intellectual is you get more and more public and less and less intellectual."

[27]Quoted in Mary Leonard, "In Land of Second Chances, an Apology Can Suffice," *Boston Globe,* Aug. 18, 1998, p. A11.

eminently forgivable actions of a "naughty boy."[28] One doesn't have to go further than the *New Yorker,* one of Clinton's staunchest media allies, to find compelling evidence of the disreputableness of the man, of his retinue, and of his tactics over a wide front.[29]

Judis and Sandel were writing, and Mikva talking to reporters, early in the crisis, before the DNA test on Monica Lewinsky's dress and before the President's grand jury testimony and television address of August 17, 1998. Sandel's description of the President's conduct as "white lies," Judis's criticisms of the press for inaccurate reporting, and Mikva's claim that the charges against Clinton rested on gossipy conversations between two women became completely untenable ("inoperative," as Nixon would have said) as Starr's investigation progressed. No retractions were forthcoming.

In the fall of 1998, well after the revelations of August 17, the *New York Times* published a full-page advertisement, signed by Ronald Dworkin, Arthur Schlesinger, Jr., Michael Sovern (a former president of Columbia University and former dean of the Columbia Law School), and other notables urging that President Clinton not be impeached.[30] The advertisement describes impeachment of the President as a "constitutional nuclear weapon" (in retrospect a hyperbolic characterization) that "should not be used unless it is absolutely necessary to save the Constitution from an even graver injury." The advertisement claims that the impeachment of Nixon would have passed this test, because Nixon "had unconstitutionally used the pretext of national security to try to cover up criminal acts against political opponents." Clinton, in contrast, "lied in order to hide private consensual sexual acts." The advertisement neglects to mention that Clinton lied under oath and engaged in related acts of obstruction of justice, in violation of his constitutional duty to take care that the laws be faithfully executed, and that once Nixon's wrongdoing was exposed and his associates packed off to jail it was no longer necessary to remove Nixon, who like Clinton

[28]It is *possible* that Wolfe was attributing the "naughty boy" view to the public without necesssarily sharing it, although that would not be the natural way to read his words.

[29]See Jeffrey Toobin, "Clinton's Other Pursuer," *New Yorker,* April 6, 1998, p. 43; Toobin, "Circling the Wagons," *New Yorker,* July 6, 1998, p. 28; Joe Klein, "Primary Cad," *New Yorker,* Sept. 7, 1998, p. 46.

[30]"An Appeal to the U.S. Congress and the Public," *New York Times,* Oct. 7, 1998, p. A13.

had two years of his second term left, in order to save the Constitution from grave danger. Nixon was forced out of office because people were outraged by his conduct (and he had not been very popular to begin with, and the economy was in trouble), not because he posed any further danger to constitutional government.

The advertisement goes on to argue that, given the parlous international situation (the international situation is always parlous), the nation cannot afford to allow "the American presidency to twist in the wind, injured and humiliated." Yet it recommends that Clinton be censured by Congress "for his actions," and it remarks approvingly on his having "now apologized on several occasions." But apologized for what? Not for obstructing justice. And so for what "actions" would Congress be censuring him? With Clinton adamant against admitting to any real wrongdoing, and confessing only to "inappropriate" sexual contact and to misleading people (implicitly, *gullible* people, who don't know him well enough to disbelieve his denials), Congress would either have had to conduct an investigation, or to accept the Starr Report in toto, or to censure Clinton for actions not grave enough to warrant censure. As grudging an apology as Clinton was willing to make could have been extracted from Nixon, who was left twisting in the wind for a year as the impeachment inquiry proceeded.

The advertisement says that censure would be "a historic act of punishment." If so, Clinton would be injured and humiliated, and our international situation worsened. But it would not be a historic act of punishment. Andrew Jackson, it is scarcely even remembered, was censured by Congress—and the censure was rescinded a few years later when his party regained control of Congress. The advertisement does not mention the possibility that legislative censure of the President would be a bill of attainder, and therefore unconstitutional.

A few weeks later, a large number of historians published another full-page ad in the *New York Times*.[31] This one says that "the current charges against him [President Clinton] depart from what the Framers saw as grounds for impeachment." No effort to support this conclusion is made; nor is there any argument that "what the Framers saw as grounds for impeachment" should resolve a current controversy. The

---

[31]"Historians in Defense of the Constitution," *New York Times*, Oct. 30, 1998, p. A15. Arthur Schlesinger, Jr., was again among the signatories.

advertisement states that "the theory of impeachment underlying these efforts [the efforts to impeach President Clinton] is unprecedented in our history." It does not say what that theory is. There are two possibilities. One is that it is the theory, for which the Nixon impeachment inquiry could be cited as a precedent, that obstruction of justice by the President is an impeachable offense. No lack of precedent there. The other possibility is that it is the theory ("political impeachment") that underlay the efforts of the Jeffersonian Republicans to impeach Federalist judges such as Samuel Chase and of the radical Republicans to impeach Andrew Johnson. That is a bad theory, but it is part of our history too. No historian who had bothered to examine the history of impeachment in the United States could have written or signed the statement that I have quoted.

One of the signers, Jack Rakove, had three weeks earlier published an article which, as the title suggests, contradicts the advertisement's central historical claim.[32] The article concludes that history cannot resolve the question whether Clinton's detractors are right or wrong in arguing that his conduct constitutes a high enough misdemeanor to justify impeachment. One wonders how Rakove reconciles the two positions.

One of the draftsmen of the historians' advertisement, Sean Wilentz, testified before the House Judiciary Committee on December 8, 1998. In his prepared testimony, he stated:

> It is no exaggeration to say that upon this impeachment inquiry, as upon all presidential impeachment inquiries, hinges the fate of our American political institutions. *It is that important.* As a historian, it is clear to me that the impeachment of President Clinton would do great damage to those institutions and to the rule of law—much greater damage than the crimes of which President Clinton is accused.[33]

This is a surprising statement for a scholar to make. How could it be *clear* to any historian, indeed to any thinking person, that "the fate of our American political institutions" hinged on whether President Clinton was impeached? A historian might speculate about these matters, but he would have to be clairvoyant to be entitled to speak with Wil-

---

[32]Jack Rakove, "Framers of Two Minds on Impeachment," *Newsday,* Oct. 11, 1998, p. B5.

[33]Emphasis in original.

entz's confidence. Several days after Wilentz wrote, Clinton *was* impeached, and the sky did not fall. No one thinks the sky *will* fall.

Wilentz went on to say that the historical record is clear that only actions taken in the performance of official duties can be the basis of an impeachment. The record is not clear, and Wilentz himself is not willing to stand by his assertion, because he admits that a President who committed murder, "even in the most private of circumstances," should be impeached and removed from office.

Wilentz says that Andrew Johnson's "impeachment helped pave the way for the Gilded Age, an age of political sordidness and unremarkable chief executives." He offers no evidence or argument in support of this vague assertion (vague because of the uncertain force of "helped to pave the way" in this context), and it is far from being self-evident. Johnson was an odd duck—an accidental President, not even of Lincoln's party, impeached by an overwhelming vote in the heated atmosphere of the aftermath of civil war, yet even he was acquitted, and his acquittal, we recall, was thought to have made it "almost inconceivable that a future president will be impeached and removed."[34] Does Wilentz believe that Ulysses S. Grant would not have been elected President in 1868 had Johnson not been impeached a few months earlier? Or that Grant's Administration would have been less corrupt? It's true that Johnson's successors as President during the remaining years of the nineteenth century were weak, but, as we saw in Chapter 5, the reasons are complex, and many earlier Presidents had been weak too.

To those who argued that failing to impeach President Clinton would allow him to get away with his crimes, Wilentz replied that it is not the business of impeachment to deal with crime (except, he forgets to add, murder, not to mention bribery, treason, and other "high Crimes and Misdemeanors") and that the President can eventually be prosecuted in the ordinary way. Wilentz makes no effort to assess the practicality of such a prosecution. Does he want to see Clinton prosecuted in 2001? Does he think Clinton would or should be convicted? If not, if Clinton "walked," like O. J. Simpson, would the rule of law be vindicated? Does Wilentz realize that Clinton might pardon himself?

[34]Michael Les Benedict, *The Impeachment and Trial of Andrew Johnson* 180 (1973). The seven Republican Senators whose defection was responsible for Johnson's acquittal seem to have been moved primarily by concern that conviction would weaken the Presidency—would "Mexicanize" our government, as one of them put it. Id. at 178–179.

Wilentz ends his statement by fairly shouting that if the members of the House of Representatives, "defying the deliberate judgment of the people whom you are supposed to represent," go through with impeachment, "your reputations will be darkened for as long as there are Americans who can tell the difference between the rule of law and the rule of politics." What is the evidence that the people have made a "*deliberate* judgment"? And doesn't the Constitution assign the responsibility for judgment to the Congress? And since when is defying public opinion polls a sign of political expedience? Is there any basis for thinking that political calculation played a smaller role in the lockstep Democratic response to the Clinton scandal and its aftermath than in the more variegated Republican response?

After the House of Representatives defied Wilentz and impeached Clinton, Ronald Dworkin chimed in.[35] In a short piece that echoes Wilentz's testimony in tone and content, he says that "we must cultivate a long memory." He means that we must be sure to remember in the year 2000 the awful thing the House has done, at which time

> we must encourage and support opponents who denounce them [the Congressmen who voted to impeach the President] for what they have done, in any way we can, including financially. The zealots will have stained the Constitution [if they succeed in forcing Clinton from office], and we must do everything in our power to make the shame theirs and not the nation's.

It is worth attending to the arguments that lead to this flamboyant conclusion. Dworkin believes that the impeachment of President Clinton shows that "a partisan group in the House, on a party-line vote, can annihilate the separation of powers." But the power to impeach, a power that can indeed be wielded by the party that controls the House, is part of the separation (more precisely the balance) of powers ordained by the Constitution. Dworkin also neglects to point out that a partisan group, namely the House Democrats, could force the impeachment decision to be made on a party-line basis simply by deciding to vote against impeachment en bloc regardless of the merits. Dworkin adds that the House ignored "the most fundamental provisions of due process and fair procedure," but he does not, and I believe he could not,

[35]Ronald Dworkin, "A Kind of Coup," *New York Review of Books,* Jan. 14, 1999, p. 61.

explain what additional process the House could have provided that would have altered the outcome without unduly protracting the impeachment inquiry, something the Democrats claimed not to want. Dworkin warns that an impeachment trial in the Senate "would frighten the markets." Wrong again. On the very day the effort to finesse the trial collapsed (January 6, 1999), the stock market reached an all-time high, and it remained at or near that level throughout the trial.

Dworkin argues that because an impeachment trial "is a seismic shock to the separation of powers," it must be reserved for cases in which "there is a constitutional or public danger in leaving a President in office." This principle, consistently applied, would have let Nixon off the hook, since the exposure of his criminal activities and the prosecution of his principal henchmen eliminated any danger that he would continue these activities in the rump of his term. Dworkin echoes Wilentz in arguing that the place to deal with Clinton's crimes is in a regular court of law after Clinton leaves office, but he does not discuss the feasibility of such a prosecution or the cloud that the pardon power places over it. He makes the familiar concession that a President who committed murder could not be allowed to remain in office, but adds that "a congressman who thinks that lying to hide a sexual embarrassment, even under oath, is on the same moral scale as murder—that it shows comparable wickedness or depravity—has no moral capacity himself." No one argues that the President's crimes are as serious as murder. The fact that murder would be sufficient grounds for impeachment and conviction does not imply that no lesser crime would be. Does Dworkin think that a President who raped women, or molested children, should be permitted to remain in office? If not, how can he rule out obstruction of justice without examining and assessing the full extent of Clinton's criminal conduct (which he gives no indication of having done)?

Dworkin calls the impeachment of Clinton a "kind of coup" because the conviction of the President would remove from office "the only official in the nation who has been elected by all the people." That is an illuminating error, as well as a good illustration of the hyperbole that permeated the public debate over the impeachment. The Vice President is also elected by all the people.[36] And this means that a President

---

[36]There is further hyperbole in the expression "elected by all the people." President Clinton was not elected unanimously. He was elected by 43 percent of the minority of

who is removed from office is succeeded not by any of the putschists but by a nationally elected member of his own party, and indeed his designated, and in this case his handpicked, successor, his ostentatiously loyal paladin. Dworkin's point would have greater force if the office of the Vice President were vacant (in which event the Republican Speaker of the House would become President if Clinton were removed from office), or if the Vice President belonged to a different faction of the Democratic Party or, as is not impossible, belonged to a different party.[37]

Moral and legal theorists like Dworkin who are constantly urging the injection of this or that moral principle into our public policy, and who think there is too much pragmatism and too little moral principle in our law, had nothing to say about the decided lack of moral principle demonstrated by President Clinton in his struggle to escape from the legal flypaper on which he had landed. All that Dworkin, whose academic writings are all about principle and integrity, would say in his January 14, 1999, *New York Review* piece about Clinton's conduct was that the President was guilty of "lying to hide a sexual embarrassment." That there was also subornation of perjury and witness tampering, and that the lying continued after the sexual embarrassment could no longer be concealed, went unmentioned.

It was surprising to find House Democrats more candid about Clinton's misconduct than leading academics, but they were. The censure resolution which they introduced in the House Judiciary Committee as

---

American adults who bothered to vote in the two elections in which he ran for President. Dworkin's talk of coups is a good example of the academic loss of cool that I mentioned in the last chapter. See also Patricia Cohen, "To the Barricades, 25 Years Later," *New York Times* (late ed.), Dec. 19, 1998, p. 9.

[37]Andrew Johnson was a Democrat, running with Republican Abraham Lincoln in 1864 on the "Unionist" ticket. Dworkin returned to the fray after the President's acquittal, with another short article. Ronald Dworkin, "The Wounded Constitution," *New York Review of Books,* March 18, 1999. He writes, with reference to the fact that "bribery" is an express ground for impeachment in the Constitution, that "a bribe [unlike Clinton's wrongdoing] induces an official to act against the public interest," id. at 8–9, but actually this depends on whether the bribe is to do an official or a purely private act. He says that Clinton "can still be indicted and prosecuted when he leaves office," but does not mention the issue of self-pardoning. He says on the same page that "Starr's behavior in this case would presumably have led to charges being dismissed in an ordinary criminal case," which we know from Chapter 2 is wrong, and that Judge Wright "had ruled the [President's] deposition [in the Paula Jones case] immaterial," which we know from Chapter 1 is wrong. Id. at 9.

an alternative to impeachment stated, far more forthrightly than Wilentz or Dworkin, that the President had "egregiously failed in th[e] obligation" to "set an example of high moral standards and conduct himself in a manner that fosters respect for the truth," had "violated the trust of the American people, lessened their esteem for the office of President, and dishonored the office which they ha[d] entrusted to him," had "made false statements concerning his reprehensible conduct with a subordinate," and had taken "steps to delay discovery of the truth."

When one thinks of the noises and the silences, of Thomas Nagel's calumnies, and of Arthur Schlesinger's bestowal of the label "gentleman" on President Clinton, it is tempting to conclude (though overgeneralization is a danger here) that the left intelligentsia lacks a moral core, while the right intelligentsia has a morbidly exaggerated fear of moral laxity. And in the response of academia to the Clinton crisis we have evidence that academic law, moral and political theory, and the study of history are soft fields despite the intelligence and toughmindedness of many of their practitioners. A hard field in the sense in which I am using "hard" and "soft" is one in which agreement on the methods for resolving disagreement enables consensus to be forged despite the differing political agendas of the practitioners. The scholarly output of such a field need not be either interesting or important, but it will tend to be objective, or at least to lack a discernible political inflection. A soft field, in contrast, is permeable to political disagreement. It is apparent that what divides a Wilentz and a Dworkin from a Frum and a William Bennett are the same things that divide the public at large in the polarized debate over Clinton: unbridgeable differences in values that have their origin in temperament, upbringing, and life experiences rather than in reasoning to divergent conclusions from shared premises.

The Legal Profession: Not Its Finest Hour

Law school deans and other leaders of the legal profession might have been expected to emphasize the importance of the rule of law in general and of telling the truth in depositions and in testimony before a grand jury, in particular, and to point out that Clinton is a member of the Arkansas bar and that the conduct in which he engaged would ordinarily result in disbarment. Dean Anthony Kronman of the Yale Law School, who has written a book deploring the moral tone of the modern

American legal profession,[38] might have been expected to rebuke his wayward alumnus. Harsh words about Clinton might also have been expected from Professor Dworkin, who is a lawyer as well as a philosopher and who is well known for advocating that law be reconceived as a branch of moral philosophy.[39] These expectations would have been disappointed.

The academic legal profession's silence[40] about the ethical dimensions of Clinton's conduct became deafening when on November 6, 1998, several *hundred* law school professors—a substantial fraction of the entire academic legal community—signed a letter urging Congress not to impeach the President. The conception of "high Crimes and Misdemeanors" advocated in the letter is similar to that urged in Cass Sunstein's statement to the House Judiciary Committee, about which I expressed reservations in Chapter 5, and repeated by Wilentz and Dworkin and others; we might call it "public acts + murder," since murder is the only example they give of a private act that might warrant impeachment.

I want to emphasize two other aspects of the November 6 letter. The first is its evasiveness about the President's conduct. It says, "*If* the President committed perjury regarding his sexual conduct, this perjury involved no exercise of Presidential power as such. *If* he concealed evidence, this misdeed too involved no exercise of executive authority." The "ifs" are italicized in the original, and the italicization conveys the impression of real doubt about the accuracy of the charges against the President. But by November 6, 1998, there were no "ifs" about the essentials of the President's conduct. The evidence of his guilt was overwhelming, and barely contested even by his lawyers. Nevertheless the letter does not criticize Clinton's conduct beyond saying that "some of

---

[38]Anthony T. Kronman, *The Lost Lawyer: Failing Ideals of the Legal Profession* (1993).

[39]See, for example, Ronald Dworkin, *Law's Empire* (1986); Dworkin, "In Praise of Theory," 29 *Arizona State Law Journal* 353 (1997).

[40]Happily not complete. See, for examples of forthright statements by law professors, Stephen Gillers, "The Perjury Precedent," *New York Times* (national ed.), Dec. 28, 1998, p. A27; Gillers, " 'Accurate Lies': The Legal World of Oxymorons," *Los Angeles Times* (home ed.), Aug. 30, 1998, p. M1; David Dahl, "Clinton Urges House to Vote by Conscience," *St. Petersburg Times,* Oct. 8, 1998, p. 1A (quoting Laurence Tribe as calling for criminal prosecution of Clinton when he leaves office). See also Philip Elman, "Shame on the Partisan Professors," *Legal Times,* Nov. 16, 1998, p. 21.

us believe that the President has acted disgracefully, some that the Independent Counsel has. This letter has nothing to do with any such judgments." I don't understand the coyness of the academic legal community about the President's behavior. Could not *all* the signatories, not just some, have agreed that the President—a lawyer engaged in behavior particularly reprobated by lawyers—acted disgracefully?

The other feature of the November 6 letter to which I want to draw attention is the sheer number of its signatories. Many, probably most, of them are not experts on constitutional law; and one wonders how many of them had actually studied either the facts of Clinton's conduct (the Starr Report alone is more than 200 pages long) or the law of impeachment. An unkind critic might describe the signing by intellectuals of petitions, open letters, and full-page ads as a form of herd behavior (the "herd of independent minds") by the animal that likes to see its name in print.

No doubt, in this age of specialization, many of the signatories of the November 6 letter know little about the law of perjury or its importance to the litigation process and don't want to take the time to find out more. But then one might expect the professors of criminal law, criminal procedure, and civil procedure to have sought to correct the misleading impression created by the November 6 letter by writing a letter of their own to the House Judiciary Committee, which they did not do, emphasizing the gravity of the President's crimes. One might expect the American Bar Association, which in recent years has taken public positions on a variety of controversial topics, such as abortion, to have taken a public position on the implications for the rule of law of a President's flouting the nation's criminal laws. Again, silence.

The silence of the bar could be thought to condone the tactics employed by the President (himself a lawyer, remember) and his lawyers, tactics that conform to the lay intuition that what lawyers mainly do is drive a wedge between law and justice. The lawyers' defense of the President against the charge of perjury was grounded in quibbling, hair-splitting equivocation, brazen denial of the obvious, truncated quotation and quotation out of context, and mischaracterization of the law. The impression that many lay observers must have taken from the spectacle was that perjury is an unimportant technical offense, that a skillful liar is beyond its reach, and that a clever lawyer can beat any perjury charge (perhaps any charge, period) by spinning a web of sophistries.

Law professors have done little to dispel this impression.[41] If anything, they have reinforced it. The evidence is not only the November 6 letter. Leo Katz of the University of Pennsylvania Law School writes: "I find it hard to be offended by the use of loopholes, be it by the President, Paula Jones's lawyers or the independent counsel. But then, I share with them the same basic character flaw: I'm a lawyer."[42] David Strauss of the University of Chicago Law School does not regard "the Monica Lewinsky matter" as a "real scandal"; it is merely a "supposed scandal," in contrast to "real scandals, like Watergate."[43] The President's conduct may or may not be grounds for removing him from office, but it was certainly scandalous. Geoffrey Stone, Provost of the University of Chicago, former dean of its law school, and co-counsel with Strauss for the President in *Clinton v. Jones*, claims that the behavior of Kenneth Starr and the congressional Republicans was "the most immoral conduct in this whole affair," "the most 'shameful' . . . aspect of this sorry episode"—"far worse than anything the president may have done."[44] (*May* have done?) Stone charges that William Bennett collaborated with Starr and the congressional Republicans and other assorted "fellow-travelers" (a McCarthyite term applied to the President's opponents three times in Stone's one-page article) "in a sordid, abusive and irresponsible effort to manipulate the levers of power to 'get' the President," an effort motivated entirely by "moral zealotry, personal vindictiveness and partisan politics" and demonstrating "the moral blindness of the Republican right." Stone even goes beyond Sunstein and Wilentz, arguing that it is well understood that impeachment is limited "to serious abuse of official authority."

Harvard Law School professor Alan Dershowitz commends Clinton for adopting a "simple and elegant" defense: "He will admit to sex and claim it is private and non-impeachable. And left [leave?] it to the in-

---

[41]Not nothing, though. See, for example, Stephen Gillers, "Clinton's Choice: Tell Truth or Dare to Gamble," *Los Angeles Times* (home ed.), Aug. 2, 1998, p. M1.

[42]Leo Katz, "All Deceptions Are Not Equal," *New York Times* (late ed.), Aug. 19, 1998, p. A31. Professor Katz's remark brings to mind Ambrose Bierce's definition of a lawyer: "one skilled in circumvention of the law." *The Devil's Dictionary,* in *The Collected Writings of Ambrose Bierce* 187, 289 (1946).

[43]David A. Strauss, "After the Clinton Storm," *New York Times* (late ed.), Aug. 6, 1998, p. A23.

[44]Geoffrey R. Stone, "Moral Zealotry Is a Worse Crime," *Chicago Tribune,* Feb. 20, 1999, p. 22.

dependent counsel to prove any impeachable offenses such as obstruction of justice or subornation of perjury. *And since there will never be stains or tapes proving obstruction or subornation, the president will prevail.*[45] The implication is that these crimes cannot be proved without either irrefutable physical evidence or taped admissions. That is false; but were it true, there would still be a difference that one might have expected a professor of criminal law to point out between not *being* guilty and not being *proved* guilty. It is an unsettling notion of "elegance" that associates it with the tactics by which guilty defendants can escape punishment.

In his testimony before the House Judiciary Committee on December 1, 1998, Dershowitz took the Republican members of the Committee to task for ignoring what he considers a more serious kind of perjury than the President's, namely perjury by police officers in criminal prosecutions. It is a serious problem,[46] but its gravity hardly mitigates the President's guilt. Dershowitz might as well say that since we largely ignore genocides (for example in Rwanda, Cambodia, and, until it was almost too late, Bosnia), we shouldn't prosecute ordinary murderers. The President, moreover, is the ultimate boss of a host of federal police forces, including the FBI, the Secret Service, the U.S. Marshals Service, the Alcohol, Tobacco, and Firearms Bureau, the criminal investigation arm of the Internal Revenue Service, the Border Patrol, the Drug Enforcement Administration, and the military police of the various branches of the armed forces. Perjury by the head cop is at least as serious a crime as perjury by the cop on the beat.

In his book *Sexual McCarthyism*[47] Dershowitz criticizes Clinton, but largely for the blunders he committed in trying to conceal his affair with Lewinsky and implicitly for not having retained Dershowitz as a legal advisor. Dershowitz is scathing in his criticisms of the tactics employed by the President's lawyers, and in particular of Robert Bennett's failure (which Dershowitz claims Bennett admitted to him in a phone

---

[45]Alan M. Dershowitz, "Testimony Key, Not the Speech," *Boston Herald,* Aug. 20, 1998, p. 37 (emphasis added).

[46]See, for example, Gabriel J. Chin and Scott C. Wells, "The 'Blue Wall' of Silence as Evidence of Bias and Motive to Lie: A New Approach to Police Perjury," 59 *University of Pittsburgh Law Review* 233 (1998).

[47]Alan M. Dershowitz, *Sexual McCarthyism: Clinton, Starr, and the Emerging Constitutional Crisis* (1998).

conversation)[48] to advise the President to default in the Paula Jones suit. There is no criticism of Clinton for committing criminal acts or for undermining the rule of law, though Dershowitz does criticize Clinton for taking a hard line on crime in general, for lacking, as it were, empathy for his fellow criminals.

The practicing bar was on display throughout Clinton's ordeal, but most conspicuously in the Senate trial. Most of the House managers and the President's lawyers had experience as trial lawyers. Their performances dramatized the asymmetry between prosecutors and defense lawyers. In our system of criminal justice, prosecutors are expected to believe in the guilt of the people they prosecute; they are not supposed to prosecute just because they think they can persuade a jury to convict. The reason is that the prosecutor's "client," the state, has little or nothing, and probably less than nothing, to gain from convicting innocent people; convicting the innocent is likely to reduce the deterrent effect of the criminal law because that effect depends not on the likelihood of a defendant's being punished if guilty, but on the *difference* between that likelihood and the likelihood of his being punished if innocent.[49] The defense lawyer's client, in contrast, has the sole goal of acquittal. Hence Clinton's lawyers had no inhibitions about making statements in the trial that, as intelligent people, they could not have believed, notably that the President had been truthful in his grand jury testimony. Both his principal lawyers, David Kendall and Charles Ruff, were emphatic that the President had told no lies to the grand jury. The only

---

[48]Id. at 19.

[49]This is clearest if punishment is imposed randomly with respect to guilt or innocence. Let the expected cost of punishment, a measure of deterrence, be denoted by EC. Then $EC = pS$, where p is the probability of apprehension and conviction and S is the sentence. The expected cost of punishment for actually committing a crime is the difference between the expected cost of punishment if the accused is guilty and the expected cost of punishment if he is innocent. That is, $EC = EC_g - EC_i$. Equivalently, $EC = p_g S - p_i S$, where p_g is the probability of punishment if the accused is guilty and p_i is the probability of punishment if he is innocent (the sentence is assumed to be the same in either case). This can be simplified to $EC = (p_g - p_i) S$, making it obvious that if the probability of punishment is the same regardless of guilt (that is, if $p_g = p_i$), the expected punishment cost for committing the crime will be zero. If, however, punishment is not imposed randomly with respect to guilt or innocence, the analysis is more complex and prediction less certain. Relaxing procedural safeguards designed to protect the innocent from being convicted might increase the probability of convicting the guilty by enough to offset the negative effect on deterrence of the increase in the likelihood of convicting the innocent.

difference was that Kendall gave no impression of believing what he was saying. Ruff, the better actor, gave a convincing impersonation of a person who believes what he is saying. The lawyers made the Senate Chamber an echo chamber of the President's untruths.

Although a high level of professional skill was displayed on both sides of the struggle from time to time, the investigation, impeachment, and trial of President Clinton was not the legal profession's finest hour. The errors of tact, taste, and public relations committed by the Independent Counsel's office and the members and staff of the House Judiciary Committee may have been decisive in the President's acquittal, while the technical acrobatics of the President's lawyers, though helpful in throwing sand in the eyes of his attackers and providing "running room" (as we shall see) for his supporters, hurt his reputation and may have tipped the balance in favor of impeachment.

The Media

The antagonists agreed only in denouncing the media for not respecting personal privacy and sexual decorum in their coverage of the Clinton-Lewinsky mess. The good old days were nostalgically recalled in which a conspiracy of silence protected Franklin Roosevelt and John Kennedy from public exposure of their adulteries. But it was not the media, not even the unfiltered Internet media, such as the *Drudge Report,* that were responsible for breaking the code of silence so far as Clinton and Lewinsky were concerned. It was the fact that a panel of judges authorized the Independent Counsel to investigate the affair, which had come to his attention through Linda Tripp, not through the media. True, they were sniffing around; the *Newsweek* article that quoted Tripp on Kathleen Willey was one of the factors impelling Tripp to tape her phone conversations with Monica Lewinsky; and Starr accelerated his investigation in the hope of getting Clinton on tape before the story of Clinton's affair with Lewinsky broke in the press. But once the investigation was launched—and at most the media affected the timing of the launch—concealing it from the public was impossible, and would have been inappropriate given the possible consequences of the investigation for the nation.

The reason the media kept mum about Presidents' adulteries in times past was not that journalists were more ethical then; to think so would be to succumb to the Golden Age fallacy. Part of the reason was that the nation was more prudish. Newspaper readers would have been scandalized by articles about the President's sexual activities. Many readers would not have believed the articles; some would have thought it disloyal, even subversive or sacrilegious, to defame the President so. The dangers for the media were palpable; even today's newspapers and television stations censor the language in their stories. But because people have become more comfortable with public discussion of sexual matters, there is less inhibition about reporting on the sex lives of public figures. Behind the media coverage of the affair and its aftermath lay not a conspiracy to increase circulation, audience, or advertising revenues, but a natural adaptation to changing mores. The people who blame the media for the crisis of Clinton's Presidency are like the people who blame it on Kenneth Starr and the "vast right-wing conspiracy" of which Mrs. Clinton hopefully spoke. They are blaming the messenger.

Second and closely related, in times past journalists, like the political scientists of the day (like many political scientists to this day), accepted the theory of Presidential mystique that I discussed in Chapter 4: the idea that a President's effectiveness depends on the public's believing that he is larger than life. Many journalists no longer believe this, and so they do not think that they are harming the nation when they expose a President's character flaws.

And third, there is more competition in the media today. Publishers don't ever want to be on a President's, or other powerful public official's, enemies list, especially if they own radio or television stations, which are valuable government franchises. Like other conspiracies, a conspiracy of silence is more fragile the greater the number of people or firms that have to be enlisted in the conspiracy for it to be effective. With the rise of cable television and the Internet, there are far more purveyors of news and information than in the old days. Internet newscasters like Drudge, Internet magazines like *Salon,* and twenty-four-hour cable news networks make it impossible for the established media to bottle up the news they would rather not carry.

The Clinton-Lewinsky saga was a bonanza for the news media, because the cost of putting together a news program is essentially invariant to the size of the audience, and programs on the saga drew huge audiences. This did not make the media "responsible" for the nation's fascination with a thirteen-month-long political and legal soap opera. The media cannot make people interested in a particular story. There is too much competition from other stories. It is not really surprising that people would become fascinated by a Presidential scandal *that they could understand* (unlike Whitewater) and that was about sex.

The media made only one big mistake in their coverage of the ordeal. That was to describe Lewinsky as a twenty-one-year-old intern, which created the impression that Clinton had taken advantage of a girl. Lewinsky was twenty-two when the affair began and only nominally an intern, since she had been hired as a regular employee, though the paperwork for the appointment had not been completed. And she was a savvy, sexually experienced young woman, not a vulnerable naif.

The media's coverage of Clinton's ordeal, though denounced as sensationalistic, should actually bolster journalism's image of professionalism. Most journalists, whether print or media, and including editorial writers, are liberal Democrats. Yet they pulled no punches in reporting and editorializing on the scandal and its aftermath even after it became clear that they were out of step with public opinion. They were less political than many academics, and less influential than conservative critics fear the "liberal media" to be.

War by Another Name

The Clinton-Lewinsky saga should teach us that we must think more systematically about the dynamics of conflict. Conflict is a pervasive feature of social life, studied by a variety of disciplines (game theory, psychology, economics, sociology, biology, and of course history) in a variety of settings. One of those settings is war.[50] No single "theory" of conflict has emerged, and perhaps conflict is too heterogeneous a phenomenon to admit of theoretical unity. But the conflict touched off by the public revelation of Clinton's affair with Lewinsky has systemic features that can be understood by analogy to the king of conflicts, which is war. The appropriateness of the analogy is underscored by Clausewitz's famous dictum that war is the continuation of politics by other means.[51] War is continuous with politics, and might even be isomorphic with it. A better understanding of the systemic features of war

[50]See, for example, Thomas C. Schelling, *The Strategy of Conflict* (1960). Schelling's emphasis is on bargaining between adversaries to avoid or limit war; mine will be on the conduct of war.

[51]Carl von Clausewitz, *On War* 69, 87, 605 (Michael Howard and Peter Paret eds. 1976).

and warlike conflict might have helped the participants in the Clinton crisis to avoid some of their mistakes.

Conflict in the sense of conflicting interests is pervasive, but the eruption of latent conflict into actual struggle is rare. Most labor disputes are settled without a strike, most litigation is settled without a trial, most international disputes are resolved short of war. The struggle phase tends to impose heavy costs on both sides and so is avoided most of the time by a negotiated settlement that gives each side an approximation to what it would have gotten by a struggle. Hence struggle is most likely to erupt when uncertainty about the likely outcome, or about the stakes that each contestant has in a particular outcome, leads to miscalculation by one or both sides.

Wars tend to impose enormous costs, even in relation to the stakes of victory, yet they do occur and often they turn out to be completely one-sided. That they occur at all, given the costs, and that when they do occur they often are one-sided, suggests that there must be radical uncertainty about military outcomes.[52] A moment's reflection will suggest why. First, war is strategic. That is, as in chess, the effect of a "move" depends on the reaction of the opponent; and since the opponent has a range of options, each of which will invite a different riposte in the second round, and so on indefinitely, the course and outcome of the struggle may be impossible to predict. Second, secrecy confers enormous advantages in war, and the institutions for dispelling it in order to facilitate peaceful settlement—institutions corresponding to pretrial discovery in litigation and to collective bargaining in labor relations—are highly imperfect; the major one is espionage. Even more important, war is at once discontinuous and technologically progressive. This makes it difficult to predict the outcome of the next war from that of the last war. In other words, war lacks good precedents.[53] And while all struggle is emotional, war is particularly so because of the fear and hatred that its violence engenders. The emotions of war make it difficult for the people or even the leaders of the warring nations to think straight, which poses a further obstacle to predicting an opponent's behavior. (It is easier to derive predictions from models that assume

[52]Again a point emphasized by Clausewitz. E.g., id. at 85–86, 101 ("war is the realm of uncertainty"), 102. No rationally governed nation would go to war if it knew it was going to be routed. So with good information, there would be no one-sided wars.
[53]Cf. id. at 112.

that human behavior is rational.) For example, it is often impossible to tell whether an attack will cause the defenders to flee in terror or to fight with redoubled fury. Because of the interaction of emotion and uncertainty, warfare is characterized by an unusually high frequency of blunders—and for the further reason that secrecy and deception characterize the struggle phase as well as the preparatory phase, complicating calculations. There is nothing in warfare corresponding to the rules of evidence or the sanctions of perjury, which are intended to reduce the role of secrecy and deception in a trial. All these considerations support Clausewitz's dictum that "everything in war is very simple, but the simplest thing is difficult."[54]

When in a civil struggle, such as that touched off by the revelation of Clinton's affair with Monica Lewinsky, the contestants are operating in conditions of radical uncertainty and intense emotionality, the struggle is likely to resemble war and to be illuminated by military theory and history. And those were the conditions of this particular struggle. The uncertainty arose in the first instance from Clinton's denials and the denials of other actual or potential targets of Starr's investigation and from Starr's reluctance to tip his hand. But it was compounded and eventually transcended by uncertainty as to how the public would respond to a Presidential sex scandal, Presidential obstructions of justice, the prosecutorial tactics of the Independent Counsel and his staff, midterm elections timed as it were to intersect with the scandal and its sequelae, and insistent media denunciations of the President's conduct and calls for his resignation. This was something so new in American political life that its course and outcome could not be predicted until too late, that is, until the principals (the President, his defenders, his attackers) had made their moves.

The struggle was riven by emotionality as well as uncertainty. As we saw in Chapter 6, the stakes seemed terribly high to many of the contestants; it seemed that their way of life was at stake. And the rules of the struggle were loose. Not so loose as in war, thank God; there was no violence and only a few threats of violence (unless the Clinton haters and the editorial writers of the *Wall Street Journal* can be believed).[55]

[54]Id. at 119.

[55]The most outlandish threat was by the actor Alec Baldwin, on NBC's *Late Night,* who said that in other countries "all of us together would go down to Washington and we would stone Henry Hyde to death! We would stone him to death and we would go to their homes and we'd kill their wives and their children." Quoted in Melinda Hen-

But lies and slanders, betrayals, and "leaks" (a kind of espionage) were treated by most of the participants in the struggle as acceptable tactics. These tactics compounded the uncertainty and intensified the emotionality of the conflict.

The conduct of Clinton's "war" exhibits a number of other warlike features. One was the pace. Fighting tends to be an intermittent rather than a continuous feature of war. Most of the time the troops are moving around, getting into position, waiting for something to happen; battles punctuate the tedium, but (in many wars) infrequently.[56] It was the same with Clinton's struggle for survival. The first "battle" lasted less than a week, from the breaking of the story on January 21, 1998, to the State of the Union address. Then there was a long period of preparation that ended with a dramatic attack by Starr—the testing of the dress—which ushered in a fierce battle that ebbed, however, following the broadcast of the President's grand jury testimony on September 21. Then came Clinton's dramatic "bloodless" victory in the midterm elections and "slaying" of the opposing general, Newt Gingrich. But to everyone's surprise, battle resumed within days. Tom DeLay picked up the fallen banner and carried the House Republicans to victory on December 19, but this was followed by another lull, and by peace feelers expected to head off the final battle in the Senate. The peace negotiations failed, and the final battle was joined in the Senate, in January.

The tale narrated in the preceding paragraph brings to the fore another analogy to war. Napoleon is supposed to have said that there is only one thing worse than a bad general, and that is two good generals. His point was that unity of command is enormously important in waging war because of the fissiparous tendencies to which the conditions of war, in particular emotionality and radical uncertainty, give rise. This factor favored the President. He was in unquestioned command of his side, although, as in most wars, his troops had their own agenda; most of his congressional foot soldiers and officers cared more about their own survival than about winning the war. His opponents lacked a single commander. Gingrich tried to play that role, but only intermittently, and with distinctly limited success. He could not survive his first defeat,

neberger, "How Henry Hyde's Resolve Was Shaped against Clinton," *New York Times,* Jan. 10, 1999, pp. A1, A14. Hyde was not amused. Id. at A14.

[56]See, for example, Rory Muir, *Tactics and the Experience of Battle in the Age of Napoleon* 7 (1998).

and he had no real successor; after his fall, command was confusingly shared by the loose-knit triumvirate of DeLay, Hyde, and Lott. Unfortunately for the Republicans, the United States has no tradition of a leader of the loyal opposition,[57] who might have commanded the Republicans in their struggle with the President and in particular might have formulated a consistent strategy, themes, and arguments.

Another warlike feature was the frequent indifference of noncombatants, and of rank and file combatants, to the issues over which the "war" was being fought. In the typical real war, many of the noncombatants just want to get out of the line of fire (many of the combatants too), while most of the rank and file combatants who do fight, who aren't shirkers, tend to fight for survival, booty, or their buddies rather than for the goals of their leaders. Public discussion of Clinton's *agon* often tacitly assumed that 280 million Americans had taken up arms, metaphorically speaking, and were fighting for the goals set forth either by the Clintonites or by the anti-Clintonites. In fact, most of the people not actively engaged in the struggle were apathetic. They didn't see what all the fuss was about, or were distracted from it by local or personal concerns of greater urgency, or shrugged it off as hopelessly confusing or irrelevant to their own lives. And among active participants many were fighting in the pure spirit of partisanship—fighting not because they thought it important for the nation that Clinton survive or go under, but because they had career stakes, personal friendships, or sentimental party affiliations on one side or the other of the fight.

A particularly Clausewitzian feature of the struggle was the extraordinary number of blunders on both sides. They began with Clinton's failure to settle or default the Jones case well in advance of Lewinsky's being drawn into it, his lawyer's slandering Linda Tripp, Clinton's trusting Lewinsky to be discreet about their affair, and the inept questioning of Clinton by Jones's lawyers, which precipitated his blunder of trying to talk his way out of their trap without committing provable perjury. The blunders continued with Lewinsky's replacing her first lawyer (the lawyer Vernon Jordan had gotten her) with a lawyer inexperienced in criminal practice[58] and with Clinton's too-emphatic public and private

---

[57]Gingrich played this role during the 1994 congressional election campaign and for a time afterward, but failed miserably in his efforts to manage the impeachment crisis.

[58]This was actually her father's mistake, not hers. The lawyer had represented her father, a doctor, in malpractice suits.

denials of the affair, his decision to lie to the grand jury,[59] his speech to the nation made while he was still smarting from that experience, and Starr's including too many graphic sexual details in his report.

The blunders culminated, it seemed—and fatally for the Republicans, it also seemed (but this was just another false dawn)—in Republican mispredictions of the outcome of the 1998 midterm elections,[60] in the House Judiciary Committee's failure to adopt a resolution (which would have been unanimous or nearly so) to conduct an impeachment inquiry before splitting over the precise timetable of the inquiry,[61] in the Committee's failure to accommodate the procedural suggestions (however mischievously intended) of House Democrats, in the Committee's decision to release the tape of President Clinton's grand jury testimony, and in the false predictions by some Republican members of the Committee that the tape would show the President losing his temper. But the House Democrats overplayed their hand as well. Their partisanship infuriated the Republicans and may have scotched any chance of resolving the impeachment inquiry, short of impeachment, by censure.[62] In the Senate the blunders were mainly on the side of the House managers. They were too numerous, too alike,[63] mistakenly emphasized the

[59]Clinton's lawyers made their own mistakes; but this one appears to have been his. "Mr. Clinton's lawyers . . . told the President that it would be suicidal for him to lie to the Federal grand jury . . . In the weekend before his testimony, lawyers for the President decided that he should make an opening statement acknowledging an inappropriate relationship with Ms. Lewinsky and then not answer any specific questions about the nature of the sexual contact. But in the four hours of grand jury testimony, the President surprised his lawyers by straying from the plan and maintaining that Ms. Lewinsky performed sexual acts on him while he never touched her." "How Republican Determination Upset Clinton's Backing at Polls," *New York Times* (national ed.), Dec. 21, 1998, pp. A1, A24. Apparently his testimony provoked the Independent Counsel's office to refer Clinton to the House of Representatives for possible impeachment. Id. at A24. Of course, this is a journalistic account and may be inaccurate.

[60]"The Democrats are doomed . . . After the voting this November 3, the Democrats are likely to be down to about 40 senators and fewer than 200 House members." William Kristol, "The Democrats' Fate," *Weekly Standard,* Oct. 19, 1998, p. 10.

[61]The Senate Republicans learned from that mistake, and did not repeat it.

[62]For some evidence in support of this hypothesis, see Henneberger, note 55 above.

[63]They were all, so far as appeared, conservative, white, Christian, "straight," physically "abled" males. The White House fielded a more diverse team of five which included a physically handicapped white male and two women, one black and the other (judging from her name) Jewish. If the Republicans couldn't have fielded a more diverse team, they could at least have finessed the lack of diversity by just having one or two prosecutors.

obstruction of justice article of impeachment, took too much time, and conducted an inept examination of Monica Lewinsky.

Despite much criticism of the quibbling, evasive, and in places perjurious character of the President's answers to the eighty-one questions propounded by the House Judiciary Committee, and of his refusal even in the face of mounting public demands to confess to perjury or at least to lying under oath (or at the very least to lying, period), I do not think that these evasions of truth and affronts to common sense and candor can confidently be judged blunders. I do think it was a mistake for him to repeat his denials after they ceased being believable, and especially on the eve of the impeachment debate. It not only confirmed the impression of him as a compulsive liar; it was a slap in the face of the moderate Republicans who wanted to trade lenity for a full confession. He should have shut up.

But the other much-criticized acts and omissions during the countdown to impeachment were as fated as they were distasteful. As the crisis ticked on, month after month, it became an increasingly unrealistic option for Clinton to come clean, to admit that he had lied repeatedly, to invite criminal prosecution, and to throw himself on the mercy of Congress. The longer he clung to the lie that he had not lied, the clearer it became that if he stopped lying it would be due not to a change of heart but to a change of tactics; if conscience was ever going to sting him into telling the truth, it would have done so earlier. By December 1998, President Clinton, if asked by anyone to recant his falsehoods, could only have replied with Macbeth: "I am in blood/ Stepped in so far that, should I wade no more,/Returning were as tedious as go o'er."[64]

As for his lawyers' tactics, which combined denying the undeniable with technical objections to the impeachment proceeding (for example, the objection that the articles of impeachment were unconstitutionally vague), they underscored rather than dispelled the impression that their client was guilty as charged. They may even have precipitated the impeachment. But they served two purposes. They avoided admissions that might make Mr. Clinton more vulnerable to criminal prosecution when he leaves office; more important (for the possibility of such a prosecution cannot be very great), they gave Democrats the same kind of running room that the Democratic Senators sought in favoring cen-

[64]*Macbeth,* act. III, sc. 4, ll. 137–139.

sure of the President for unspecified misconduct over a finding that he had committed specific crimes. To any constituent who asked how a criminal President could be allowed to remain in office, a Democratic member of Congress could answer that Clinton's lawyers had raised genuine if perhaps technical doubts as to whether the President was guilty of any crimes. The lawyers who defended Andrew Johnson in his impeachment trial also relied very heavily on technical legal arguments,[65] and this enabled the seven Republicans who voted against conviction, and so against their own party, to argue that their vote was determined by legal considerations.[66] It is always a comfort to be able to hide behind the law. But the President's lawyers probably overdid the technicalities and scorched-earth tactics. Such tactics sometimes succeed, but they are a sign of desperation.

We must be careful in our evaluations to distinguish between *ex post* and *ex ante,* or between hindsight and foresight: between tactics that reasonably seemed best at the time but turned out badly (or seemed bad at the time but turned out well, which may be the ultimate verdict on the pettifogging defenses thrown up by the President's lawyers) and tactics that should have been recognized in advance as probably unsound. The best example of the divergence between the wisdom of hindsight and the wisdom of foresight may be Clinton's initial emphatic public denials of any sexual relationship with Lewinsky. In retrospect it may seem that he would have been better off to come clean immediately. But apart from Dick Morris's poll-driven advice that the people were not ready to accept the enormity of the President's conduct, retrospect knows about the dress, and prospect did not. Because so many people wanted to believe Clinton, or at least wanted not to have to acknowledge their disbelief, it is possible that had it not been for the result of the DNA test he simply would have brazened out the scandal, as he looked to be doing until shortly before his grand jury appearance in August. (In commending denial as a tactic, I do not mean to imply moral approval.)

My next point of comparison between Clinton's struggle to save his Presidency and a real war is that the blunders so often took a favorable bounce for the blunderer, which is what one expects under conditions

[65]See Michael Les Benedict, *The Impeachment and Trial of Andrew Johnson* 146–167 (1973).
[66]See id. at 174–178.

of extreme uncertainty. An example is the inept questioning of Clinton by Jones's lawyers. Had they asked questions that he couldn't possibly dodge (which would have been easy to do), he might have decided on the spot not to answer the questions. This would have led to a default judgment, and though it might not have turned off the Independent Counsel's investigation, which had been launched from the Tripp tapes that implicated the President in witness tampering and subornation of perjury before he testified, it would have deprived the investigation of its richest fruits.

A second example is the ineptitude of Lewinsky's malpractice-turned-criminal lawyer, which by delaying her cooperation with the Independent Counsel protracted the period of Clinton's denial and caused an enormous expansion in the evidentiary record created by the investigation, a record highly unfavorable to Clinton. A third example is Clinton's decision to testify before the grand jury and allow his testimony to be taped, as a result of which he committed perjury before an audience of tens of millions of people. But that broadcast may have been the turning point in the struggle—Clinton's Stalingrad—because while it did his reputation enormous damage, it turned the public against impeachment. This was partly because of Clinton's charm and pluck, and the sinister and disagreeable impression made on the television audience by his faceless inquisitors, and partly because the inaccuracy of the Republicans' advance description of the tape made them seem partisan and unreliable.

Both the turning point (the broadcast of Clinton's grand jury testimony) and the apparent but illusory *coup de grâce* (the midterm elections) illustrate the danger, in a struggle, of failing to reach an announced goal, even if the goal is intrinsically irrelevant. It should not have mattered to Clinton's impeachability whether he lost his cool when questioned before the grand jury or whether the Republicans picked up additional seats in the midterm elections. These things mattered because there was so much uncertainty as to how the struggle would end that the public looked to the antagonists for signals of what *they* thought were the milestones. Evidently the Republicans thought that Clinton's losing his temper on television was important and likewise their gaining a larger majority in Congress. Otherwise they wouldn't have predicted these things.[67] That at least is a natural inference when there is nothing

[67]Conceivably, the Republicans were trying to influence the public reaction—hoping

else to go on. The Tet offensive in 1968 was basically a failed suicide attack. But it proved to be the turning point of the Vietnam War because the United States had denied the possibility of such an offensive. The public didn't know how badly the Vietcong had been defeated; all it knew was that our government had underestimated the enemy's strength.

The emotionality of warfare produces false dawns, generating dangerous overconfidence. The defeat of the French charge on the left flank of the British early in the Battle of Waterloo is a case in point. The British cavalry counterattacked with such élan that their charge carried them to within point-blank range of the French cannon, where they were slaughtered. Something like this happened to the Republicans during Clinton's crisis. At first they thought it best to step back and let the Democrats determine Clinton's fate; if he survived, he would be a weakened and disgraced President and the Republicans would be in a good position to pick up seats in the 1998 midterm elections and win back the Presidency in 2000. But as Clinton reeled under Starr's blows, the Republicans began to think they could knock off Clinton, win big in November 1998, cast Vice President Gore as Clinton's doomed twin, and perhaps pull him down too with an independent counsel investigation of campaign fundraising abuses. So they pushed hard, lost their own balance, and provoked a backlash that led to the fall of Gingrich. They look dumb in retrospect, but allowance should be made for the compounding of uncertainty by emotionality that leads to rapid mood swings that impair judgment. If Gingrich had had Clinton's resilience and had delayed his resignation by a few days, he might have survived.

Another point related to the emotionality of warfare is that warring parties tend to lose sight of their original war aims and to adopt more ambitious, often more vengeful, aims as the war proceeds, so they'll have more to "show" for their sacrifices. In other words (and this is another point emphasized by Clausewitz), wars tend to escalate. In the *Iliad*, a war to recover Helen becomes a war to destroy Troy. The emancipation of the slaves emerged as a war aim of the North in the Civil War. A defensive war against Germany and its allies became a war to "make the world safe for democracy" and redraw the map of Central Europe (World War I). Destroying the Communist regime in North Ko-

---

that if they told the public that it would see Clinton losing his temper, that is what the public would see.

rea emerged as a war aim of the United States in the Korean War, though it had soon to be abandoned. Similarly, what began, from the Republican point of view, as a skirmish designed to weaken President Clinton, but not to oust him and so give Vice President Gore an incumbent's advantage in the 2000 election, became an all-out effort to oust the President regardless of political cost. Part of the reason was simply that his stubborn defense infuriated his attackers and made them redouble their efforts.[68] The "war" took a personal and political toll on them and they became desperate for revenge and heedless of the cost.

My last three points are related to one another and also to the earlier point about the importance of achieving an announced goal however intrinsically trivial. They are the intertwined phenomena of premature claims of victory,[69] defeat as the *acceptance* of defeat (a point made by Montaigne and repeated by Clausewitz),[70] and victory as dependent on an end-game strategy. Because of the uncertainty and emotionality of war, and the resulting fear that it may be interminable or inconclusive, the contestants find it tempting to define in advance a sufficient condition for victory, so as to create an attainable goal, an intelligible focus, and a definite terminus of the struggle. But often this is just a convention, which the enemy is free to refuse to accept. It was "understood" in 1812 that if Napoleon captured Moscow, the war would be over; the Russians would admit defeat. But they didn't, and within months Napoleon's army was destroyed. It had been assumed in World War I, probably correctly, that if Germany conquered France it would have won the war; and when in 1940 Germany did conquer France, it was widely believed that it *had* won the war and that the British would sue for peace. But the British refused to admit defeat and eventually the Germans were defeated. Even France need not have admitted defeat;

---

[68] Again see Henneberger's article, note 55 above.

[69] An example is the shower of congratulations that descended on the President's lawyer in the Paula Jones case when the district court dismissed the case in April 1998. See, for example, John Aloysius Farrell, "Despite Scrapes, Bennett Emerges without a Scratch," *Boston Globe* (city ed.), April 2, 1998, p. A28. (There were naysayers—and they were prescient. See Lloyd Grove and David Segal, "The President's Lawyer: Bennett Jumps a Hurdle on His Victory Lap," *Washington Post* [final ed.], April 3, 1998, p. A34.) Six months later—by which time it was the conventional wisdom that the case could and should have been settled or defaulted years earlier, at a probable cost of no more than $25,000 and a probable gain of avoiding the entire Lewinsky investigation—the President settled the case for $850,000.

[70] Clausewitz, note 51 above, at 90.

though metropolitan France was occupied, the nation could have continued to fight from its colonial empire.

Twice in the course of the struggle touched off by the public revelation of Clinton's affair with Lewinsky it seemed that Clinton would be forced out of office. The first time was the first few days after the scandal broke into the open. The second was the period between the President's grand jury testimony and speech of August 17, 1998, and the televising of his grand jury testimony on September 21. At both times he seemed so totally disgraced as to make his continued occupation of the Presidency unthinkable. A weaker person, or a nobler person, might well have quit. But if, as happened, he refused to admit defeat, his opponents did not actually have the power to bring about his defeat. Those who were confident that he was defeated and that he would *have* to admit it and get out failed to study carefully the moves that would be necessary to end the game. Wholesale desertion of the President by the Democratic Party, the Cabinet, and the White House staff might have done the trick, but how likely was that? The sudden, wholesale repudiation of a President by his party, Cabinet, and staff would be unprecedented in American history and might destroy the Democratic Party. But failing that (something that would be closer to a real coup d'état than impeachment and conviction of the President), Clinton could be removed from office only by impeachment and conviction. Conviction by the necessary two-thirds vote was always a long shot; one just couldn't identify 67 likely votes, for there were only 55 Republican Senators and not all them—and very few Democratic Senators—seemed likely to vote to convict.[71] The only realistic possibility was that there would be a huge groundswell of popular revulsion against the President that would change opinion in the Senate. On the morning of September 21, waiting for the tape of the President's grand jury testimony to be broadcast, that still seemed a possibility. By the evening of that day, it had vanished. It was like the Battle of Midway. For a few minutes after the fighters from the Japanese carriers had shot down wave after wave of U.S. attack planes without loss, it seemed that Japan had won the war. Then the dive bombers from the *Enterprise* arrived and sank the Japanese carrier fleet, writing *finis* to Japan's hopes.

The broadcast was not, to continue the parallel, the end of the war. President Clinton's evasive and perjurious answers to the House Judi-

---

[71]In the end, no Democratic Senators voted to convict the President.

ciary Committee's questions set off a downward spiral in his fortunes that bottomed out with his four-minute Rose Garden speech of December 11, delivered minutes before the House Judiciary Committee voted on the first of four proposed articles of impeachment. Looking like a whipped dog, the President delivered still another evasive and unconvincing apology for his elusively unspecified wrongful words and deeds, then walked silently back to the Oval Office, ignoring the shouts of the journalist-hounds demanding that he confess to lies and perjury. A week later the impeachment debate began on the floor of the House, and the following day he was impeached.

The parallel between the war against Japan and the Republicans' war against Clinton is imprecise. One reason is the dissimilarity of the positions of the United States in the world of the 1940s and President Clinton in the politics of the United States in 1998. The United States was a rising nation in the forties, Clinton a lame duck in 1998. His position resembled that of Great Britain in World War II. Britain's victory was essential, heroic, glorious, but also Pyrrhic, accelerating the nation's decline. Clinton's fight against removal from office was an impressive tribute to his toughness, resilience, and verbal skills; but it also wounded him grievously, and a lame duck, further wounded, is apt to be a helpless cripple. I am speaking not of the wound to Clinton's reputation, the severity of which must be referred to the judgment of the future, but of the wound to his effectiveness as President. Already in a weak position by virtue of his inability to run again and the control of both houses of Congress by the opposite party, he has suffered so large an additional loss of authority by virtue of the investigation and impeachment that he may become completely ineffectual on any plane other than the rhetorical.

For we now can see that the Democrats had their own false dawn. It was the November 1998 midterm congressional election. It had been billed as a referendum on whether to impeach the President. The Democrats did better than expected; the President had "won" the referendum; it was confidently expected that the President would not be impeached. But the Republicans, like the Russians after Napoleon captured Moscow, refused to admit defeat. In the face of the incredulity of the media pundits, they pressed on with the impeachment inquiry. Like the Russians, they had discovered the advantages of a war of attrition. The steady drumbeat of accusation of the President took its toll, reinforced rather than diminished by the increasingly contorted and desperately ingenious legal sophistries of the President's lawyers. They could not beat back the charge of perjury. Public boredom with the impeachment inquiry molted into public indifference to the President's fate. His moral authority oozed away. He was impeached, and less than a month later put on trial before the Senate.

CHAPTER 8

———————•———————

The Balance Sheet

The public life of the nation in 1998 and the first six weeks of 1999 was dominated by President Clinton's struggle to retain his office. The struggle was deeply and not merely pruriently or dramatically interesting, though it *was* high drama—Wagnerian in intensity and protraction, with wonderful actors, the Clintons, in the lead roles, a supporting cast of hundreds, dramatic revelations aplenty (the tapes, the dress, the sex lives of Republican Congressmen), a splendid libretto by Kenneth Starr,[1] a Greek chorus of television commentators; plus hapless walk-ons, clandestine comings and goings, betrayals, suspense, reversals of fortune, hints of violence (supplied by the Clinton haters), a May-December romance as it might be depicted by an Updike or a Cheever, a doubling and redoubling of plot, a *Bildungsroman,*[2] even allegorical commentary (the movies *Primary Colors* and *Wag the Dog*) and a touch of comic opera (Chief Justice Rehnquist's costume out of *Iolanthe*). It was the ultimate Washington novel, the supreme and never to be equaled expression of the genre and the proof that truth is indeed stranger than fiction.

But putting its entertainment value to one side, are we better or worse off for the experience? It is too soon to tell; it is especially premature to say that we are worse off.

[1] On the Starr Report as (almost) "a novel in the classic tradition," or a "moralizing narrative," see Adam Gopnik, "American Studies," *New Yorker,* Sept. 28, 1998, p. 39.

[2] I have in mind the metamorphosis of Monica Lewinsky from the giddy pizza-bearing sextern of November 1995 to the poised and articulate young woman whose videotaped testimony was shown to the Senate and the world on February 6, 1999.

We are surely better off in some respects. We have learned a lot about the mischief of the independent counsel law and about the pitfalls of Presidential impeachment. Unlike other recent nonfiction entertainments (the death of Princess Diana for example, or John Glenn's reentry into outer space), the ordeal of Clinton's Presidency has gotten people thinking seriously about important issues—issues of law, morality, constitutional structure, public opinion, and political behavior. It has thus made people more civic minded, although one cannot know how long the civic lessons will be remembered. It has also contributed to a franker public discourse on matters of sex, which I think is good. The idea that it has loosened parental control over their children's moral development is unproven and implausible. Young children do not understand what Clinton and Lewinsky did, and teenagers understand without being told. It is too soon to tell whether oral sex will become a more popular sexual practice as a result of the incessant public discussion of the President's taste for it, but, if so, it would not be the end of the world; offensive though the practice is to some religious people, it is, at least, securely contraceptive and only rarely a conduit for disease. Phone sex is better yet on these dimensions, though I imagine that William Bennett would fall off his chair if he read a page of *Vox*. If some people have been encouraged by Clinton's survival in office to commit perjury and obstruction of justice, others, for whom these crimes had no resonance or visibility, have learned that one can get into a lot of trouble by committing them. The stripping away of the privacy not only of Clinton and Monica Lewinsky but of a number of the supporting characters in the Clinton-Lewinsky drama, including several Republican House members, may have neutralized scandal-mongering as an electoral tactic by revealing that a high percentage of politicians have skeletons in their closet, and may thus have contributed to a refocusing of electoral competition on substantive issues.[3]

The drama has demonstrated the resilience of the American government. For despite everything, government ticked along in its usual way through thirteen months of so-called crisis. No doubt there was distraction. But the idea that the federal government (which is by no means the whole of American government) was *seriously* deflected from a productive engagement with international financial or political issues, or

[3]John Harwood and Jeanne Cummings, "Tactical Retreat: One Likely Casualty of the Clinton Years: The Scandal Gambit," *Wall Street Journal*, Dec. 11, 1998, p. A1.

domestic crises such as Social Security and health insurance, is unsupported. Some of the problems that the government was asked to solve, or at least to make progress toward solving, in 1998 are insoluble by the federal (perhaps any) government; some are not problems; some were addressed in the usual way. Others would have been pushed to the back burner anyway in the twilight years of a lame-duck President facing a Congress both houses of which are controlled by the opposition at a time when peace and prosperity and at least a temporary abatement of some of the nation's most acute social problems, coupled with the toll that scandal and scandal-mongering have taken of public confidence in government, disincline the American people to support active government. Clinton, a proponent of active government, by his antic behavior damaged public faith in it. We have learned that the President of the United States, like Tolstoy's Napoleon, is to a certain extent a cork floating on the ocean rather than the moon controlling the tides.[4] We have also learned about the strength of weakness. International terrorists may have maintained a lower than usual profile during Clinton's struggle for survival, knowing that Clinton was eager to demonstrate strength and change the subject *(Wag the Dog)*. I do think that the Supreme Court was playing with fire when by the combined effect of its decisions in *Morrison* and *Jones* it exposed the President and the nation to the ordeal that began on January 21, 1998; but a lucky conjunction of circumstances has spared the nation from the worst consequences.

Resilient our institutions may be, meaning they can take a lot of punishment; but they are also flawed. The crisis of Clinton's Presidency, like the Vietnam War decades earlier, revealed feet of clay in a number of departments of the American Establishment—the media pundits (though not the working journalists), the political consultants and forecasters, the public intellectuals,[5] the Washington bar, Supreme Court Justices, the members of Congress, the White House groupies and toadies, and, above all, the President. But it has done so at a time when we

[4]Cf. Stephen Skowronek, *The Politics Presidents Make: Leadership from John Adams to George Bush* (1993).

[5]Especially those whom Stanley Fish calls " 'rent for a day' intellectuals or 'cameo' intellectuals—persons brought in either because they are considered authorities on a particular issue (the media equivalent of an expert witness) or because they hold a position on that same issue that can be theatrically opposed to the position of another

can learn the lessons at relatively low cost because we are in a period of calm between the crises that punctuate history.

We have learned that powerful, intelligent, articulate, well-educated, and successful people who would like us to submit to their leadership whether political or intellectual are, much of the time, fools, knaves, cowards, and blunderers, just like the rest of us. That is to say, they are ordinary people, with all the ordinary vices, whom luck, or specialized, compartmentalized talents have propelled into positions of power or influence in which they preen and strut until some unexpected event strips away their masks, demolishes their carefully constructed, imperturbable-seeming public selves, and exposes them in their full ordinariness and inadequacy.

We have learned that professionalism, whether in law, scholarship, or politics, is no guarantor of being able to cope with novel challenges. Rather the opposite. The tendency of professionalism is to a productive narrowness. The professional masters the proven techniques for dealing with a familiar category of problems. When something comes along to knock him out of his groove—in the case of the Clinton-Lewinsky business a political, legal, and cultural phenomenon without precedents to steer by—the limitedness of his professional skills, training, and experience is revealed.

We have learned that too much law can be a bad thing. We do not need to be able to sue our Presidents during their term of office, and we do not need an independent counsel law.

The mystique of the Presidency became a casualty of the narration in the Starr Report and of the public interrogation of the President by a grand jury before a global audience. It is one thing to know in the abstract, as everyone does, that Presidents have bodies and private lives that include bodily functions, have private embarrassments and lapses of taste (a President who collects *frogs?*) and character flaws aplenty, and make egregious errors of judgment. It is another thing to know in riveting and exact detail the normally hidden and in this case disreputable private life of the very President we have now, not some dim historical figure, so that when Joan Didion speaks cuttingly of the President as embodying "the familiar predatory sexuality of the provincial adolescent" and remarks "the reservoir of self-pity, the quickness to

well-credentialled professor." Stanley Fish, *Professional Correctness: Literary Studies and Political Change* 118–119 (1995).

blame, the narrowing of the eyes, as in a wildlife documentary, when things did not go his way,"[6] there is no one to deny the justness of her observations. Her reference to wildlife is apt. Animals have no privacy.

The mystique of the Presidency was damaged, maybe destroyed; but the mystique of the other branches of the federal government was not compensatorily enhanced—indeed was also damaged. The role of the courts will be remembered for the fiasco of *Morrison v. Olson* and *Clinton v. Jones,* and for the stripes on Chief Justice Rehnquist's robe; and we have learned that the Senate of the United States, no less than the House of Representatives, is too politicized an organ of government to play the judicial role in Presidential impeachment that the Constitution assigned it.

The role of the courts in the fiasco will soon be forgotten; and no one who knows Congress could have thought it a judicial body. The most abiding effect of what I have called the ultimate Washington novel may be to make it difficult to take Presidents seriously, as superior people, for the same reason that an even greater novel, *The Remembrance of Things Past,* made it impossible by dint of its riveting detail to take aristocrats seriously as superior people. For those who think that authority depends on mystery, the shattering of the Presidential mystique has been a disaster for which Clinton ought of rights to have paid with his job. They may be right about the dependence of effective political leadership on mystique. My guess is that they are wrong, that Americans have reached a level of political sophistication at which they can take in stride the knowledge that the nation's political and intellectual leaders are their peers, and not their paragons. The nation does not depend on the superior virtue of one man.

[6]Joan Didion, "Clinton Agonistes," *New York Review of Books,* Oct. 22, 1998, p. 16.

Acknowledgments

I want to thank Susan Burgess, Ryan Hanley, Dimitri Karcazes, Christopher Ottele, and Christopher Snell for excellent research assistance and Eldon Eisenach, Philip Elman, Jean Bethke Elshtain, Israel Friedman, Jack Goldsmith, Sanford Levinson, Lawrence Lessig, John Mearsheimer, Martha Nussbaum, Charlene Posner, Eric Posner, Stephen Schulhofer, Cass Sunstein, and Timothy Wu for many helpful comments on portions of the previous draft. I particularly want to thank my long-time editor at Harvard University Press, Michael Aronson, for countless rounds of helpful comments and suggestions. Needless to say, no one but myself is responsible for any of the opinions expressed in the book.

Index